Starting and Managing
Fee-Based Information Services
in Academic Libraries

FOUNDATIONS IN LIBRARY AND
INFORMATION SCIENCE, Volume 40

Editor: Murray S. Martin, *University Librarian and Professor of Library Science Emeritus,*
Tufts University

Foundations in
Library and Information Science

Edited by **Thomas W. Leonhardt**, *Director of Library Technical Services, Bizzell Memorial Library, University of Oklahoma* and **Murray S. Martin,** *University Librarian and Professor of Library Science Emeritus, Tufts University*

Starting and Managing Fee-Based Information Services in Academic Libraries

by Suzanne M. Ward
Technical Information Service
Purdue University

 JAI PRESS INC.

Greenwich, Connecticut   *London, England*

Library of Congress Cataloging-in-Publication Data

Ward, Suzanne M.
  Starting and managing fee-based information services in academic
libraries / by Suzanne M. Ward.
      p.   cm – (Foundations in library and information science :
v. 40)
  Includes bibliographical references (p.   ) and index.
  ISBN 0-7623-0225-9
  1. Academic libraries—United States.   2.   Fee-based library
services—United States.   I. Title. II. Series.
Z675.U5W33   1997
025.1'977–DC21

                                                    97-4997
                                                      CIP

Copyright © 1997 JAI PRESS INC.
55 Old Post Road, No. 2
Greenwich, Connecticut 06836

JAI PRESS LTD.
38 Tavistock Street
Covent Garden
London WC2E 7PB
England

ISBN: 0-7623-0225-9

Library of Congress Catalog Number: 97-4997

Manufactured in the United States of America

CONTENTS

Acknowledgments

Writing this book would have been impossible without the support of many people. Many thanks to:

Bill Corya, for reading and commenting on a draft of the manuscript and for his encouragement

Gordon Law, for his instrumental role in establishing the Technical Information Service and for his recommendation in 1987 to hire me as its first information specialist

All the Technical Information Service staff, past and present, who taught me what it truly means to work in a team environment

Purdue's Interlibrary Loan staff, for obtaining dozens of books and articles unavailable locally

Colleagues at Purdue who have graciously shared their collections and their subject expertise to support the TIS mission of providing information services to the business community

Colleagues in other fee-based information services who have over the years shared both their "war stories" and their triumphs

Emily Mobley, whose vision of excellence in academic library service includes meeting the corporate community's information needs

Preface

As the manager of the Purdue University Libraries' Technical Information Service, one of the largest and most successful fee-based information services in a U.S. academic library, I receive one or two calls or letters a month from colleagues at other institutions. Sometimes the conversation starts like this:

> Our library budget has been cut drastically this year. Our director just read an article about fee-based information services, and we're interested in starting a service like yours in order to generate some income for the library. Can you give us some tips on getting started?

I have the impression that the caller hopes by the end of a 10-minute conversation to be able to open a fee-based service next week, rapidly generating thousands of dollars with which to bolster the library's battered budget.

The opening lines of other conversations sound more like this:

> Our library has been offering informal, limited research services to non-campus patrons for the past few years. We've noticed an increasing demand for these services, and we'd like to be able to respond to these requests without diminishing our ability to meet the demands of our primary clientele. Establishing a fee-based information service looks like a good way to accomplish this goal. Please send me some information about your fee-based information service.

I hope this book will guide librarians from whatever point and viewpoint they begin contemplating the possibility of a fee-based information service at their institutions. The book's intent is to define the issues and challenges, as well as to offer suggestions for dealing with the dozens of questions that arise at all stages, from submitting the initial proposal to the library administration to managing an established service. Starting or managing a fee-based information service is very much like starting and running a small business, with all the accompanying headaches and triumphs, but with the additional challenge that the parent institution is often not flexible enough to meet all the special needs of an entrepreneurial unit.

Starting and managing a fee-based information service is not an easy job but, if done well, it is immensely rewarding.

As the title indicates, this book's emphasis is on academic libraries, but many of the same issues and challenges exist for librarians beginning fee-based information services in public, corporate, or association libraries, or indeed for entrepreneurs starting information services as small businesses. Most academic fee-based information services report to the library, but there are services operated by a library school, a university's economic development office, a university's business school, and a university's engineering department.

One of the biggest controversies in the library profession over the past few decades raged around the great "fee or free" debate. Is it necessary, desirable, or even ethical to charge users for library services? For all services and all users or only for selected ones? Which ones? If libraries charge fees, are they discriminating against or disenfranchising users who cannot afford to pay? What about the fact that the American Library Association's Bill of Rights "opposes the charging of user fees for the provision of information services that receive their major support from public funds"? ("Economic Barriers" 1993, p. 137).

Hundreds of articles and dozens of books and journal special issues have been devoted to this topic over the past few decades. I shall not attempt to summarize the many points of view and opinions on the subject of charging fees to users. My assumption is that most of this book's readers already agree with the position that an important part of meeting external users' information needs is to offer special services in a cost-recovery environment that does not diminish the library's ability to respond to the basic needs of its primary clientele.

For several reasons, I enjoy a unique perspective for writing a book about managing fee-based information services. First, I came to Purdue in 1987 when the Technical Information Service (TIS) was just starting and, with my supervisor, Gordon Law, made or influenced many of the early decisions. These decisions ranged from marketing strategies for attracting clients to what color paper to use for our document cover sheets. Second, through 10 years at Purdue, I have helped TIS grow from a small service serving only Indiana clients into one of the largest U.S. academic fee-based information services with a full-time staff of nine assisting clients from Indianapolis to Istanbul. Third, I have been involved in the library fee-for-service arena through conference presentations, published articles, private consulting, and professional meetings. Finally, just as the information industry has grown and changed over these years, so has TIS grown and changed to keep up with client demands and expectations.

CITED REFERENCE

"Economic Barriers to Information Access: An Interpretation of the Library Bill of Rights." 1993. *Newsletter on Intellectual Freedom* 42(5): 137.

Chapter 1

What Is A Library Fee-Based Information Service?

AN HOUR IN THE DAY OF A FEE-BASED INFORMATION SERVICE

"My boss is going into a meeting in 30 minutes. He absolutely has to have a copy of this article by then. Is there any way you can fax it to me by 10:30?" pleaded a librarian from a company a 1,000 miles away.

The clerk never missed a beat. Within minutes, a student assistant walked into another library several buildings away to photocopy the article specified on the retrieval form. By 10:20, the copy hummed through the fax machine.

The clerk took another call. "Sure, we can get you a copy of a Japanese standard. Would you prefer an English translation, if it's available? Do you need rush or regular delivery?"

The supervisor, an information specialist, finished sending an electronic mail message to a document supplier in Finland for a copy of a paper from a conference held in Switzerland but sponsored by a French professional association. Then, the information specialist started jotting down the search strategy for a database search on trends and projections for the black walnut industry and made a note to check for any trade associations, government agencies, or academic research institutes that might compile information on the subject.

The fax beeped again. A paralegal sent in a list of 20 articles and four books about the health effects of asbestos that one of the firm's attorneys wanted on his desk the next morning. The paralegal asked that the material be sent via overnight courier to the attorney in Connecticut, but that the invoice be sent to the firm's main office in South Carolina.

The information specialist's next phone call was from a new client. "I know there were a few articles published in the 1970s about carpeting used in airplanes. When they burned, the carpets released toxic fumes. Can you identify these articles and send me copies by tomorrow?"

The information specialist set the walnut search aside and logged into Dialog to search *Compendex* and the *Aerospace Database.*

As she finished, the clerk handed her another request. "This client asked for a chapter from *Methods in Enzymology,* volume 107, but the article doesn't appear on the pages he listed. Would you please verify it?"

The specialist gave the clerk the airplane carpet citations from the *Compendex* search and asked her to prepare document retrieval forms. A quick author check in *Biosis* revealed that the client's handwritten request for volume 107 should have been for volume 109. The specialist handed the order back to the clerk for completion and picked up the walnut search again.

Five minutes later, another document assistant appeared at her elbow. "Where can we get copies of nuclear regulations?"

A few hours like this may represent business as usual in a corporate library, but to many academic librarians it sounds like a nightmare. Yet, for the staff in academic fee-based information services around the country, the scenario also describes a typical hour. In some ways, work in a fee-based service may be even more challenging than in a corporate library, because clients come from all types and sizes of companies and represent widely different levels of education, expectations, information literacy, and information needs. While an academic library represents an asset in terms of the depth of its library collections, it may also be a liability in terms of some of its constraints—for example, a university policy that cannot accommodate billing clients' credit cards for library services.

THE NATURE OF FEE-BASED INFORMATION SERVICES

What is a library fee-based information service? It is a library department or unit with the express mission of providing information services to the library's non-primary clientele. These are value-added services, individually tailored to meet each client's unique needs. The two major services offered are generally research and document delivery. The department's staff usually have full-time appointments in the service, although the manager or administrator may have a split assignment.

Staff bill clients on a cost-recovery basis. Cost-recovery means billing to recover the costs associated with a specific project, such as database charges, staff time, and overnight courier fees, as well as at least some of the overall costs associated with operating the service, such as general office supplies and database documentation. Every fee-based information service's parent institution has different criteria about what constitutes indirect costs for which it wants to be reimbursed. Some services struggle to meet all or a portion of general overhead costs or fringe benefits as well as salaries. Others need only pay for the supplies, equipment, and services (paper clips, fax machines, phone calls) they consume directly. Some services strive to make a profit.

Fee-based information services can be successfully organized in many different ways (Peinaar 1994), but they also share common characteristics. This book defines the major characteristics of fee-based information services as:

- A separate unit or department;
- Exclusively or largely staffed by people with full-time appointments in the service;
- Offering services for a fee, usually on a cost-recovery basis; and
- Providing information services mainly for the library's non-primary clientele.

By this definition, a library whose reference staff occasionally run database searches for a few local firms or whose circulation department sells borrower's cards to nonaffiliated users does not qualify as a true fee-based information service. Neither do those libraries that organize a slightly more formal arrangement in which information services for non-primary clientele are solicited and provided on a cost-recovery basis, but almost exclusively handled by existing staff who juggle demands from external users along with their regular duties. Simply charging fees in exchange for providing some services does not necessarily mean that a library has a true fee-based information service. Joan B. Fiscella and Joan D. Ringel differentiated between a firm's "physical access to research collections and intellectual access to people with expertise in the structure of information sources" (Fiscella and Ringel 1988, p. 135). A library fee-based information service has as its primary focus the provision of intellectual access to information.

Although a library fee-based information service is usually operated on a non-profit basis, it shares many characteristics with a small business. Staff work with members of the corporate community who expect a businesslike attitude from their suppliers. To be successful, the service must:

- Attract and keep clients;
- Consistently meet deadlines and other commitments;
- Provide quality services and products at competitive prices;
- Manage a budget;
- Resolve occasional customer complaints;
- Pay its bills on time;
- Issue its own bills in a timely and accurate manner;
- Monitor client payments;
- Maintain records;
- Manage an office;
- Hire, train, evaluate, and reward staff;
- Keep up with the latest developments in the information industry;
- Grapple with internal and external regulations;
- Break even (or in some cases, make a profit);

- Evaluate and improve current services;
- Plan for the future;
- Meet crises and challenges calmly, flexibly, and creatively;
- Fulfill its mission; and
- Meet larger institutional goals or expectations.

WHAT DOES A FEE-BASED INFORMATION SERVICE DO?

A library fee-based information service fills many roles. For many of its customers, the fee-based service acts like a corporate library for companies that do not have resident information specialists or formal library collections, or that have only occasional research or document needs. Fee-based services also provide back-up services for companies with corporate libraries, more typically with document delivery but also with occasional work completing database searches for which the corporate librarian may not have the time, the access to an appropriate database, or the experience in a particular file, to handle quickly and cost effectively in-house. A successful fee-based information service may also fill document orders for commercial information or document brokers. It may also offer its clients other information products or services. Although it works largely with the institution's non-primary users, it may occasionally also handle projects for local patrons who request expedited or customized services and who are able to pay the service's fees.

Fee-based information services vary in many details, but Lee Anne George has listed three common characteristics. First, fee-based information services are "library based and have ready access to the library's resources." Second, the services "respond to requests from the library's non-primary users." And finally, "fee-based services are client centered" with customer satisfaction as the major goal (George 1993, p. 42).

WHY DO BUSINESSPEOPLE CHOOSE FEE-BASED INFORMATION SERVICES?

Unlike librarians, who view information as a service, most businesspeople view information as a commodity, a good, or a product. Like machine parts, software, telephones, staples, and labor, information is a simply tool or supply they need to get the job done. They may not need specialized information every day, or even very frequently, but when they need it, they need it quickly. "Information ... is a desirable good, one for which the individual wants, needs, and is willing to pay" (Weinland and McClure 1987, p. 54). But businesspeople do not want raw information any more than they want a general laborer when they requested a precision machinist. Just as they are used to calling an agency to hire on a short-term basis an employee with specialized skills, so are they willing to pay for the professional skills needed to identify, synthesize, assemble, and ship relevant information. "The businessman has to place only one telephone call in order to set up a chain reaction of information access procedures that results in the information being presented on his desk when he needs it, in the format that he needs it, and at a cost that bears a relationship to its value to that person concerned" (White 1980, p. 84).

For most clients, the fee-based service represents a reliable, accurate, and cost-effective way to get information and documents sent directly to their desks within a matter of hours or days, rather than requiring that they personally go somewhere or learn something to meet their information need. It is almost always less expensive for a busy professional to hire an experienced information specialist to handle a request than it is for the professional to take the time to locate and acquire the information directly. Clients appreciate access to information specialists who, because of their training and experience, already know or can easily find out where to get information or documents in a fraction of the time and at a fraction of the cost it might take the client:

> [T]he information user wants external specialists to gather information for him for a fee. It saves him time and money while he does more important things. ... Many users don't want to be bothered with the nuisance or cost of operating a terminal, or maintaining and training a staff of searchers. They don't really care where the answer comes from—just so they get the right information at the right time at the right price (Gaffner 1976, pp. 39-40).

Potential customers include a wide variety of people, including medical professionals, consultants, lawyers, engineers, publishers, manufacturers, business owners, entrepreneurs, and corporate librarians, as well as the staff who support them, such as paralegals and administrative assistants. For reasons generally having to do with speed, time, and cost, these people choose not to do their own research or document procurement. Instead, they outsource some or all of their information needs. There is an ever-growing assortment of companies and organizations eager to meet these information needs. What makes some people choose a fee-based information service rather than one of the many other types of information providers?

Lee Anne George summarized clients' needs with the phrase "quality service" and further explained that corporate clients seek a full range of services, reliability, responsiveness, and individualized attention. These factors are generally more important to clients than the strengths of the local library collection and the price (within reason). When a businessperson finds a service able to provide all these features, coupled with speed, the customer is likely to place repeat orders (George 1993a, pp. 41-42).

Elizabeth Lunden wrote that a university-affiliated information service "suggests permanence, integrity, expertise, academic excellence, a fine collection of resources, and very importantly, a non-profit public service motive. There is an immediate bond of trust with the client" (Lunden 1983, p. 126).

INSTITUTIONAL BENEFITS

An institution and its library gain many benefits from establishing and maintaining a fee-based information service. One manager notes that the service enhances the library's image within the institution by drawing attention to the library staff's competence in serving business clients (Grund 1992, p. 120). Douglas J. Ernest wrote that:

> libraries are all but invisible to people engaged in commerce and industry. Fee-based services offer the promise of bringing libraries and librarians more to center stage.
>
> Fee-based services carry an important symbolic weight that goes beyond the rather modest role they play in library operations at present. These agencies allow librarians to view themselves as providers of valuable information for which others willingly pay a fee. The activities performed by these librarians in gathering and packaging information adds value to the final product and enhances their self-image as well as their image with others (Ernest 1993, p. 401).

"Most libraries regard the charging of fees as a way to expand the range of products and services they can offer their publics, without compromising fundamental library services" (Coffman and Josephine 1991, p. 33). Reference staff have somewhere to refer non-primary clientele with in-depth or rush queries. Interlibrary loan staff may refer some types of queries, such as document requests from selected international addresses for which prepayment is required or requests from individuals who are not associated with the home institution and who prefer to handle their document needs directly instead of through a local library. Individual academic or research departments, whose secretaries have little time for handling requests from the public for technical reports or other local publications, are usually happy to transfer calls to the fee-based service.

There may be some library collection development benefits: for example, the fee-based service might contribute towards the cost of a specialized reference work or the back file of a serial title or a piece of equipment that it needs to meet clients' requests but that the library might not otherwise be able to afford. The service also may sometimes purchase books to lend to clients and then donate the items to the library as gifts.

A less tangible public relations benefit is that, from the client's perspective, the fee-based service represents the institution; a responsive, well-managed fee-based service shapes the institution's image in the clients' mind.

One manager cited several benefits. First, the fee-based information service enhanced the library's corporate donor program, because corporate donors received special services. Second, the library was able to buy resources and equipment that were made available to primary users as well as the fee-based service's clients. Next, cooperation and networking improved. The service also increased general awareness of the library. And finally, the library was able to offer special services, such as rush document delivery, that formerly were not available at all (Kallunki 1990, pp. 19-20).

If the service is run on a for-profit basis, benefits include additional revenue for equipment, collections, and other resources that benefit not only the service's clients but also the academic community (Grund 1992, p. 120; Williams, Lemkau, and Burrows 1988, p. 321).

Some fee-based information services are associated with their universities' industrial liaison programs and, thus, form a part of the institutions' plans to provide academic resources to the community. Caren and Somerville wrote that "fee-based access to collections and services is now perceived as a valuable product for attracting small corporations and businesses into town-gown partnerships" (Caren and Somerville 1988, p. 38). Services without connections to other campus programs demonstrate to the institution that the library plays a vital role in providing information resources to business.

INSTITUTIONAL RISKS

Starting and operating a fee-based information service is not without risks. The library commits to significant start-up costs for staffing, equipping, and promoting the service. Setting prices, estimating demand, and reaching clients are all difficult tasks that, if done improperly, may jeopardize the service's success. Any service, and especially a new one, is subject to larger economic, legal, and institutional forces over which it has little or no control.

This book's premise, however, is that by planning and implementing a well-designed service, the library minimizes its risks. The potential benefits, both to the clients and to the institution, far outweigh the possible risks.

WORKING IN A FEE-BASED INFORMATION SERVICE

As for the staff in a fee-based service, the ones that survive the initial shock of entry into what is essentially a fast-paced corporate library setting are usually convinced they have the best jobs in the library. They enjoy working in an academic environment, but in a businesslike way with businesspeople. The pace can sometimes be punishing, but the payoff is contact with a wide range of clients with varied and interesting information needs. Every day brings a new challenge. Very little work is routine. There are few rules, except to meet the clients' needs as quickly and cost-effectively as possible. In a well managed service, support staff are empowered to think creatively, solve problems, make decisions, choose suppliers, and try alternatives to satisfy clients and keep them coming back. Professional staff relish the knowledge and skills they gain answering questions in a wide range of subject areas. Work in a fee-based service represents the best aspects of teamwork combined with the chance to make more daily independent decisions than staff in many traditional library units make in a month. The work is fast and hard, but it is also fun and rewarding.

CITED REFERENCES

Caren, L., and A. Somerville. 1988. "Issues Facing Private Academic Libraries Considering Fee-Based Programs." *The Reference Librarian* 22: 37-49.

Coffman, S., and H. Josephine. 1991. "Doing It for Money." *Library Journal* 116(17): 32-36.

Ernest, D.J. 1993. "Academic Libraries, Fee-Based Information Services, and the Business Community." *RQ* 32(3): 393-402.

Fiscella, J.B., and J.D. Ringel. 1988. "Academic Libraries and Regional Economic Development." Pp. 127-136 in *Libraries and the Search for Academic Excellence,* edited by P.S. Breivik and R. Wedgeworth, Metuchen, NJ: Scarecrow Press.

Gaffner, H.B. 1976. "The Demand for Information-on-Demand." *Bulletin of the American Society for Information Science* 2(7): 39-40.

George, L.A. 1993a. "Fee-Based Information Services and Document Delivery." *Wilson Library Bulletin* 67(February): 41-44, 112.

Grund, D. 1992. "Fee-Based Information Services: Serving Business/Strengthening the LRC." Pp. 113-121 in *Community College Reference Services,* edited by B. Katz. Metuchen, NJ: Scarecrow Press.

Kallunki, S. 1990. "To Fee or Not to Fee." *The Unabashed Librarian* 75: 19-20.

Lunden, E. 1983. "Marketing the R.I.C.E. Operation." Pp. 113-127 in *Conference on Fee Based Research in College and University Libraries.* Greenvale, NY: Long Island University Center for Business Research.

Pienaar, R.E. 1994. "The Organization of Fee-Based Services." *Fee for Service* 1(4): 49, 51-53.

Weinland, J., and C.R. McClure. 1987. "Economic Considerations for Fee Based Library Services: An Administrative Perspective." *Journal of Library Administration* 8(1): 53-68.

White, M.S. 1980. "Information for Industry: The Role of the Information Broker." *Aslib Proceedings* 32(2): 82-86.

Williams, T.L., H.L. Lemkau, and S. Burrows. 1988. "The Economics of Academic Health Science Libraries: Cost Recovery in the Era of Big Science." *Bulletin of the Medical Library Association* 76(4): 317-322.

Chapter 2

Is a Library Fee-Based Information Service Right for Your Library?

INSTITUTIONAL MISSION

Universities typically have three major missions: education, research, and service. Academic libraries support the first two of these missions very well, first by helping educate students in the use of information resources and supporting the teaching faculty's curriculum needs, and second by supporting the faculty's research needs by acquiring or otherwise obtaining the indexes, books, databases, articles, and other documents they need. These services are provided to users on a no- or low-cost basis. Community service takes on a special role in an institution at least partly supported by state funding. Citizens often feel entitled to some personal, tangible return in exchange for their annual tax bill. Libraries are often at a loss to support this service aspect of their institution's mission, apart from offering general reference services and a visitor's library card to members of the community who walk into the library.

In an academic setting, the library staff's primary responsibility is to provide information services to the campus community, in support of the institution's educational and research missions. The staff has a further goal of teaching patrons how to make the most effective use of proliferating sources of information. Traditionally, when local businesspeople walk into the library, staff are glad to show them the sources that answer their question, but then leave them to plow though the material themselves. At some institutions, a nonaffiliated member of the public can request a database search, or, more rarely, interlibrary loan services. However, these services are often not delivered as quickly or as comprehensively as the businessperson would like. The major reason for this failure to meet customer expectations is because the academic librarians' first job is to meet commitments to the students and faculty. Some businesspeople, on offering to pay for services or for expedited delivery, have been baffled by the librarians' response that because the institution has no policy or staff for handling the request, there is actu-

9

ally no mechanism for billing them or for accepting payments for the services they need. No matter how much the staff may want to help the patron, there is no way of recovering the costs associated with the search.

WHY ESTABLISH A FEE-BASED INFORMATION SERVICE?

Why would a college or university library decide to offer information services to the public for a fee? To the uninitiated, the logical first response is: "To make money." But, in my opinion, making money, in the sense of making a profit, should not be the primary motive. A successful fee-based service can certainly generate invoices totaling hundreds of thousands of dollars. By 1996, Purdue's nine-year-old Technical Information Service (TIS), staffed by a quarter-time manager, three and a half professionals, five support staff, and four full-time equivalent (FTE) student assistants, annually completed over 500 research projects and shipped over 17,000 document delivery orders to clients around the globe. But even although TIS is one of the highest-volume academic fee-based information services in the United States, its goal is simply to break even at the end of each year. Every dollar generated in fees goes to pay the expenses incurred in operating the service. In addition, TIS is a non-profit unit of a non-profit state institution and, as such, cost-recovery, not profit, is its goal.

If the best a library can hope for is a balanced budget at the end of the year, especially during the first few years of operation, why start a fee-based information service at all? The answer is the same reason many of us chose library careers in the first place: to provide excellent information services to users. A fee-based information service serves users for whom traditional or routine academic library services are not mandated (nor adequately funded or staffed) to serve: non-primary clientele. A fee-based service also provides the library with the chance to enhance public relations between the university and the business community. In a publicly supported university, a fee-based information service provides a convenient mechanism for providing value-added information products and services to its citizens.

Helen Josephine listed the elements essential for establishing and maintaining a successful fee-based information service:

1. A dedicated innovative team manager with vision who sets self-determined goals;
2. An administrative environment that encourages autonomy and rewards innovation; and
3. An institutional environment that embraces the objectives of the service and incorporates them into the overall goals and mission statement (Josephine 1989, p. 156).

Managers' Views

Several managers and other librarians have written about their insights in starting fee-based services. Frances K. Wood identified four factors for starting a service and pointed out that the final decision is based on at least one of them:

> the service can bring in additional, needed revenue; overwhelmed by outside user requests for information, the library or information center staff needs to have some of the pressure removed (charging fees may cut down on the number of requests and/or generate money for additional staffing); the service can be a good public relations/outreach vehicle; and since everyone else is selling information, the administration wants to get into the act (Wood 1987, p. 25).

Diane Richards mentioned that the service at North Dakota State University Libraries started to handle increasing demands by non-primary clientele to respond both to a statewide economic development effort and to the university's interest in providing academic resources to the business community (Richards 1991, p. 15). Other managers cited imposing fees as a means of discouraging, controlling, rationing, or reducing use by non-primary users (Carter and Pagel 1984, p. 245; Downing 1990, p. 59; Franks and Montgomery 1991, p. 15; Roeder 1987, p. 172). Carlton Rochell suggested that libraries should provide information services at competitive, not bargain, rates for customers who "recognize and treat information as a commodity, and who use it for profit" (Rochell 1985, p. 22). Librarians at the University of Rochester noticed that local information brokers used the library to meet their customers' needs, and decided to make their own resources available to the business community. A local company also approached the library requesting services for a fee (Caren and Somerville 1988, pp. 39-40).

At an urban law library, not only was the collection heavily used, but a survey also showed that a large percentage of reader space was being occupied by secondary users. This library sought to restrict physical access to the premises, as well as to implement fees for certain services (Carter and Pagel 1984, p. 247). Other librarians specifically mentioned "service to alumni" and the need to alleviate "pressure on reference staff from external users" (Ernest 1993, p. 398).

For-Profit Motivation

The literature documents cases in which profit was a major reasons for establishing fee-based information services. For example, librarians at the Louis Calder Memorial Library at the University of Miami School of Medicine reported that they developed their fee-based service specifically to "obtain continuing sources of support for recurring expenditures" (Williams, Lemkau, and Burrows 1988, p. 319). This library not only charged corporations, individuals, and hospitals for information services but also billed the institution's primary clientele, the medical school faculty. Since the same people who staffed the library also provided the fee-based services, it seems likely that income did not have to cover salaries and fringe benefits. Thus, this service more easily made a profit from its fees. A service such as this one, that charges both internal and external users, operates under a slightly different definition of a fee-based information service than the kind described in this book.

TREATING INFORMATION AS A COMMODITY

Supplying information as a commodity usually requires a philosophical shift in the way most academic librarians regard their service mission. How easy will it be to attain and sustain the new attitude of providing premium services at a premium rate for paying customers? Are there people already in the system, or can the library easily attract, the kind of people who meet the requirements for working in an entrepreneurial unit operating on a business, not academic, model? Voigt described the characteristics of successful information providers for the corporate community:

> They are very much like a reference librarian in that the individual must understand that information is power; must understand the actual needs of the user; must have excellent listening, communicating, and interviewing skills; must be flexible and adaptable; must be able to organize, synthesize, and interpret information; must be able to teach and work with users unfamiliar with library materials; and must have some administrative ability. In addition, a logical, analytical mind is important in doing research together with self-confidence, a retentive memory, perseverance and patience, and efficient work habits. Skills needed in addition to the above librarian skills include business expertise in statistics, public relations, and sampling (Voigt 1988, p. 24).

Can the library and university system adapt to the needs of such a unit, in terms of sharing its resources and providing financial, administrative, and computing support in a fast and flexible manner?

FIRST STEPS

The impetus for considering establishing a fee-based information service may come from one of several directions. Sometimes an upper administrator wants to investigate the feasibility of having a service and delegates the background investigation to another librarian or to a task force. Sometimes the idea comes from further down the administrative ladder, from a branch library or department head, from an individual, or from a group of librarians who perceive a need for responding in a systematic and organized way to requests from the business community. No matter who originates the first idea, most librarians would concede the wisdom of some preliminary research before putting a microcomputer into an empty office and printing up business cards.

The analogy of a fee-based information service as a small business is especially valid in the initial planning stages. No savvy entrepreneur would rent and equip an office without first carefully planning the business. Likewise, no library should make the investment required to launch a fee-based information service successfully without first:

1. Ascertaining the institution's reaction to the suggestion;
2. Checking the feasibility of operating a service in the local institutional environment; and
3. Preparing a solid business plan outlining the service's goals and how they will be attained.

While it is true that a fee-based information service will generate income, it is virtually impossible to begin a service without first allocating some resources to establish it. Bob Norton commented that "before resource allocation comes the question of defensible and justified resource attraction" (Norton 1988, p. 19). No matter how philosophically supportive the library administrators, they will almost certainly require convincing evidence that allocating funds, space, and staff to the program is fiscally justifiable.

HOW SHOULD THE LIBRARY START ITS INVESTIGATION?

There are a number of ways that libraries approach the planning stage of a fee-based information service. Reported methods include:

- A six-month planning period during which the structures of existing fee-based services were compared (Franks and Montgomery 1991, p. 15).
- Establishing a task force to write a policy statement and to determine "service definition, administrative organization, staffing needs, clientele, and fees" (Richards 1991, p. 15).
- Making decisions about key issues, conducting a marketing survey, and setting policy (Wood 1987, pp. 25-26).
- Developing a business plan (Grund 1992, p. 115).
- Offering services on a trial basis to selected clients, using existing staff and resources (Caren and Somerville 1988, p. 40). I do not recommend this approach.
- Hiring a corporate services librarian to assess external users' needs, and to develop and implement a business plan (Josephine and Reneker 1989, p. 378).
- Writing a proposal (Beaubien 1983).
- Undertaking market research, and forming a steering group from local business to gather opinions from potential clients (McGuire 1993, p. 125).

- Interviewing selected local business professionals and corporate librarians (Richards and Widdicombe 1985, p. 61).

I recommend a two-stage approach to the initial investigation: first, a proposal, and then, following a strong indication of administrative interest and support, a detailed business plan.

THE PRINCIPAL INVESTIGATOR

The first step in beginning this planning process is to appoint the principal investigator. This investigator may be self-appointed, acting either independently at the proposal stage or on the basis of an initially positive general discussion with an immediate supervisor, typically a department head or assistant director. If the initial interest sprang from the library administrators, they may name an investigator with little knowledge or preparation (or even initial interest).

The administration should choose the investigator carefully. The investigator should be someone who, if not already familiar with the concept, would be likely to be enthusiastic about it. This librarian should not be someone who is strongly opposed to charging user fees. Good organizational, research, and writing skills are essential, as is a strong customer service orientation. The investigator should have been with the library long enough to be familiar with the institutional environment and to know how to use it advantageously. Colleagues should respect the investigator. The administrators should be prepared to negotiate with the investigator's immediate supervisor for short-term release time to prepare the proposal, with the understanding that more substantial release time will be required if a business plan is later requested.

The investigator, whether self-appointed or named, should have a clear understanding of the role throughout the planning process, and later in the early stages of establishing the fee-based service. Resolve questions such as:

- Are the only tasks to review the situation, complete the preliminary groundwork, and make recommendations for setting up the service?
- Will the investigator work independently on both the proposal and the business plan, or will there be the option (or mandate) of working with a small group on the plan?
- To whom is the investigator responsible for completing this work, if not to the usual supervisor?
- Does the investigator, or the administrators, anticipate a further role for the investigator when the service is established? If so, what is that role?
- Do the administrators envision the investigator on the staff of the new service, and if so, in what capacity? As an information specialist? As the manager? As the person to whom the service reports? Or just as an advisor during the first year of operation?

- Is the investigator comfortable with any anticipated or expected role, or is there an expectation for more (or less) than the administration seems willing to consider?

Unclear expectations or vague statements at this point may lead to misunderstandings or discontent later, so it is important that all parties agree about the investigator's anticipated role from the beginning. Everyone may later agree to change that role, but a clear initial understanding will prevent future discord. Although hiring a consultant may be appropriate at a later stage, I recommend that the initial proposal be prepared by one of the institution's librarians.

THE PROPOSAL

Even if a small team will later be assigned to research and write the business plan, the proposal might best be prepared over a few weeks by the principal investigator, either working alone if self-designated, or with the guidance of the appointing administrator.

The main virtue of the proposal is that it should be short. Ten pages should be sufficient. The proposal states the reasons why the library should consider starting a fee-based information service and points out the benefits to the library, the university, and the potential clients. It may highlight the successes enjoyed by established fee-based services in similar institutions. It offers to conduct an in-depth investigation (the business plan) and briefly presents the major issues that must be discussed and resolved as a result of that further investigation. The proposal's major goal is to paint a broad and positive picture. It demonstrates that the investigator has identified the major issues and is willing and able to explore them further but has not invested time to propose specific solutions before the administration has approved the concept. The proposal concludes by asking the administrators to indicate their interest in the idea by approving a small budget and some release time for conducting further research and preparing the business plan.

The investigator submits the proposal to the library administration to gauge the interest and support that such an idea generates. If it elicits little enthusiasm, the time might not be right to pursue the matter further. On the other hand, if the administrators indicate interest in seeing a more detailed study, the investigator then begins the second stage, preparing the business plan.

CITED REFERENCES

Beaubien, A.K. 1983. "Michigan Information Transfer Source: Fee-Based Information Service." *Library Hi Tech* 1(Fall): 69-71.

Caren, L., and A. Somerville. 1988. "Issues Facing Private Academic Libraries Considering Fee-Based Programs." *The Reference Librarian* (22): 37-49.

Carter, N.C., and S.B. Pagel. 1984. "Fees for Service: The Golden Gate University Law Library Membership Plan." *Law Library Journal* 77(2): 243-274.

Downing, A. 1990. "The Consequences of Offering Fee-Based Services in a Medical Library." *Bulletin of the Medical Library Association* 78(1): 57-63.

Ernest, D.J. 1993. "Academic Libraries, Fee-Based Information Services, and the Business Community." *RQ* 32(3): 393-402.

Franks, J.A., and K.K. Montgomery. 1991. "LINE: The Fee-Based Service at the University of Central Florida Library." *Mississippi Libraries* 55(Spring): 15-17.

Grund, D. 1992. "Fee-Based Information Services: Serving Business/Strengthening the LRC." Pp. 113-121 in *Community College Reference Services*, edited by B. Katz. Metuchen, NJ: Scarecrow Press.

Josephine, H.B. 1989. "Intrapreneurship in Fee-Based Information Services." *Journal of Library Administration* 10(2-3): 151-158.

Josephine, H.B., and M.H. Reneker. 1989. "In Defense of FIRST and Freedom of Access to Information." *College and Research Libraries News* 50(5): 377-379.

McGuire, K. 1993. "Information Direct: Birmingham Library Services' Fee-Based Business Service." *Law Librarian* 24 (September): 125-126.

Norton, B. 1988. *Charging for Library and Information Services*. London: Library Association.

Richards, B.G., and R. Widdicombe. 1985. "Fee-Based Information Services to Industry. Pp. 59-64 in *The Future of Information Resources for Science and Technology and The role of Libraries*, edited by N. Fjällbrant. Göteborg, Sweden: Chalmers University Technology Library.

Richards, D. 1991. "Starting a Fee-Based Service in a Rural Area." *The Bottom Line* 5(1): 14-17.

Rochell, C. 1985. "The Knowledge Business: Economic Issues of Access to Bibliographic Information." *Information Reports and Bibliographies* 14(4): 17-23.

Roeder, C.S. 1987. "Access Fees in a Hospital Library: A Program for Pharmaceutical Company Representatives." *Bulletin of the Medical Library Association* 75(2): 171-173.

Voigt, K.J. 1988. "Computer Search Services and Information Brokering in Academic Libraries." *The Reference Librarian* (22): 17-36.

Williams, T.L., H.L. Lemkau, and S. Burrows. 1988. "The Economics of Academic Health Science Libraries: Cost Recovery in the Era of Big Science." *Bulletin of the Medical Library Association* 76(4): 317-322.

Wood, F.K. 1987. "When Do Dollars for Information Service Make Sense? The Wisconsin ISD Experience." *The Bottom Line* 1(4): 25-27.

Chapter 3

Background Research: Preparing the Business Plan

Once library administrators review the initial short proposal and indicate that they are receptive to the idea of establishing a fee-based information service, the investigator's next challenge is to write the business plan. Preparing the business plan accomplishes several objectives. It provides the enthusiastic investigator with a reality check, driving home the fact that planning and establishing a fee-based information service properly will be both time-consuming and expensive. The plan also forces the investigator to gather concrete information on issues such as the potential client base, estimated start-up costs, staffing, marketing, institutional requirements, and the competition. The purpose of preparing the plan is to provide enough information so that library administrators can make an informed decision, based on the local situation, about whether to make a firm commitment to establish a fee-based service.

An administrator may ask if hiring a consultant to prepare the business plan would be cost-effective. In my opinion, this option is neither cost-effective nor desirable. A librarian already familiar with the local environment can much more quickly and efficiently (and cheaply) gather and summarize the information needed. The investigator usually has a stake, or at least a strong interest or enthusiasm, in the proposed service, as well as knowledge of the university and its libraries, that an outside consultant, no matter how skilled in preparing business plans for fee-based information services, will be unable to acquire in a short campus visit. However, it can be advantageous to hire a consultant at a later stage, after administrators have reviewed the business plan but feel reluctant to make the final commitment without an outside expert opinion. The next chapter discusses working with a consultant to obtain independent confirmation that the budgets, strategies, and goals presented in the business plan are indeed accurate, reasonable, and necessary.

The investigator may work alone, or the administrator may appoint a small team of investigators. In the case of a team approach, designate one of the members as the principal investigator. The principal investigator's responsibilities are to:

- Establish a time line for completing the business plan;
- Assign each team member's area of investigation;
- Call meetings;
- Keep the investigation on track;
- Coordinate writing the plan; and
- Present the final document to the administration.

Reviewing several handbooks on proposal preparation may be helpful. The final document consists at least these three major parts:

1. An executive summary;
2. The text—a narrative section covering the major points discussed in this chapter; and
3. A projected budget for the first few years' operation.

The plan may also include relevant appendices and a bibliography.

GETTING STARTED

A good way to start is to prepare a rough outline of the text listing the major areas to be included in the business plan. The executive summary, despite being the first element of the business plan, will be written last. The sections following "The Business Plan" heading in this chapter provide a basic beginning outline. Set up a series of folders, each labeled with a heading from the outline. As the investigator finds pieces of information about each heading, add them to the appropriate folder.

Prepare two additional folders or notebooks, one for jotting down questions and another for noting the costs of the various elements needed to start and maintain a fee-based information service. These notes for the budget should not consume a lot of time or energy during the first half of the investigation, but as the investigator learns facts such as the recent price paid for a fax machine or the starting hourly rate for a billing clerk, make a note of them.

Guard against the tendency to focus too heavily on promotional issues at the beginning of the investigation. Marketing is certainly a key issue, and most people agree that developing promotional materials is one of the most fun and creative aspects of establishing a fee-based information service. However, I advise against considering it in detail until after having made some of the less glamorous, but equally critical, recommendations in areas such as defining services, writing the mission statement, and drafting a budget. As the investigator discovers in reviewing standard texts, marketing involves many more activities than simply mailing out brochures and waiting for the orders to roll in.

The business plan lays the marketing foundations. If the investigator has already defined what services to offer, for example, at least some of the questions regarding the target client base will have been answered. Once the target client base has been defined, then some of the marketing questions will have answered themselves. The reality of potential funding will drive other marketing decisions. So curb the urge to write the promotional brochure at the outset of the investigation. By the plan's final draft, the investigator will have made recommendations for marketing and promoting the fee-based information service, but time spent developing a brochure is much better invested in the implementation stage.

THE BUSINESS PLAN

The following sections cover the major issues that the business plan addresses. Even though many of the issues are interrelated, it may be helpful to review them in the order presented below. This chapter asks a lot of questions but does not necessarily answer all of them directly or definitively. Many of the answers depend on the unique situation at each institution. A solution that works well at Purdue's Technical Information Service, for instance, may be impossible or impractical to implement at another university because of local policies and regulations. This chapter guides the investigator through the issues; the job is to discover the answers that will work in the local situation.

A final point to remember is that while the investigator asks all these questions and makes recommendations about the answers, everything need not be decided or implemented at once. For instance, the investigator might suggest that while offering document special orders would be desirable in the long term, in the short term the service should initially fill orders from the local collection only. As another example, although offering clients options such as deposit accounts or credit card payment may eventually be desirable, the immediate goal is to establish a monthly billing procedure.

Basic Research

The first step involves general information-gathering or background research, a task that should not daunt an investigating librarian. For a general overview of issues about fee-based information services, begin with a review of the literature. This book's references provide an overview up until the time the manuscript was submitted for publication. For other or more recent citations, check the LISA database, ERIC, and *Library Literature*. Look for articles about starting an information broker business as well as about managing fee-based information services. Contact the current editor of *FISCAL Facts*, the newsletter from FISCAL (Fee-

Based Information Services Centers in Academic Libraries), an American Library Association discussion group, and ask for a few of the most recent back issues. Also ask which fee-based service currently sells the *FISCAL Primer*, a varying compilation of assorted brochures and promotional material from a variety of fee-based information services. Subscribe to FISC-L, FISCAL's listserv. Purchase the recent edition of the *Burwell World Directory of Information Brokers* and the *Internet-Plus Directory of Express Library Services* with some of the funds requested in the proposal (see Chapter 2).

Contacting Established Services

The basic research will identify general articles and directory listings about fee-based information services (and it will not hurt to read a few articles that react negatively to the notion of charging fees for library services). Identify services similar to the one planned locally and compile a list of five or six ones of the same type and size of institution, in a similarly sized metropolitan area, and/or with similar local industries.

Make initial contacts with the managers of these services with brief phone calls. This preliminary information-gathering stage is *not* the time to send lengthy questionnaires or engage in hour-long phone conversations. The investigator explains the local institution's interest in establishing a fee-based information service and asks for the standard packet of promotional materials that the service sends to new or prospective clients. This promotional material will answer many basic questions.

The time to ask specific questions such as what accounting software another service uses or how the service reports copyright comes later, after the library has given the green light for establishing the service and implementing the business plan (see Chapter 5). The investigator thanks the managers for their time and, when reviewing the materials they sent, notes any specific questions to ask later.

Fee-based service managers are usually glad to help colleagues, but remember that they essentially run businesses. Thirty minutes on the phone with the investigator means 30 minutes that they are unable to spend on income-generating work their clients have requested. Most managers will not grudge this time when properly approached as described in Chapter 5, but many will be understandably reluctant to spend a lot of time outlining basic issues that the caller can easily find out with a little research. It is always a nice touch to send a brief thank you note after receiving the promotional packets. When the investigator contacts two or three of these managers again at the implementation stage, they are more likely to remember the encounter favorably if they received a short note after their response to the initial request. Also remember that these established services may one day become document suppliers and/or customers of the investigator's new service. The business plan stage is not too soon to begin establishing professional contacts with potentially helpful colleagues.

Reviewing the Promotional Packets

Most of the promotional packets contain at least a general information brochure listing fees and describing services available to potential clients. Some packets include additional items, such as a newsletter, reprints of staff-written articles, an annual report, or a promotional giveaway item such as a bookmark or calendar.

Evaluating the design and layout of the promotional pieces comes later in the marketing section of the business plan. While working through the next few sections, refer back to the articles and promotional materials to see how other fee-based services have successfully solved some of the issues under investigation.

Basic Texts

Now is the time to review a few basic textbooks on starting small businesses, writing business plans, and marketing, especially for non-profit organizations. Not everything in these books will apply to setting up a non-profit, cost-recovery fee-based information service in an academic library, but a basic understanding of the major concepts will enable the investigator to prepare a thorough and comprehensive business plan. Although the references at the end of this chapter suggest several books on these topics, the astute investigator will identify and read other helpful titles.

Follow-up Research

After completing the basic background research, the investigator may feel overwhelmed and unsure about what to do next. Should investigating possible funding sources come first, or figuring out how to reach prospective clients, or worrying about staff or copyright or what brand of fax machine to recommend? All these issues are important, and many of them, such as potential clients and marketing issues and basic services, are so closely related that it is difficult to consider them separately from one another. Despite being overwhelmed, the investigator may also feel even more excited about the prospect of developing a local fee-based service.

Keep the idea firmly in mind that the current task is to prepare the business plan. While filling in more detail than the initial proposal, the plan still paints the picture in fairly broad strokes. While it is appropriate to point out that the new service will need a fax machine and to provide cost estimates for it in the suggested budget, agonizing at this stage over which model to buy will only sidetrack the investigator from the task at hand. Whenever the investigator feels the research going off track, ask: "Is resolving this issue part of the planning process, or is it a detail better left till the implementation stage?"

Mission, Goals, and Objectives

Draft a mission statement, along with the goals and objectives necessary to fulfill that mission. The mission statement provides the framework for the rest of the investigation. Generally, the mission statement answers these questions:

- Why is the institution offering the service?
- Who are the customers?
- Where are the customers?
- What are the customers' needs?
- How will the fee-based information service meet these needs?
- Who are the major competitors?

The goals and objectives section addresses issues such as:

- How will the service raise the funds and other resources to support it?
- Who is eligible for service?
- What segments, if any, of the total potential user group are part of a target group?

The mission will be a sentence or two defining in broad terms what the service plans to do. Although the investigator sketches out specific goals and objectives at this point, it will almost certainly be necessary to return to the list later in the investigation. Further research will probably suggest at least some different, or revised, goals and objectives.

Although most fee-based information services share the same mission of meeting the business community's information needs, no two services will have identical goals and objectives. A service operating out of a medical library, for example, will have a slightly different mission and a vastly different target customer base than a service intended to assist the general business community or the region's law firms.

Analyzing Resources and Defining Services

Many marketing textbooks rightly suggest that the reader first identify the market, then segment the market to target specific groups, and finally develop products or services that meet the needs of those segments. In developing a library fee-based information service, however, it makes more sense to reverse the procedure by identifying those products and services that the proposed information service could deliver well, and then identify the market segment that would form the potential client base for those services. If, for example, the library's resources in computer science mainly support the undergraduate curriculum, it would be a mistake to target software development companies whose engineers need research-level material.

In the first place, there is a fairly limited range of services that can be offered, and second, a major part of those services, at least initially, will probably be document delivery from the local library collection, and the collection, if defined as a product, is an element over which the service's manager has little control.

Scope of Services. After reading or skimming the major articles identified during the basic research stage above, the principal investigator has begun to form an idea of how a fee-based information service would function in the local institution. One of the first tasks is to assess the strengths and weaknesses of the local resource base. Will the service attempt to cover virtually all subject areas? Or will it concentrate on a single area such as business, medicine, law, or engineering? The answer to this question may be a foregone conclusion if, for example, the investigator has a clear mandate from the health science library's administration to check the feasibility of starting a specialized medical fee-based service. In other cases, the vision calls for the creation of a fee-based service that cuts across most subject disciplines.

Having a clear idea of the service's potential subject scope early in the investigation drives other issues such as the potential client base, desirable skills of the proposed professional staff, and which other libraries in the system would be most affected by the presence of a fee-based service drawing on their resources. The subject scope naturally reflects both the library's collection strengths and the anticipated information needs of the expected client base.

There are pros and cons for either decision. A specialized service usually draws on a collection in a single library, a collection that the staff will come to know better than if they tried to learn the quirks and specialties of a dozen or more branch libraries on campus. Professional staff in a specialized service will be expected to have significant experience and skills providing information services solely in that subject and, in general, one would expect their information skills in the specialized discipline to be better than those of a generalist.

Drawbacks include the fact that the specialization may limit the potential client base. In addition, many subjects have become multidisciplinary. An experienced medical searcher, for example, might not have the training to search a patent database effectively to identify patents for a particular medical device or have the experience to follow up with a search through the business literature to find articles and reports about the potential European market for that device. The in-house collection might also be strong in clinical medicine titles but weaker in related subscriptions for biomechanics or chemistry.

Remember, however, that in an electronically connected library world quickly changing from ownership to access, a fee-based service can retrieve information from non-locally owned sources almost as fast as it can from a building across campus. Weaknesses in some areas of the collection need not necessarily preclude the ability to provide information services in that discipline. It is true that even a specialized academic library collection, developed specifically to meet the educational and research needs of students and faculty, will not contain all the material necessary to support industry's needs. However, a fee-based information service's success rests in part on its staff's ability to obtain quickly any items unavailable locally. In fact, this argument against starting a service—that the collection cannot support the clients' needs—becomes woefully thin as libraries' budgets prevent them from collecting some of the material necessary to support their primary users' needs. In addition, commercial information brokers have availed themselves of academic collections for years and found them adequate.

A fee-based service that aspires to comprehensive subject coverage faces different challenges. With a potential client base of virtually every company in the region, it can be difficult to decide how to begin the marketing program, especially when the early start-up months are so critical. Managing a document delivery service ranging over a large campus takes more staff time and ingenuity than does a similar operation in a single library building. Information professionals must have the flexibility, creativity, and skills to handle queries on everything from commodity futures to the solubility of polypropylene.

Will the service be comprehensive except for one or two disciplines? Purdue's Technical Information Service (TIS) strives to "cover the waterfront" as a client once said, with the exception of legal and chemical questions. In the case of legal questions, we felt that since there was no law school on Purdue's West Lafayette campus and, hence, no law collection, we would not be able to answer clients' questions well enough. So we have no subscriptions to specialized legal databases, and the professional staff accept requests no more complicated than document delivery for laws and regulations. We also recognize our limits in the area of chemical information. None of the information specialists on staff have advanced searching skills or education in chemistry, so we have opted to recognize that our limitations in this area mean we are unable to research questions much more complex than the environmental fate of a chemical. In the cases of both these types of questions, we refer clients to other fee-based services with legal and chemical information experts on staff.

Basic Services: Research and Document Delivery. After deciding whether the new fee-based service will specialize or attempt comprehensive coverage, the next consideration involves services. Traditionally, fee-based information services offer both research services and document delivery, but the ratio varies widely. At Purdue's Technical Information Service, the pattern for years has settled at 25 percent research and 75 percent document delivery. A few other services find that these proportions are reversed. At least one other service now outsources almost all of its relatively low number of document delivery requests and concentrates on research. Another outsources its research questions but fills document delivery orders.

At the business plan stage, the principal investigator will not know the best local mix of services, but I recommend that the plan include the intention to provide both research and document delivery. Although some clients will only use one or the other of these services, many will use both. The two services are in many respects complementary. Research projects frequently generate document delivery requests, and some document delivery orders require at least basic research skills, usually to identify a vaguely defined item ("My boss needs a copy of the first building code published in our state, but we don't know the title, publisher, or publication date"), but sometimes even to obtain it.

With document delivery as part of the mix, consider the following issues:

- Will the service draw on the local collection only?
- Will the service handle special orders for documents that the institution does not own?
- How will the service fill document special requests?
- What is the best way to build supplier relationships with other fee-based information services?
- How reliable are commercial document delivery firms?
- How many document suppliers should the service use?
- Does the service aim to be comprehensive in obtaining special order documents, or will staff check a few standard sources only, such as OCLC and one or two commercial suppliers, and then cancel any document requests unavailable through these sources?
- How can the staff gain expertise in acquiring specialized documents?

Some services build a thriving customer base drawing on the resources of the local collection only; others, like TIS, pride themselves on going almost literally to the ends of the earth to obtain obscure international documents. Still others find a middle path.

Consider the question of providing document delivery from outside sources carefully. Almost all services will want to offer special orders eventually, but decide whether the new service wants to get involved with it at all during its start-up months. Establishing procedures for filling orders from the local collection will be complicated enough without adding the pressure to identify and obtain items from other sources as well.

In the TIS case, this decision was made for us. Our initial funding in 1987 and 1988 came entirely from a state economic development grant that stipulated that we were not to charge clients (Indiana residents only, at that time) for our services. With no cost-recovery mechanism in place and with only limited grant funds available, we could only afford to fill orders from the Purdue Libraries collection. Since clients at that time received Purdue items free, they did not complain too much when we explained that we were unable to obtain other documents for them. During this 18-month period, TIS staff were able to develop and refine most basic procedures (except billing). When TIS made the transition to cost-recovery operations in early 1989, adding a special order component was much easier to implement.

Librarians with no in-depth interlibrary loan or document delivery experience sometimes underestimate its complexity. There is a tendency to regard it as the relatively simple process of sending student assistants all over campus to photocopy articles. While a high percentage of document delivery requests are straightforward, a significant minority of them require intervention or handling by the professional staff or by support staff with advanced training or experience in document delivery.

Potential difficulties include requests for documents with one or more of the following challenges:

- Poor handwriting or typographical errors;
- Foreign languages;
- Abbreviations;
- Conferences cataloged as serials, as monographs, as journal special issues, or some combination of these;
- Government documents that change titles, agencies, frequency, or format;
- Government publications that are not part of the document depository program;
- Journal titles that change name, publisher, frequency, or volume numbering;
- Items that libraries catalog as serials or not at all, such as standards, specifications, patents, or technical reports;
- Specialized publications that no libraries ever acquired or cataloged; and
- International publications with no national holdings.

Clients usually have no additional information other than their original scrambled citation. They expect the fee-based service staff to identify and locate the material, often on a rush basis. These expectations define the value-added component of document delivery. The investigator notes that staffing requirements will include some professional time for handling difficult document requests.

Other Services. The investigator considers other services that the proposed fee-based information program might offer. Is there something unique or unusual about the local collection that can be offered to clients? The New Mexico State University library, for example, built its service around the Southwest Center for Codes and Standards. Does the institution offer any special services, programs, databases, or expertise that can be connected with the service? Could specialized expertise be built into the fee-based service? Possible additional services include:

- Acquisitions
- Analytical reports
- Bibliographies
- Cataloging
- Conference planning and organization
- Consulting

- Editing
- Identifying experts
- Indexing or abstracting
- Instruction in the use of information resources
- Newsletter publishing
- Primary research (e.g., surveys, questionnaires)
- Seminars or workshops
- Setting up corporate libraries
- Speech writing
- Technical writing
- Translating

The investigator considers the options carefully before recommending additions to the service mix. Would the benefit of adding a service be worth the extra costs for hiring or training staff and for marketing the special services? Extra services usually mean more staff, as few people are both crackerjack database searchers and experienced questionnaire designers as well. Offering translation services, for example, would be a mistake unless the service had access to reliable translators experienced in translating specialized subjects such as medical reports or technical manuals. Indexing and cataloging are so labor intensive, and thus so expensive, that it would probably be best to refer the few clients who inquired about it to organizations specializing in these activities. Offering to analyze research gathered from secondary sources leads to complicated liability questions. However, a series of seminars for local businesspeople on Internet access and navigation may both generate revenue and attract new clients.

While it would be unwise to offer too many additional services on opening day, the investigator lists all the reasonable options, recommending one, or at most two, extra services that are important enough to offer first, based on expected market needs and staff expertise. Identify which services are outside the scope of the proposed program, and mention others that might be offered later.

At this stage, the investigator need not agonize over which services might be appropriate but should spend enough time to identify a range of services that might be offered, and to prioritize the most important ones. Keep in mind, however, that many successful fee-based information services thrive offering just document delivery and research, or even only one of these two. Extra offerings are not essential to success, although in a later stage of development they may be the key to growth. At the beginning, "it may be easier to start with a few well-defined services than to overextend and become overwhelmed" (Caren and Somerville 1988, p. 41).

Potential Clients and Their Information Needs

Once the mission statement has been drafted and the major service mix identified, determining the potential client base is an easier task. One important question to answer is "Who are the potential clients?"

- Will clients come primarily from particular industries (e.g., manufacturers, or more specifically, plastics manufacturers) or services (e.g., law firms or environmental consultants)?
- Will clients come from a mix of industries or services?
- Will it be best to target firms at a local, state, regional, or national level?
- Will the proposed fee-based service offer such specifically tailored services that it needs a national client base to support it?
- Are there certain groups it would be politic to include or exclude?
- Should any special considerations be made for alumni?

It is tempting to suggest that the proposed program will serve anybody willing and able to pay for services. Although the service may evolve to embrace this philosophy, an investigator narrows the field to a clearly identifiable, appropriate, and reachable target audience selected to match the strengths of the collection and other resources upon which the service will draw.

The target market should also be one that can both afford information services and provide repeat business. To survive, the service needs to cultivate clients with frequent information needs. These clients are more often found in easily identifiable medium and large companies. An investigator facing constraints due to administrative idealism, funding agency mandates, or other issues insists that at least half the marketing effort be directed towards large companies in the target user group. Balance demands for social responsibility with the vital necessity for generating enough income to survive.

What do these clients need? In most cases, if a library is considering a fee-based service at all, there has already been at least a low level of demand for services from local people unaffiliated with the institution. Who are they and what do they need? Are they paralegals grumbling about the hours spent with the patent collection, engineers checking out industry standards, secretaries copying articles, or junior executives searching the CD-ROMs? Are they unidentified business callers wondering about the gross national product of Thailand or how many corporate jets were in service last year? Conversations with the investigator's colleagues in the campus libraries reveal some general information about these types of queries. Remember to ask the weekend and evening reference staff, especially if professionals do not work these shifts in some branch libraries.

The main point to remember is that although the potential client base is virtually limitless, the fee-based service cannot possibly identify and meet everyone's needs. Trying to do so invites failure. Especially when starting out, concentrate on serving a few people well rather than a wide range of clients in a mediocre fashion. By focusing on a specific, easily identifiable, easily reachable target client base, especially at first, the service builds both reputation and expertise in a well-defined area. The manager will also be better able to determine if the service is meeting its goal of attracting a particular type of client that its mission mandates it serve. The service may certainly accept orders and projects from people outside the target client base, and may later expand its marketing efforts to include other specific groups, but be sure to define the initial focus clearly.

For example, Purdue's Technical Information Service focuses on serving small- and medium-sized Indiana manufacturers, especially for research projects. This mandate comes from the state economic agency that provides part of our funding, but it also makes sense in terms of focusing on a particular client base. We search the appropriate database files by selected Standard Industrial Classification (SIC) codes and company size codes to produce a mailing list of target companies to which we send marketing letters and brochures. The trade journals in which we might advertise form a relatively small, finite group. As a result of the marketing strategy suggested by this mandate, three-quarters of the research work we complete is for Indiana companies in this size range.

However, our mission does not preclude us from serving other types of customers who learn about TIS and request services. We ran a patent search for a local dentist who later patented the dental device he had invented; we occasionally track down obscure international documents for Purdue graduate students or faculty when the items they need are outside the scope of our interlibrary loan department to obtain; and we fill the document requests arriving from around the world from individuals, companies, and universities addressed to "Library, Purdue University, Indiana, USA." Although we serve these types of clients when they find us, we do not specifically include them in our marketing efforts.

Market Research

Should the investigator suggest, or even implement, extensive market research to determine the potential level of business that could be expected from the target audience? Some fee-based information services, including Purdue's Technical Information Service, were founded and have successfully operated for years without formal market research ever having been done (Wood 1987, p. 26). In other institutions, the administrators may feel more comfortable if the results of a small research project indicate enough positive local interest to justify establishing the service.

Implementing market research is more involved than writing a quick questionnaire to send to the presidents of half the local companies with more than 50 employees. Surveys are, in fact, only one of several market research techniques that might be appropriate. Investigators deciding to recommend or undertake a market research project review at least several books about how to design, distribute, and tabulate meaningful surveys or other marketing studies. Corporate respondents will not take the time to work through a long survey with the same diligence or interest that librarians expect from academic colleagues. Getting some advice from an expert in the university's business school would be a good idea.

One approach to this question is to regard the finished business plan itself as a result of market research. The investigator will have compiled a lot of information about everything except the likely response of local businesses to the new service. However, the very existence of both fee-based information services and various similar commercial enterprises proves to a great extent that the market for these services exists. In addition, even when fee-based information services focus most heavily on local or regional business and industry, they also assist clients all over the country and sometimes all over the world. Getting the local industry's reaction to proposed services may not paint the whole picture.

An acceptable solution may be to skip formal market research during the investigative phase. A study can be conducted later if, after they review the completed plan, the library administrators ask the implementer to conduct one.

Competition

Traditionally, librarians have not been trained to identify competitors, to research their strengths and weaknesses, and then to offer a new or different mix of services to lure customers away from the competition and build loyalty to the library. In the past, we knew that the library was a good thing and that the local citizenry, even if they were not all patrons, would also recognize the library as a worthy institution and continue to support it with their tax dollars. Although the economic climate has changed, academic libraries, particularly publicly supported ones, have been partially insulated. Budgets and hours have been cut, but in general not as drastically as those in some public libraries. With the mission of education and research to fulfill, universities pare but generally do not cripple or eliminate their libraries. Still, students and faculty can meet at least some of their information needs from other sources, such as bookstores, the Internet, copy shops, and commercial document delivery firms offering databases and easy ordering options.

A fee-based information service faces even more competitors:

- Local information brokers;
- Larger information brokers with regional or national clienteles;
- Public libraries;
- Other fee-based services in academic, public, or trade association libraries;
- Document delivery firms of varying sizes;
- Firms offering any of the same other services that the investigator proposes the library also offer to clients;
- The local institution's interlibrary loan department; and
- Internet or other electronic sources that invite end users to do their own searching.

Taking the issue of competition to extremes, corporate libraries can even be viewed as competitors. So can other programs at the parent institution, since these projects compete for the same limited funding available to establish and maintain university programs.

The issue of competition should not carry an exclusively negative connotation. Evaluating the industry is an important piece of a business plan for any business. By asking for other fee-based services' brochures, the investigator has, among other things, checked out the competition. As a result of canvassing the competition, the investigator learns:

- What types of services have been successful elsewhere?
- What prices are clients apparently willing to pay?
- What turnaround times seem to be the industry average, the turnaround that the proposed new service must at least meet, if not beat?
- What other similar services compete for the same local or regional clientele that the new service would approach?
- How can the proposed service differentiate itself from these competitors?
- Are there some services that the proposed fee-based service could provide better or less expensively?
- What services would the proposed service *not* be able to provide at all, as efficiently, or as economically?

One potentially sensitive issue is that of unfair competition. How will the library address possible accusations from for-profit information brokers that the university-based, non-profit fee-based service competes unfairly with them?

Institutional Requirements

Every library and every university has its own way of handling issues such as space allocation, establishing new staff positions, and billing for services rendered. At this point, the investigator may encounter higher levels of frustration than in any of the previous areas; many universities are not set up to respond quickly or, it often seems, reasonably, to the needs of an entrepreneurial unit.

Space. To identify potential space for the fee-based information service, the investigator works with the library administration or, depending on the institution, with the university space planning or facilities department. The space need not be a prime public service area. Most clients will contact the fee-based service by phone; only a very small percentage of them will ever visit the office in person. Services affiliated with urban institutions may see more drop-in visitors and client couriers. Purdue's Technical Information Service, located in a relatively rural area, sees only a handful of non-campus clients each year in the office. The fee-based service needs an office and standard office furniture, supplies, and equipment. It should be wired, or wiring should be easily able to be installed, for all types of communication that will be needed.

Do not overlook storage space. The office will need much more storage space than a shelf for a box of letterhead and a pile of paper clips. Printing costs are lower when orders for brochures and envelopes are placed in the thousands, but then storing these items becomes a challenge. While writing the business plan, it may be hard to imagine a time when the staff need to order Federal Express envelopes in boxes of a hundred, but that time may come faster than expected. Boxes of bubble envelopes devour space. And no matter what computer system is chosen, there will be at least two or three pieces of paper associated with each order. These paper records should be kept easily accessible for at least a few months, in case clients question their invoices. After these initial few months, additional, and possibly remote, storage must be provided. Not only may some clients question an unpaid invoice over a year later, but the institution probably has standards based on federal requirements about how long supporting documentation for financial transactions must be kept. There is also the possibility of internal audits. The relatively massive storage requirement for promotional materials, bulky office supplies, reference books, database documentation, and back-up paperwork was one aspect of managing a fee-based information service that did not occur to me until our first office was bursting with boxes piled to the ceiling.

It will be more cost-effective in the long run to establish the office in the same building as the library from which the highest level of document delivery is expected. Is this location possible? Does the proposed space need any structural or cosmetic changes, such as closing off a hallway or painting the walls? How much will this cost, and who pays for it? What is the lead time for having the work done?

When the investigator encounters difficulty getting space assigned in the first place, it may be easy to overlook the issue of growth. If the fee-based service is spectacularly successful, then 18 months after Day One, the area that comfortably housed an information specialist, two clerks, and four student assistants will be hopelessly cramped for double or triple that number.

Negotiate for space for potential growth from the outset. Even if the request is not initially successful, the seed has been planted in the administrators' minds; when the manager requests additional space later, the request will not come as a complete surprise. Relocating the office later may be an option, but too-frequent address changes result in lost clients, lost productivity, and increased costs.

If necessary, dip into the planning budget and purchase a 50-foot metal tape measure. Measure each of the proposed office locations. Buy a pad of graph paper and borrow or buy a plastic template with shapes for standard office furniture. As the investigator considers staffing and equipment more fully in the sections below, sketch possible office layouts to see how the furniture will fit into each space. Consider using office layout software if the graph paper and pencil option proves difficult or tedious.

Staffing. As in any library operation, the quality of the staff is perhaps the most critical issue in starting and managing a fee-based service. Having a strong collection, access to hundreds of databases, a superbly equipped office, and a classy brochure will not spell success if the staff is not dedicated to filling clients' needs promptly, professionally, and accurately.

The investigator considers:

- Who will work in the fee-based information service?
- What qualifications should they have?
- How will they be recruited?
- What kinds of specialized training will they need?
- To whom will they report?
- How many employees will be needed during the initial implementation stage and on opening day?
- What mix of employee classifications is optimal?
- How easy and how fast will it be in terms of both space and personnel issues to add staff if demand for services booms?
- Can the service manager offer overtime to the support staff if meeting client demand means working a few additional hours now and then?
- Can temporary staff be easily hired over semester breaks, to fill vacancies, or to handle special projects?
- If the service starts with only one professional, what is the contingency plan if that person is sick or takes vacation or leaves town on a marketing trip?

Finding the right people is often complicated by the fact that the fee-based service's income usually funds the staff's salaries. The library may agree to subsidize the first few start-up months or years, but after that, continued employment usually depends on generating sufficient revenue. For this reason, staff in fee-based information services are usually risk-takers.

I cannot emphasize strongly enough that the staff in a fee-based information service should have one job, and one job only. They should be hired to work in the fee-based service as their only employment responsibility. Trying to staff a service with people who also have major responsibilities elsewhere in the library system is a recipe for failure, rapid staff burnout, or both. For the service to succeed, the staff must concentrate solely on the task of providing quality information services and document delivery to clients.

For similar reasons, the professional staff positions should be not be tenure track. While it may be desirable for the professionals to be involved in a few general library activities, such as serving on one or two committees, it will be extremely difficult for them to do justice both to their own careers and to their clients' needs if they must also meet tenure requirements. This issue may be moot in cases where continuing employment is based largely on sufficient income, since the institution can hardly guarantee continued employment as a tenured faculty member if it cannot also guarantee funds to pay the salary. Some institutions try to circumvent this issue by assigning split appointments to the tenure-track professionals. I have seen several colleagues at other fee-based services burn out with the strain of managing a demanding fee-based information service on a part-time basis, perhaps combined with interlibrary loan or with reference duties, while also struggling to publish, serve on myriad committees, be professionally active, and maintain a satisfactory personal life.

Finding a manager is the first critical task. This is the person who will review the business plan and other background work prepared by the investigator, launch the promotional program, and shape the policies and procedures by which the service will operate.

There are two types of managers for fee-based information services. The first type acts in an administrative or advisory capacity. This type of manager works on a few client projects but for the most part does not participate in the service's daily operation. The manager oversees the staff and administers the program. Purdue started out with this arrangement, with the principal investigator acting as a quarter-time TIS Coordinator.

The second type of manager puts a full-time effort into the service, handling the administrative duties but also spending a significant percentage of time working directly with client projects. Typically, the manager reports to an assistant director.

There are pros and cons for both models. An on-the-spot manager can see some client needs and trends more easily, and can observe office interpersonal dynamics directly. The manager can also become so involved in meeting the constant stream of clients' needs that it is difficult to take the time to stand back and view the whole picture, evaluate the service, and make long- and short-term plans. A manager less involved in daily activities may be in a better position to assess the service and to plan for the future, but compiling statistics alone can never entirely capture the intangible essence of the service, the clients it serves, and the needs it meets. This manager's knowledge of the service becomes anecdotal, rather than actual.

The Manager

Of all the positions, the manager is the most critical. The right combination of skills and attributes is especially essential for the first manager of a new service.

Type of Manager. As explained in previous section on staff, there are two types of managers for fee-based information services. The business plan clearly states what type of manager the position will be: a hands-on (usually full-time) manager or an administrative (usually with a split assignment) manager.

I strongly recommend a hands-on manager for a new service. The staff need someone available in the office most of the time to guide them through the first difficult months. A hands-on manager will be better able to guide the service's development through all the early crises and triumphs, providing everything from practical advice about how best to set up the office filing system to suggesting ways to fine-tune the marketing program.

However, for various institutional reasons, a hands-on manager may not be an option, at least in the beginning as the service establishes itself and proves that it can support this full-time position. In the interim, appoint an administrative manager. This person is usually someone already employed at the library and may be a department head or other librarian interested in or qualified for the responsibility.

The investigator may strongly recommend a hands-on manager but realize that economic or other necessities dictate an administrative manager. The business plan spells out what percentage of the manager's salary, and fringe benefits if required, will be paid from the fee-based service's account and what percentage from library funds. The plan states whether the administrative manager position is intended as a permanent job or as a temporary one with a later transition to a hands-on manager planned for the future after the service establishes itself. If an existing staff member will be the administrative manager, how will the remaining portion of this person's job be covered? If the manager is to be the hands-on type, does the library plan to name an existing staff member, perhaps one of the investigators, as the manager? Will there be any options available for this person's current job to be held open for a specified period in case the manager wants to return to it later?

A Manager's Qualifications.   Chapter 5 includes a list of attributes found in effective managers. The implementer need not draft a full job description for the manager's position, but the business plan outlines the recommended minimum professional qualifications for this position. They will vary somewhat depending on the type of manager recruited, but the plan recommends both minimum and desired qualifications for:

- Educational attainment;
- Subject and level of degrees;
- Years and type of professional library experience;
- Reference, research, and database searching abilities;
- Computer literacy;
- Supervisory experience (of support staff as well as of professionals);
- Experience in a cost-recovery environment;
- Marketing or promotional experience;
- Experience with budgets; and
- Written and oral communication skills.

Which qualifications are essential and which are desirable? If the manager will be recruited from outside the organization, the plan includes suggestions about places to advertise for candidates and the start-up or first year's budget includes realistic costs for advertising the job, as well as for bringing finalist candidates to campus for interviews. Remember that there are some places to advertise that might not be used for regular academic library jobs but might be appropriate for attracting candidates with corporate library experience. Most job-hunting corporate librarians do not read the *Chronicle of Higher Education*, for example; they check the listings in the Sunday classified sections of major local metropolitan newspapers, they scan online joblines, and they read the Special Libraries Association newsletter *The SpeciaList*.

Besides suggesting places to advertise the position, the library's personnel office can provide background information to answer other questions such as:

- What is a reasonable salary to attract qualified candidates for the position, but still remain in the range for jobs with similar department head responsibilities within the library system?
- How long, on average, does it take the institution to hire a professional librarian?
- What are the requirements for a search committee?
- Are there other recruitment considerations?

The plan also includes a recommendation for the point in the implementation process at which an externally recruited manager starts work. If the manager begins as soon as possible after the library administration approves the business plan, this person would then be charged with implementing the plan. This manager would be better prepared for opening day if writing the brochures, overseeing their production, hiring the staff, setting up accounts with database vendors, and choosing and customizing the software had been handled personally. However, this recommendation also means that the library commits itself to paying a professional salary for three months or more before the first invoice goes out.

Choosing the option of hiring a manager closer to opening day means that although there will be some salary savings, someone else will have to spend the time making all the preliminary decisions and arrangements. The manager might not initially be as comfortable with staff and equipment selected by someone else, but this reason is not critical since a new manager joining an established service will face some of the same challenges.

The Manager's Place in the Library's Structure. As a department head, the manager reports to one of the library's top administrators. This place in the reporting structure underscores to the rest of the organization the value and importance with which the administrators view the fee-based information service. James Thompson pointed out that this arrangement "will lend the department weight in its dealings with other departments, and will reduce the possibility of peer or supervisory lack of cooperation and support" (Thompson 1982, p. 70).

Other Professional Staff

If the office starts with an administrative manager, a full-time information specialist is essential if the service will offer research as well a document delivery.

Even with a hands-on manager, another professional in the office will be extremely important, especially during the first months when the manager plans frequent marketing trips and meetings.

Many of the same criteria used for recruiting a manager will apply for selecting additional professional staff. Strong research and communication skills are critical. Length and type of professional experience are not as crucial; after a few months on the job, a fairly recent library school graduate may be as good or better as someone with years of experience. Someone with less experience, however, might be better paired with a hands-on manager rather than left to flounder with little direct contact with a supervisor during the new service's important first months.

Barbara Whyte Felicetti made an important point about information brokers that applies equally to information specialists in fee-based information services. "Brokers aren't experts on everything. The expertise of a broker lies in being an expert on information, in knowing how to find information, in knowing how to extract information" (Felicetti 1982, p. 12). Unless a service caters to a very specialized market, such as law, it is probably not essential for the specialists to hold degrees in relevant subject areas.

Tim C. Green conducted a study to "determine those competencies that practicing independent information professionals rate as essential for individuals entering the information brokering field" (Green 1993, p. 165). These skills or competencies are equally critical in the professional staff, entry level or beyond, of fee-based information services. The top competencies on Green's list are:

- Apply effective interpersonal skills with clients;
- Provide accurate estimates for services/accurately price products;
- Develop a search strategy;
- Define market(s) for services/products offered;
- Communicate effectively in writing reports, proposals, and so forth;
- Operate personal computing equipment;
- Apply effective personal time-management techniques;
- Apply knowledge of marketing techniques;
- Develop and follow an ethical code of conduct; and
- Effectively search online databases (Green 1993, p. 166).

One special consideration for the professional staff (except the manager) is whether the library will require a masters degree in library science (MLS) for the position. Over the years, TIS has hired two information specialists with bachelors degrees and with extensive professional experience in special libraries but without MLS degrees. If permissible at the local institution, consider proposing that the job descriptions be worded "bachelors degree required; MLS preferred." The search committee can then consider an outstanding candidate with the right experience and other qualities, but without the academic credentials.

The business plan clearly describes what the other professionals' supervisory responsibilities, if any, are towards the rest of the support staff. Avoid inadvertently creating a situation in which a professional, who is given no written supervisory responsibility or authority, works closely with several support staff. This situation is most likely to occur with a part-time administrative manager, especially one whose office is located at some distance from the fee-based information service office. Even in a cooperative team environment, difficulties may arise if there is no clear leadership role, and no adequate compensation or recognition for that role.

Support Staff

Finding support staff is generally easier than filling professional positions. The investigator's job is to recommend the right mix of support staff to perform the new service's tasks. The major job functions to be covered are:

- Office manager;
- Accountant;
- Marketing support;
- Document delivery (internal and external);
- Occasional support for research projects, under an information specialist's direction;
- Software, network, and computer equipment support;
- Receptionist;
- Student assistant supervisor;
- Shipping clerk;
- Filing clerk;
- Data entry clerk; and
- Billing clerk.

Many of these job functions will be logically combined; for example, one person might answer the phone, handle some document delivery orders, train students, and supervise mass mailing marketing activities. Other job functions may be farmed out to other library or university departments to some extent, such as part of the accounting or billing procedures or computer support. Still others, such as filing or shipping, might be delegated to selected student assistants. A new service would probably be lucky to start with two support staff, so most of the job functions listed above would be divided between them.

Graduate Assistants

Several services, especially those located at institutions with library school programs have discovered that "graduate assistants ... who have completed part of their training and education, provide a valuable pool of talent for part-time work"

(Grant 1987, p. 243). Avoid the temptation to rely too heavily on library school students, however. The turnover is generally higher than for permanent staff. Continuous training programs rob time that other staff could be spending on client projects. Clients may perceive a lower overall quality of service if every few months different people handle their projects. While it is an admirable practice to provide librarians-in-training with valuable experience, the investigator realizes that the service's primary goal is to provide skilled and dependable research and document delivery services to customers. Clients paying premium prices for information expect professional results.

One service used a graduate business student to develop marketing support (Grant 1987, p. 246). Purdue's Technical Information Service hired a graduate business student for a one-year project to conduct a management audit and to oversee a client satisfaction survey. Over several years, TIS has hired graduate students as computer support technicians. Employing graduate students for supplementary support may be a wiser course than hiring them to handle high-profile client contact projects.

Student Assistants

An academic fee-based information service planning document delivery as one of its major cost-recovery activities will very likely depend on student assistants for a significant percentage of its labor force. A possible exception might be a service that draws almost exclusively on a single library's collection, such as in a medical or law library. In these cases, it may be less expensive in the long run to hire clerks whose major job responsibilities are to retrieve, prepare, and ship documents.

However, in most libraries it will be less expensive to hire students, because their hourly rate is lower and the institution usually does not have to pay many fringe benefits for part-time casual employees. In a large, multi-library system such as Purdue University's, it is essential for a fee-based information service to have a large, relatively flexible work force able to travel to collections around campus to retrieve books, to make photocopies, and to handle various office functions such as filing and recording transactions in the copyright log.

Using student help requires careful management. Staff must train students adequately so they can work independently without asking too many questions of the regular library staff. Student work must be monitored. Hiring and other personnel procedures take time. The staff must look ahead to breaks in the academic schedule when many students may not be available. Some students do not take their part-time work seriously and call in frequently with excuses about why they cannot work the day's shift. However, most student assistants are hard-working people who take pride in their jobs and make every effort to work quickly and accurately.

Initial Staffing Mix

What should the staff complement be on opening day? If the service offers both research and document delivery, there should be at least one full-time professional (either the hands-on manager or a combination of an administrative manager and a full-time information specialist), one or two full-time clerks, and several hours a day of scheduled student assistant time. Business may be very slow for the first few weeks or months, but the staff can spend the time coordinating mailings and other promotional activities, familiarizing themselves with office software, setting up a filing system, modifying office forms, and so on. If the service opens with more than one clerk, clearly designate one of them with the responsibility for implementing the billing operation.

Staff Training and Development

The investigator notes training and development that staff will need. Training ranges from sending the clerical staff to half-day workshops introducing standard software packages to advanced database training, often in other cities, that information specialists need to become more effective searchers. Although more training sessions may be needed during the initial implementation phase, write training into annual budgets as an ongoing investment in keeping the staff's skills current to provide clients with excellent service. Change is constant and inevitable, especially in the computer-related skills staff in fee-based information services need to continue providing fast, efficient, and effective service. Off-campus training is often expensive, but it is usually more cost-efficient in the long run to pay for specialized, concentrated training sessions taught by experts than to rely on departmental staff squeezing 30 or 60 minutes out of their schedules here and there to train a new staff member in advanced techniques.

In addition, plan for expenditures for professional staff development. This staff development includes at least partial reimbursement for attending professional meetings. Do not confuse professional development expenses with the cost of travel for marketing purposes. Marketing expenses should be paid for or reimbursed in full, whereas institutional policies on professional development reimbursement may mandate only partial reimbursement.

Equipment and Supplies. Having reached a conclusion about how large a staff to recommend for opening day, the investigator next plans how much equipment, furniture, supplies, and related items will be required. Will the equipment be new, or will the service depend on hand-me-downs? I strongly urge that new equipment be purchased unless financial constraints are so severe that the service cannot be started unless it accepts castoffs. The staff work with the business community; if businesspeople receive spotty photocopies or if the fax machine breaks down several times a week, many clients will switch to another information provider who sends clear copies and prompt faxes. The look of the finished products is part of the overall promotional effort. For example, if a client has a choice between one service's excellent search results from a dot matrix printer and someone else's slightly less comprehensive results produced on a laser printer, the client may choose the provider perceived to have the better professional image. Many clients will, to some extent, equate appearance with quality. Another argument for new equipment is that it is generally faster and more reliable than older, used models. Fast printing, faxing, and computing mean that staff can be more efficient, finish tasks more quickly, and bill more documents or projects than they could with slower equipment.

The investigator recommends equipment and furniture on the assumption that the library will purchase new pieces. The library administrators will indicate if the costs are unrealistic. First list all the equipment, furniture, and supplies in the categories designated by the local institution. Remember to calculate the costs of both maintenance agreements and routine maintenance.

Each permanent staff member should have a workstation, complete with the best microcomputer and telecommunications connection that the library can afford. Staff can share laser printers. Consider what would happen if one of the machines needed repairs or became inoperable. Could that staff member still do most of the job? The answer is probably no, so think about emergency back-up equipment. Would a portable PC meet most emergency needs? Should the service purchase one and load it with all the appropriate software, or does the library have laptops that can be borrowed? Are there enough loaners so that the service could be almost sure of getting one for a week while a machine was being repaired? Should there be an extra workstation in the office anyway, both for emergencies and for some processing that student assistants might be trained to do, such as reporting copyright over the Internet to the Copyright Clearance Center? Be sure to provide telecommunications connections for all machines, and consider larger-than-average monitors, such as 17-inch ones. The staff will spend a lot of time in front of their screens and, especially if the tracking and billing software forms become dense, will appreciate having the larger screens. Larger monitors are also less expensive if ordered with the rest of the microcomputer set-up than months later as separate items.

Based on the network configuration recommended, determine the best way to provide back-ups for electronic files. This ability is essential. There will inevitably come a day when, through accident or error, one or more critical files will be irretrievably lost or corrupted. Having back-up files to replace the lost ones is critical. Reentering a day's worth of data is bad enough; reconstructing months of billing information or a 3,000-name client list represents a disastrous drain on staff time and morale, as well as days or weeks of impaired ability to provide good customer service. At a minimum, plan to make daily back-ups of changed data on all machines, and weekly back-ups of the whole system.

Along with the microcomputers, choose adjustable workstations, desks, and chairs. Every staff member will have different ergonomic requirements or preferences when it comes to things like keyboard height, wrist rests, foot rests, back support, lighting, and distance from the monitor screen. Spending a few dollars to accommodate these differences in the early stages may prevent expensive worker's compensation claims later, as well as ensure the staff's ongoing physical comfort on the job.

A fax machine, perhaps with add-on memory, is essential. Insist on a fax machine for the exclusive use of the fee-based information service. Most orders will arrive by fax; when the machine is not receiving orders it should be free for transmitting rush requests back to clients. It is a mistaken economy to think that the service can share a fax with another department. Some clients will stop sending orders if they hear a busy signal too often, or if staff cannot tell them whether a certain order has arrived yet because the fax machine is located on another floor, or if rush orders are delayed because someone from another department is transmitting a 30-page report to Argentina. In fact, it may not be long before the new service needs two fax machines, one for receiving new orders and another kept open for transmitting rush requests back to clients. Fax machines can be configured so that incoming messages divert from a busy machine to a back-up unit.

An Internet-based scanning workstation, such as Ariel, is not essential for start-up and may not be essential equipment even as the service matures. Most business clients, except a few of those working in very large corporate libraries, do not have Ariel machines themselves. Even those with Ariel equipment will generally accept articles delivered by more traditional means. The fee-based service may be able to use the interlibrary loan department's Ariel scanner in those few cases where clients prefer Ariel transmissions.

Add phones at each desk. Besides the costs of the instruments themselves and the initial installation, there may also be an annual charge for each line. When calculating the number of lines the office needs, remember to count all the phone, modem, and fax lines.

An office copy machine may not be essential at first, if staff have relatively easy access to one in another office or in a nearby library; most article photocopying is handled by student retrievers out in the campus libraries.

A start-up operation will probably not require expensive **CD-ROM** equipment and networks. Easy access to existing **CD-ROM** networks may be possible, but it may not be advisable if the current **CD-ROM** titles have been purchased or leased with the understanding that they shall only be used to support the educational or research efforts of the campus community.

However, the investigator considers a local area network (LAN) so that the all the staff can access or update the office electronic files. If the investigator is not personally experienced or knowledgeable about the computer requirements for the office, enlist the aid of the library's microcomputer specialist. The specialist will make recommendations about the computer-related equipment, as well as provide average or recent costs for these pieces. Ask if the specialist knows about the types and amounts of discounts the library can expect from certain suppliers. What software would the specialist suggest for meeting the service's requirements for a client list, a document or research project tracking and billing database, and a spreadsheet? It would certainly be helpful to choose a software package for which the microcomputer support department already provides technical support, but the investigator notes if the supported packages do not meet the service's major requirements, and if other packages should be reviewed.

Besides the tracking and billing/accounting software, the investigator includes cost estimates for word processing and telecommunications software. Besides the standard office telecommunications software, the investigator also considers specialized software for connecting to and searching selected database vendors' files, such as the Dialoglink package for searching Dialog. Suggest buying enough copies to load every office microcomputer with the same versions of the same software. One reason is that it is often less expensive to buy multiple copies at the same time. It is also wise to make each workstation similar to its mates in case of an emergency. For example, the investigator may not envision the billing clerk ever searching Dialog from that workstation, but if the information specialist's machine needs repairs or adjustments, then the specialist can at least run a search or two on the other machine while the clerk is at lunch. Balance the need for an array of software with the inevitable high learning curve if staff must master too many different packages.

Minor supplies include an adding machine with a paper tape attachment for the staff member responsible for billing. A scale that weighs packages up to 20 or 25 pounds will be necessary if couriers such as United Parcel Service or Federal Express ship the service's packages. Consider a heavy-duty stapler and rolls of wide shipping tape. A spiral binding machine for neatly packaging long photocopied documents like theses and government documents is a helpful device; the binding process also requires specially printed folder covers and a large assortment of plastic binder combs. Access to a typewriter may be the most cost-effective way of preparing mailing labels for the daily shipments and for labeling file folders. Lockable filing cabinets are essential to limit access to confidential client records. At least a few bookcases will be necessary. The professional staff will start collecting database documentation. Having at least some major reference books such as *Ulrich's International Periodicals Directory* and Gale's *Periodical Title Abbreviations* at the staff's fingertips will save hours of time. Will climate control be a problem in the office, especially if modifications such as enclosing a corridor have been made, thus possibly interfering with the previous airflow pattern? Will staff need fans or heaters? If the institution is located in the snow belt, will there be enough pegs to hang coats for the full-time staff as well as for the student assistants?

The library staff member responsible for overseeing the equipment and supplies purchasing procedure may be able to estimate how much it will cost to establish each new employee with those relatively small, one-time purchases such as a wastepaper basket, stapler, in-basket, and Rolodex. This person may also know approximately how much the average staff member needs each year in terms of consumable supplies such as pens, diskettes, and transparent tape.

The fee-based service will also use some specialized supplies, not all of which need be available to begin operations, but that will eventually be both helpful and also project an efficient, professional image for the service. For example, the Technical Information Service staff use:

- Rubber stamps, such as "BEST COPY POSSIBLE" or "CANCELLED" to add to word processed forms, as appropriate, after they have been printed;
- 9 by 12 inch white envelopes with the logo and return address preprinted on them;
- Inexpensive stiff blue folders with the name and logo on the front for providing extra protection for photocopies during shipping;
- Sturdier, glossy folders for packaging search results;
- Customized address labels;
- Long colored paper bands to wrap around books on loan, indicating the TIS address, the due date, and order numbers associated with the request; and
- Return address labels for clients to use when mailing back loaned material.

Many of these specialized supplies were ordered several months or years after TIS began operating. A new service does not need to have all these items on hand by the launch date.

Revisit the space issue at this point. Where will the boxes of 5,000 brochures be stored? The 300 bubble envelopes? Twenty or 30 or 50 reams of paper in various colors? Are any special storage units needed for some of these items, either in the office or in a remote storage location?

Once again, the investigator should not focus too closely on brand names or exact costs at this point but should compile a list of equipment and supplies with approximate or average prices. Some of the equipment can be labeled as essential (e.g., chairs) and other pieces can be designated as desirable (e.g., binding machine).

Suppliers. The new fee-based information service needs to have several types of suppliers already in place on opening day. At least one major database vendor should have been selected, an account opened, and the professional staff comfortable with searching, saving, downloading, editing, and printing that vendor's files using whatever telecommunications software has been selected. The investigator calls at least four or five major database vendors and files their promotional literature for the manager to review later.

The investigator should not assume that the U.S. Postal Service can meet all the service's shipping needs. A more reliable and flexible, although more expensive, alternative is to negotiate with an overnight courier service. Most of these services offer standard as well as express delivery, and, for a modest additional fee, will send a driver to the office late each afternoon to pick up the day's packages. However, using a single courier service will probably still not offer enough shipping flexibility. The Technical Information Service ships most packages via United Parcel Service (UPS), with Federal Express as a supplemental courier for clients who prefer having rush orders shipped on their own company's Federal Express account. Before making a recommendation for the final selection, the investigator checks the institution's policies for overnight couriers. Can the service establish a separate Federal Express account, or must it use the institution's account number for having items shipped directly either to itself or to a client?

The investigator also briefly addresses the issue of shipping material to international clients. Airmail delivery is adequate for shipments to some countries, but using an overnight courier service is more reliable for sending packages to others.

Spending a lot of time dwelling on shipping questions at this stage is unproductive since, in most cases, shipping costs will be billed back to the clients, either as a separate fee if the service ships an item on its own Federal Express number, for example, or bundled into the document delivery base price. For internal calculations, the Technical Information Service assumes that most packages contain at least two documents and weigh less than a pound.

If the service will offer document delivery services from outside its collection, the investigator identifies several potential document suppliers. The subject focus of the proposed service will have an impact on the selection of document suppliers, but the five to eight recommended suppliers include:

- Several other fee-based information services located in institutions whose collections complement the local one;
- One or two specialized services, if appropriate, such as Chemical Abstracts or the National Technical Information Service (NTIS), or a patent service;
- One or two commercial firms; and
- Perhaps one or two smaller information brokers who send runners to major libraries such as the Library of Congress or the National Library of Medicine.

Some of these suppliers operate on a pay-as-you-go basis; others are much easier to work with if the fee-based information service establishes a deposit account in advance of the first order. The initial deposits can usually be fairly small ones of perhaps $500 each, but figure this expense in the final budget. These expenses are, of course, recovered when staff order documents on clients' behalf from these suppliers.

If the service should be lucky enough to be granted an institutional credit card by opening day, the necessity for some of the deposit accounts will disappear. However, business officers are usually nervous enough about the prospect of a fee-based information service without issuing credit cards with an available balance of several hundreds or thousands of dollars to a service without a proven track record. It is also easier to reconcile a detailed, monthly deposit account statement from a supplier than to identify individual documents from a credit card invoice that might bundle the prices for several documents shipped on the same day into a single amount. Since the manager will select the initial combination of suppliers, the investigator need only identify a few in each category.

Relationships with Existing Library Units. The investigator considers the expected impact that the proposed fee-based information service will have on existing library units. Issues include interpersonal dynamics as well as changes in work flow and pricing. Staff in existing units may perceive the advent of a fee-based information service as a long-overdue savior for handling some types of work they barely have time to complete, as a usurper encroaching on their turf, or as anything in between.

A fee-based information service will almost certainly want to define its relationship with the interlibrary loan office. The business plan describes the difference between the services that the ILL department provides and those that the fee-based service will provide (Marvin 1988, pp. 147-149). The library must avoid the confusing and unfair scenario in which company A sends a photocopy request over OCLC to the ILL department and pays $10 for the article, whereas company B pays $15 for a similar item filled through the fee-based information service. The Purdue Libraries solved this problem by arranging for the Technical Information Service to fill nearly all requests sent to ILL by for-profit organizations.

Over time, TIS has picked up more business that Purdue's increasingly busy ILL unit finds little time to handle: requests from all international addresses except Canada, requests from nonreciprocal libraries for rush handling, requests from individuals unaffiliated with the university, and occasional requests from campus patrons who need fast service purchasing international or other difficult-to-obtain items. Some of these categories of requests may be ones that can be shifted to the fee-based information service at the outset.

If the institution has a database or electronic services coordinator, the advent of a fee-based information service may have an impact on this person's job.

- Will some nonaffiliated customers be asked to switch from the database office to the fee-based service?
- Can fee-based information service staff share or consult some of the database documentation the coordinator has assembled?

- Can the coordinator act as a back-up searcher in emergencies?
- Will the coordinator be involved in any aspects of training the new fee-based services staff?
- Will the database coordinator's unit be compensated for activities that support the fee-based service?

The library development officer is someone else to consider. Will there be any formal relationship between the library development office and the fee-based service? The development office will have built up a list of corporate donors over the years.

- Is it possible or desirable to send mailings about the new service to the people on the corporate donors list?
- If so, is it politic to solicit business from donors?
- Should the mailing be more informational than promotional?
- How will the fee-based service respond to a donor who suggests that since the donor's company wrote a generous check to the institution last year, the articles employees need now should be sent gratis?
- Once the fee-based service has established its own corporate mailing list, should the development office be allowed access to it?
- If the fee-based service guarantees or implies confidentiality to its clients, will some of them be irritated to find their in-boxes stuffed with letters urging them to make generous donations to the institution?

The circulation department may be asked to issue library cards to the new service's staff to facilitate checking out the books to be sent on loan to clients. How will overdue notices and fees be handled? If the service proposes a membership program with one of the benefits being client library cards, how will the impact of corporate patrons affect circulation functions and policies?

Almost every other library public service unit will feel the impact of a new fee-based information service. On the positive side, reference librarians will have a place to refer non-primary patrons who have in-depth research questions or who need an article or industry standard mailed to them. Circulation staff can suggest that the fee-based service mail a book on loan rather than requiring that the caller drive to campus. Less positive impacts include inevitable events such as a campus patron needing a book that has been shipped to a client 2,000 miles away, or a client losing or irreparably damaging an out-of-print book, or the undeniable but immeasurable increase in wear and tear on the collection and photocopy equipment. One could argue that these events would have happened even without a fee-based information service: patrons check out books that other patrons want; patrons lose books; ILL sends books all over the country; people inadvertently break the spines of tightly bound periodical volumes.

Other perceptions are harder to answer. Some colleagues view charging any fees for information services as a breach of professional ethics. Others will point out that it is unfair that corporate clients get faster and sometimes more extensive services than the campus community. Why, they ask, should a company get an Australian technical report on a rush basis within a week, when a faculty member approaching ILL might be told either that it will take a month or two to obtain, or, because there are no holdings in North America for the report, it is unavailable through interlibrary loan at all? The reply that the company is willing to pay $150 for the rush international purchase while the professor's budget is $25 does not mollify the questioner. After all, isn't the faculty member's need as great as the company's? Isn't the library's mission to serve the faculty? Why can't the library pay the $150 bill to get the report rapidly for the professor?

Although the investigator realizes that some colleagues may never change their minds about the benefits of having a fee-based service, it is important to include a section in the business plan showing how the library staff will be kept informed during the implementation stages. Misinformation or insufficient information breed confusion or resentment.

Relationship with Other University Departments. Most universities sponsor a number of departments or programs that work with the community. A central office often publishes a brochure or booklet that lists these programs and briefly describes each one. While it would be an unnecessarily large task to contact all these departments, the investigator reviews the list and determines which selected program directors to visit. Does the university sponsor a small business development center, an industrial liaison program, or a project to assist regional firms sell their products overseas? Remember to ask colleagues; the business or engineering librarians probably know which one or two of a list of a dozen programs in their subject area would be the most beneficial to visit.

There are a number of reasons for becoming familiar with other local services offered to the business community. For one thing, it would be unwise for the fee-based service to offer a service that another university department already provides. When the service is established, the staff should know when and where to refer appropriate queries to other programs, and the manager ensures through periodic visits, phone calls, and mailings that the directors of these other services know about and understand what the library's fee-based information service does. There may be opportunities for joint marketing efforts if one program's services complement another's. Some programs may wish to include a brief description of the fee-based service in their own promotional material. As with the internal library staff, other program directors who understand the fee-based information service's mission will be less likely to view it as a potential threat or as just another program competing for the same scarce institutional dollars.

Marketing

The investigator may be surprised to learn that many of the issues investigated up to this point laid the groundwork for some of the more interesting aspects of marketing. For example, the mission and goals have been defined, the services to be offered identified, and a target client base suggested. The final step involves recommending how to reach those clients.

The marketing aspect of planning and, later, implementing a fee-based information service is often one of the most exciting. However, the investigator remembers that the job at this stage is to offer marketing suggestions, not develop a full-blown marketing strategic plan. For example, in the planning stage one points out that an advertising campaign is a potentially useful promotional strategy and collects information about representative advertising vehicles and the costs for ad insertion in each; however, designing and placing the actual ad are activities that belong in the implementation phase.

Target Audience.   In light of what has been learned so far, the investigator reexamines the target audience designated earlier in the planning process.

- Is the target audience either too broad or too narrow?
- If one target is engineering consultants, for example, can large firms and one- or two-person operations be differentiated?
- Can different sizes of firms be identified?
- For large firms, what are the job titles of the people most likely to use the service? The CEO, the head of R&D, or the individual researchers or engineers?
- How easily can these people be identified and reached?

Reaching the Target Audience.   There are many marketing tools for reaching the target audience. In the planning stage, the investigator's task is to identify these tools, to collect information about the relative effectiveness and the average costs for each of them, and then to recommend the ones most likely to meet the goals of reaching the target audience. Chapters 5 and 6 discuss at greater length most of the marketing tools that at least some fee-based information services have found to be effective.

Some of the tools, such as developing effective brochures, are as essential in the start-up phase as they are for a mature service. Others, such as conferences and exhibits, are better employed by a growing service than by a new one. A partial list includes:

- Brochures
- Stationery
- Mailing lists
- Advertisements in print media

- Networking
- Campus contacts
- Press releases
- Personal speaking appearances
- Supplemental printed promotional pieces
- Conferences and exhibits
- Articles
- Client visits
- Radio

The Brochure. Whatever kind of advertising or promotion strategy the manager eventually implements, every new information service needs a brochure describing its services and products, and presenting its fee schedule. In the first weeks of the new service, the brochure may be the only official promotional piece available. A single-sheet price list, no matter how nicely formatted with eye-catching fonts and graphics, simply will not project a professional image.

Now is the time for the investigator to pull out the brochures obtained earlier from other fee-based information services. While the job of drafting or designing the brochure lies in the future, the investigator selects one or two representative samples and finds out how much similar brochures would cost.

Look first at the layout and overall design. Which ones are best? Why? Look at the paper, the ink, the fonts, any illustrations or photographs, the format, the colors. Are any too slick, too tacky, too "busy," too full of library-ese? Which ones would be more likely to catch the eye of a busy business executive? Find out if the library uses a graphics design department on campus, and get cost estimates for the design work on similar brochures. How much will it cost to print 2,000 or 5,000 or 10,000 brochures? The price per piece usually decreases dramatically with higher print runs, but larger print runs also involve larger cash outlays and possible storage challenges.

When figuring costs for attracting clients, the investigator remembers the importance of marketing the service within the institution. The library administrators and professional librarians should all receive at least an annual reminder about their fee-based information service. Other campus administrators, directors of selected other university programs, and people who have shown an interest in or helped with various aspects of the service will also be added to the campus mailing list.

Mailing Lists. The investigator considers ways of distributing the brochure to members of the target audience. One of the best ways is to use direct mail marketing, but this strategy almost certainly involves a commitment to purchasing mailing lists. The business plan recommends and provides cost estimates for implementing this part of the marketing strategy. The operation raises a number of questions:

- Should the brochure be sent alone, or should it be accompanied by a letter? If alone, will it be designed to travel by itself through the mail, or in an envelope?

- How will the service obtain mailing lists for members of the target audience? Possibilities include trade and professional associations, professional licensing bureaus, trade journal subscriber lists, and the local institution's alumni office. The service can also buy company lists, but it may be less effective to send mail addressed to the "R&D Director," for example, rather than to people's names.
- How much do these lists cost? Can they be customized? For example, can the service buy names for just one or two states?
- Will the mailing list provider send labels or a disk?
- How much will it cost to send 1,000, 2,000, 5,000, or more pieces of direct mail? First class mail with commemorative stamps yields better response rates, but bulk mail is less expensive.
- How many pieces will be sent out at a time?
- Will the service send several pieces to the same people over time? If so, how often? How will the timing of the mailings be tracked?
- Should the manager develop a different follow-up piece, or send multiple mailings of the same promotional material?
- How does the local institution process bulk mail or large first class mail orders?

Advertising. Even if the investigator's final recommendation is that the new service should not place media advertisements in its initial start-up phase, gather representative information about this marketing strategy. The library administrators will probably ask to see it if it is not there.

- Should the service advertise?
- If so, who will develop the ad and what are the design costs?
- What types of publications and/or specific titles are appropriate for placing the ad?
- How often should the ad appear?
- Should the ad vary depending on the publication in which it appears?
- How much does advertising cost? Are there discounts if the ad appears frequently in the same publication?
- How will the manager know if the advertising draws customers?
- What about advertising in the telephone book's yellow pages? At least one service found itself facing a potential lawsuit over a local independent information broker's allegation that the academic fee-based service represented unfair competition by advertising in the yellow pages.

Marketing Recommendations. The business plan's final recommendations present an approach that balances easy or less expensive ways of reaching a particular audience with the usually more expensive methods that have proven more effective in attracting clients serious about placing orders. The new service should not depend solely on one marketing strategy nor, at the other extreme, should the eager staff try half a dozen techniques simultaneously.

In the happy event that the service's manager will enjoy a robust marketing budget, the investigator avoids the trap of thinking that more is better. Two hundred brochures mailed to a carefully selected target group of potential clients may generate more business than thousands of brochures mailed to every engineer who graduated from the institution over the last five years.

Online Marketing. Electronic marketing, online marketing, and cybermarketing are just three of the terms used to describe advertising on the Internet or the World Wide Web. While cybermarketing may eventually become an integral part of the established service's marketing mix, the investigator would be wise to mention it in the business plan only as a possible future option. Consider electronic marketing after the newly launched service is confident in its abilities to attract and respond to clients using traditional methods.

Financial Considerations

After gathering information about the topics above, the investigator certainly realizes by now that starting a fee-based is not a cheap proposition.

Talk with the Business Officer. Some conversations with the library's business or financial officer are next on the agenda. It will be helpful if, in advance of the first meeting, the investigator briefly describes the goals of the investigation, and provides the business officer with a copy of the initial proposal, along with any memos indicating administrative approval for proceeding with the business plan.

It is also unrealistic to expect to answer all the business-related questions in a single meeting. For one thing, even after working for the library for years in increasingly responsible positions, the investigator may not know all the institutional constraints that determine financial policies and procedures, especially for non-university clientele. Second, the business officer may need several sessions before becoming familiar, if not immediately comfortable, with the financial needs of a fee-based information service. Library business officers typically supervise the annual disbursement of several million dollars in salaries, equipment, and materials acquisitions but generally see very little income other than a trickle from overdue fines and interlibrary loan fees. The prospect of handling several hundred thousand dollars of potential income per year, especially income that must be closely monitored against expenditures, may be daunting at first.

For-Profit or Not-for-Profit? The decision about offering services on a for-profit or not-for-profit basis may be dictated by the institutional type. A publicly supported institution might not be allowed to offer for-profit services of any kind, but only services that more or less break even by charging fees that cover their operating costs. The business officer explains whether the institution allows a choice. If the for-profit option is available, then further questions arise.

- What happens to the profit, if any?
- Is it plowed back into the fee-based service, as it would be in a company, for new equipment, new staff, or an expanded marketing program?
- Would some or all of the profit be channeled elsewhere? Where?
- What happens if the service fails to make a profit over several months or years?
- Can the profits be saved or rolled forward from one year to the next so that the surplus from a good year can be used to meet the payroll in a bad year?
- Is the library willing to·support the new service, at a loss if necessary, while it establishes itself during its first few years?

Related questions involve the distinction between cost-recovery and cost-subsidy. Must the service recover every dime it takes to operate, or are some costs covered by the parent institution or other sources? True cost-recovery means generating enough income to pay for everything, both direct and indirect costs.

In practice, every academic fee-based service I know about is subsidized to some extent, even if the library pays for only a few of the indirect costs. Most fee-based services describe themselves as operating on a cost-recovery basis, but due to local institutional quirks, constraints, and philosophy, every fee-based service defines cost-recovery differently. Almost all of them price their services to cover direct expenses such as supplies, equipment, photocopy expenses, postage, database charges, and document procurement costs. Most services also recover staff salaries, but not all of them also recover fringe benefits, which may run an additional 30 to 40 percent over the salary figures. Some libraries cover travel to professional meetings from the general travel budget; others expect the fee-based service to pick up the tab for its information specialists. Some libraries require that the fee-based service reimburse them a certain percentage or a certain amount to cover overhead, such as office space, janitorial services, heat, and electricity. I have not yet heard of any institution presenting a bill to its fee-based service for the small percentage of time that other staff, such as the personnel officer, the business officer, or staff from the microcomputer support department, spend meeting the service's needs in these areas. The service usually does not pay to draw on the collection from which it derives its document delivery income, although at least one service pays back the appropriate branch library one dollar for each document it photocopies or lends from that location.

Other financial issues such as initial funding, pricing, and billing are addressed later in this chapter. The investigator plans several discussions with the business officer to ask specific questions about each of areas. The more knowledge and understanding the business officer has about the proposed fee-based information service, the better the financial aspects will function smoothly and efficiently.

Estimating the Budget and Setting Prices. Having completed all the research listed above, the investigator probably feels ready to begin work on drafting the price list. However, before setting the fees, it is important first to calculate the true cost of providing services. Harriet Zais described pricing as an art and wrote that "pricing decisions reflect a blend of intuition, past experience, and sophisticated analysis" (Zais 1977, pp. 89-90). Pricing may pose a particularly big challenge to an investigator who has no past experience because the service is not yet established and who may also be unfamiliar with sophisticated cost analysis methods. At the same time, the library administrators want a pricing recommendation based on more than intuition.

There are two major cost categories to consider. Labor and supplies form the first category of direct costs. These costs can usually be calculated fairly accurately, even though the level of demand is hard to predict. Remember that "supplies" covers everything from pens to database charges to document procurement fees to copy machine toner to postage to printing.

The indirect or overhead costs, such as utilities, comprise the second category, but in general the fee-based service's use of these indirect costs will be a percentage of the entire library's use.

There are many methods of calculating costs and making pricing decisions. Some of the references cited at the end of this chapter discuss methods of calculating costs and of pricing information services. While reviewing standard business texts on the subject will be helpful, the investigator bears in mind that these texts assume the reader's objective is profit maximization. While costs are calculated the same way in both for-profit and non-profit environments, the resulting pricing decisions based on those costs may be very different. Check first with the library's business officer to learn if there is a locally preferred method for calculating these costs. Also ask if the administrators prefer an implementation or start-up budget separate from the first year's projected budget.

Have a clear understanding about whether the library expects the service to recover all labor costs (salaries and fringes, or just salaries?) or any overhead costs. Then determine the break-even point for each of the services to be offered.

The next section examines the question of what specific costs to include in the price. But as a simplistic example of calculating a break-even point, suppose the library requires the service to cover all staff salaries (but not fringe benefits), all the supplies, materials, and equipment it uses, and to contribute $2,000 a year towards general overhead. The new service will offer document delivery and research, with document delivery expected to account for 60 percent of the total income. The investigator makes two sets of calculations, one for document delivery and one for research projects.

For example, suppose the investigator estimates that the annual salary cost for document delivery will be $40,000 (one document clerk, a small percentage of a professional's time, student retrievers, and part of the billing clerk's time). The investigator further expects that an additional $20,000 will be necessary to pay for supplies (envelopes, postage, photocopying, a fax machine, printing brochures, any copyright fees not passed on to the client, etc.). Finally, there will be $1,200 in overhead expenses (the remaining $800 being calculated into the projections for research projects). Estimated document delivery costs thus total $61,200:

Salaries	$40,000
Supplies	20,000
Overhead	1,200
Total	$61,200

If the service charges $10 per document, it must provide 6,120 documents that year to cover its costs. However, if it charges $13 per document, only 4,708 document orders need be filled to reach the break-even point.

In reality, many things complicate these calculations. For example, the fax machine will be purchased in one year, but used over several. How should this cost be amortized over five years? In addition, some unknown percentage of orders will require rush handling at higher rates, thus generating more income. A small percentage of orders will prove unfillable for various reasons. The costs of handling these cancelled orders should be included in the final price for completed orders. Clients will balk at paying costs for documents that they never received.

Larry Herman stressed that "what a service costs may not bear any relationship to what the library chooses to charge for it" (Herman 1990, p. 27). So even if the calculations reveal a break-even point of $11 per document, for example, there may be good reasons for settling on a published rate of $10 or of $15. Reasons might include:

- Bringing the service's rates in line with those charged by competitors;
- Charging a premium for a particular service to enhance its value in the customers' minds;
- Making a profit;
- Ensuring sufficient income to cover unforeseen expenses;
- Creating revenue to pay for future expenses (e.g., equipment or advertising);
- Meeting non-monetary goals, such as providing a segment of the client population, such as alumni or donors, with lower-priced services;
- Offering a particular service as a "loss leader" to attract clients in the hope that they will later order other, more expensive services; and
- Avoiding the possibility of customers perceiving the service as inferior because the price is set too low.

Alice Sizer Warner wrote that the final prices for information services reflect the local institution's goals. Since each institution's goals are different, merely copying the competition's prices is not wise (Warner 1990, p. 34). H.E. Broadbent outlined three methods for pricing for market structures. The first, cost-oriented pricing, is a cost-plus technique in which users are charged for the actual cost of a database search, for example, plus an additional charge to cover fixed costs. The second method, competition-oriented pricing, is "a popular means of pricing, especially where the services or products are not distinctive . . . because it tends to reflect the collective wisdom of the industry." Finally, demand-oriented pricing allows price discrimination based on "a number of different factors: customer, product version, place, or time" (Broadbent 1981, pp. 103-105).

Johan L. Olaisen described five pricing models:

1. Optimal pricing where substantial profit is made;
2. Pricing according to value allowing both profit and loss;
3. Full cost-recovery where all costs are covered;
4. Marginal cost pricing where subsidies are needed; and
5. Free distribution of services where full subsidies are needed (Olaisen 1989, pp. 256-262).

Chapter 6 in Harry M. Kibirige's book *The Information Dilemma* provides detailed information about pricing information services and products, including definitions of cost concepts (average variable cost, marginal cost, etc.) and explanations of cost-based pricing, demand-based pricing, competition-based pricing, and optimum pricing (Kibirige 1983, pp. 105-118). Harriet Zais' article lists other models for costing and pricing information services (Zais 1977).

Sally F. Williams provided a very helpful section on guidelines for fees in her 1987 article. Among the nine common sense guidelines are the points that fees should be:

• Realistic
• Logical
• Inexpensive to implement
• Predictable
• Based on actual costs
• Periodically adjusted (Williams 1987, pp. 131-133).

I advise drafting projected budgets for the start-up year and the two following years. Some of the estimates will be very rough, of course; the investigator cannot hope to provide very accurate figures for postage or copyright payments three years into the future, for example. However the budgets should clearly show that many of the first year's costs are one-time start-up expenses that will not be repeated in subsequent years. Replacing existing equipment should not be a concern until the program reaches its fourth or fifth years, unless the service starts out on a shoestring with cast-off equipment meant to be replaced as income allows.

The budgets for the second and subsequent years will reflect increased income, fewer large one-time purchases, and a sense of the typical ongoing annual expenses. Increased income, however, means some increased expenses, such as costs for shipping, copyright, and certain supplies. These increases simply reflect the fact that paying copyright fees for 8,000 documents will cost more than paying them for 5,000. Projecting too far into the future, however, may be both dangerous and misleading. The investigator may certainly hope that the service fills 15,000 document requests by year five but has no facts or trends on which to base these figures.

Confer with the library business officer to determine what style of finished budget the administrators prefer to review. There may be a standard format for grouping various kinds of similar expenses, such as personnel costs or supplies. Ask the business officer to review the draft budgets for style, consistency and accuracy. The business officer may not be able to catch omissions, such as the investigator's oversight in not including a line for equipment maintenance, but may provide valuable suggestions for formatting the budgets into a style to which the administrators are accustomed.

Appendix A shows a sample budget outline for Purdue's Technical Information Service. Keep in mind that this sample budget not only profiles a mature service's annual financial picture but also presents a format that may not be a preferred style at another institution.

Add up all the projected expenses for each year. It may also be wise to add in an additional 5 or 10 percent for contingencies, and to allow between 1 and 2 percent of the income for bad debt, beginning in the second year. Certainly for the first year, the expenses will vastly overshadow the income because of the high start-up costs. The budget indicates the origin of the funds to cover these expenses, and also indicates how any short fall will be paid. If the start-up funds or the initial few years' short falls need not be paid back, then the budget can be presented to show either a zero balance at the end of the year (expenses equal income) or a small positive balance to be rolled over into the next year's budget, if the institution allows this. If some of the start-up costs must be paid back over time, the first year's budget notes that fact. Subsequent budgets then include a line for the annual amount due back to the funding source until the debt is paid off.

Pricing Document Delivery. By now, the investigator has a relatively firm list of the services that will be offered to the business community: research, document delivery, and perhaps one or two related services. The investigator also knows what costs the institution expects the fee-based service to recover, and whether there will be any extra leeway the first year or two. From the preliminary draft of the expenses side of the budget, the investigator has cost estimates for most of the major categories of expenses, and also knows the prices of similar services offered at other institutions.

Does the local service have to break even, or come out ahead? Even if the objective is to break even, the service might shoot for a goal of breaking even plus a few percentage points. There will always be unexpected expenses, and the income must also be sufficient to cover a small amount of bad debt.

How can the investigator put all this information together to establish a fee schedule that will cover all the costs, be accepted by the clients as reasonable, and also be easy to explain and to implement? Begin by determining what the final price in each category will cover. For document delivery:

- Will the final price include photocopying and shipping for regular handling?
- Will there be a per page photocopy charge added to the base price, plus the shipping cost, plus the copyright fee?
- Will copyright fees always be an add-on cost, or will the base fee include copyright charges up to a certain threshold?
- Will copies of extremely lengthy documents such as theses or technical reports cost extra?
- What kinds of rush services will be available, and how much will each cost?
- What percentage of document requests will be rush orders?
- Will there be additional charges for shipping items outside the country or the continent, even for regular service?
- Will there be extra charges for lending multi-volume sets or especially heavy items?
- What will be the standard fee for handling a special order? A rush special order?

Pricing Research Projects. It is generally easier to establish prices for research projects. Most fee-based information services charge an hourly rate, usually divisible into 15-minute increments. Some services set a minimum fee for a research project. Most services then add database charges at cost. Staff often bill rush projects at time-and-a-half, plus database costs, plus any rush delivery costs incurred.

When setting the hourly rate, remember that although each professional may work eight hours a day, not all of those hours can be counted as billable time. Searchers spend a lot of time on non-billable activities such as giving clients cost quotes, handling administrative duties, supervising staff, marketing, and attending meetings. They also devote time to cost-recovery activities such as verifying poor citations or pitching in to help with document delivery for which they do not bill an hourly rate. Vacations and sick leave also whittle down the number of billable hours. To calculate a break-even point while developing the fee schedule, a reasonable estimate would be billing the hourly rate for two to four hours a day for each information specialist. The actual number of hours will be lower during the new service's first few months. Of course, the income recovered from the billable hours must cover the non-billable ones, too.

Revising the Budget. If the first draft of the budget shows a large discrepancy between estimated expenses (other than items representing start-up costs) and expected income, the investigator must reconcile the two amounts realistically. Simply increasing the anticipated income figure until the budget balances may not be a realistic solution. The investigator considers:

- Can any purchases be downsized, postponed, or trimmed?
- Might the service function with one position reduced from a full-time to a half-time one?
- Even though 10,000 brochures ordered this year will cost less apiece than 5,000 printed over each of two years, will two print runs a year apart help bring the budget in line?
- What corners can be cut without irreparably cutting quality? For example, perhaps the service could use plain manila envelopes the first year, and order envelopes with its logo the next year.
- What would the difference be if the base document price was raised by one dollar or if other fees were adjusted upward slightly?
- Is there another potential source of additional start-up funding?
- Will a combination of several changes result in a balanced budget?

Initial Funding

After drafting the budget for the fee-based information service's first few years (and a separate implementation budget, if required), most investigators discover that a substantial investment for start-up costs, and possibly also for the first year's operating costs, is necessary. At least some equipment, furniture, supplies, promotional material, and staff must be in place before the service begins advertising and meeting clients' requests. Helen Josephine pointed out that "most services take from three to five years to break even" (Josephine 1992, p. 323).

- How will the library pay for the fee-based information service's start-up costs?
- Does the director have some discretionary funds?
- If these funds are used, will the service be expected to repay them? Over what time period? With interest, and if so, at what rate? What are the penalties, if any, if the service cannot meet the deadlines?
- Are there major gifts to the library that could be earmarked for starting the service?

- Would a current corporate donor be interested in making a special donation, perhaps in exchange for special rates?
- Does the university provide start-up funds or loans for new programs?
- Would a currently established university program be able to contribute toward the start-up costs in return for an agreement that the fee-based information service provides certain services to the program or its clients at a reduced rate?
- Are there any local, state, regional, or federal funds for which the service could apply?
- Would these be potentially ongoing funds or one-time allocations?
- What would the funding agencies expect in return? Quarterly and annual reports? Extensive analysis of the use made of the funds and the economic impact of the services provided to business? Deep discounts or preferential treatment when staff from the funding agency need services?

Even in a cautious economic climate, the tenacious investigator should be able to identify several potential sources of funding. After determining how much the library is willing to give or lend, the investigator carefully weighs the remaining options. What are the tradeoffs for accepting funds from a particular agency? What are acceptable and reasonable compromises? For example, the investigator would probably not want to commit the fee-based service to providing a funding agency with free document delivery, even for a specific time period, such as a year, without any prior knowledge about the volume and variety of documents that the agency needs. A better, less open-ended solution might be to provide a specific number of documents per month from the local collection at no charge or at a reduced rate for regular delivery. Make the agreement in writing and indicate a specific date to reconsider and renegotiate the terms.

The Fee Schedule.   I recommend as simple a fee schedule as possible. For one reason, it is usually easier to gain administrative approval and university rate approval, especially at the time the service is established, if the schedule is very easy to follow. The staff will also be able to explain the rate structure easily to clients if there are not too many exceptions. The manager will also be able to translate a relatively uncomplicated fee schedule into an easily readable and easily understood section of the brochure. It will be much more appealing to clients than densely printed columns outlining many potential add-on charges.

For an investigator coming from an academic library background, it may be initially daunting to think of charging $10 to $15 for a single document, especially one that may be only one or two pages long, or of charging $50 or more an hour for research time. Many experienced managers, however, agree with Stephen Marvin that "a high price means a higher perceived value of the product" (Marvin 1988, p. 146). Cautiously charging an artificially low price at first may leave prospective clients with the impression that there must be something wrong if the prices are so low.

Marvin's use of the word "product" in reference to document delivery is important. Clients perceive an article or a book loan as a product and expect to pay a standard price for each one they order. Georgia Finnigan pointed out that "what in fact is happening, is that a service is being provided, the costs of which are variable and difficult to anticipate in advance. ... Document delivery is both a commodity and a service" (Finnigan 1995, p. 23).

As a customer of other information services, I prefer those with a slightly higher base fee that includes most aspects of standard delivery for an average document. At the Technical Information Service, staff have learned to avoid using those services that advertise a low document fee and then silently add on postage, photocopy charges, and copyright fees, none of which can be estimated in advance because they rely on initially unknown quantities such as weight and article length. When a seemingly straightforward document order arrives with an unexpectedly high invoice, clients are justifiably unhappy.

Some handling charges are unavoidable, but are also both expected and accepted. These include extra fees for rush handling and citation verification, and a handling fee added to the supplier's charges for obtaining special orders.

The staff should have the prerogative and the flexibility to make occasional, individual exceptions to the fee schedule to fit varying circumstances. For example, the current TIS fee schedule states that regular delivery of a photocopy or a book loan from the Purdue Libraries collection to a North American address costs $14. If a client orders a two-volume set, we charge for one-and-a-half documents: $21. The additional fee offsets our additional shipping and handling costs. Our fee schedule does not explicitly mention pricing for multi-volume sets, but fortunately our university accepts our judgment to make reasonable adjustments to the fee schedule to meet unusual or infrequent circumstances. Likewise, if a tightly bound journal results in a readable photocopy that is not up to our usual standards, we clearly mark it "best copy possible" and charge half price. If we order a document from an international supplier who bills us in the local currency, we charge back to the client the $15 international check fee that the bank charges Purdue when TIS requests a check to pay the supplier. This infrequent fee does not appear in our rate approval document or on our fee schedule but would be included in the cost quote we provide the client before placing the order.

A fee schedule is also adjustable. No matter how efficient the service becomes, as it matures many costs will slowly increase over the years. Periodic price increases are inevitable, whether from increased costs or from the realization that some prices were initially set too low. While it is not advisable to adjust prices too often, changing the fee schedule later is one way to increase revenue to cover expenses.

Ask the business officer what happens next when the library administration approves the pricing structure. Can the service just print up and distribute a fee schedule, or are more formal steps required for rate approval? Will the service be required to charge sales tax to in-state clients? Are federal business income taxes due? If so, how are these taxes calculated, paid, and audited? What categories of clients, if any, would be exempt from having to pay the local or state sales tax? What documentation should the staff see before granting clients tax-exempt status?

Billing, Payments, and Collections. The investigator stresses the desirability of offering services to clients on a ship now, pay later basis. Many clients may request only one search a year or several documents a month; they will be justifiably irritated if they must send advance payment before any work is done, especially if they need documents on a rush basis or if they request a service, such as a search, for which the total cost cannot be exactly calculated in advance. Handling credit card purchases, especially for a lot of relatively small amounts, is time-consuming.

If the institution insists on some form of prepayment before work begins, a fairly high percentage of potential clients will turn to other information services with less stringent requirements. However, the investigator asks if the institution might eventually consider accepting credit card payments or client deposit accounts in selected cases, though neither of these need be available on opening day.

Some fee-based information services operate on an annual membership or subscription basis (Burrows and LaRocca 1983; Cady and Richards 1982; Caren and Somerville 1988; Carter and Pagel 1984; Downing 1990; Roeder 1987; Williams, Lemkau, and Burrows 1988). This option may be attractive for high-volume clients, especially in urban areas where many companies send couriers to the library. Membership in the fee-based service might include visitor or corporate library cards, multiple cards, a parking lot pass, or other services. However, a professional, especially one who works too far away to make use of a library card, will hesitate to send in a membership fee to a service used only a few times a year. To address this potential problem, many services that prefer membership clients also provide documents or searches at higher rates for non-members.

How will invoices be issued? Can the fee-based information service issue invoices directly to its clients and collect the payments? If this is an acceptable option, the service will almost certainly need an experienced billing clerk on staff from the beginning. How will the service report summaries of its financial activity to the library or the university business office? Who is ultimately responsible and accountable for the billing operation, especially if the service processes incoming checks?

How often will the invoices be sent? Some services send invoices with each daily package, a practice I would discourage. While this procedure might be acceptable to clients who only use the service occasionally, it may prove a burden to the staff and a nuisance to higher volume requesters to handle several invoices a month for the same company. On busy or short-staffed days, some packages might not be shipped at all if the invoice is not prepared in time. In addition, many special order documents will be handled by suppliers who bill monthly, so the service will not know the actual cost to bill back to its own clients until weeks later. Thus, some packages to a client might contain an invoice covering all or part of a shipment, while some documents would be shipped, but not billed, until later. In short, monthly billings are probably best both for the service and for the clients.

If the service issues its own invoices, what will they look like? They should clearly state the service's name, address, and institutional affiliation. They should be dated. Each item the client ordered should be clearly indicated, showing the date each order was received and citing the service's internal document tracking number as well as any identifying numbers that the client may have provided. Clients, especially ones who order documents for several other people at their companies, do not like bills that simply announce: 84 documents for March: $1437.29. Identifying information about each item, such as journal or article title, is helpful but not essential. Some services' invoices break down all the charges individually, showing not only the base document fee but also each individual add-on fee such as copyright costs or rush charges. Other services simply provide the bundled total for each document. Clearly indicate the payment due date.

Some services, like the Technical Information Service, have no control over the invoice format since local regulations allow only the university accounts receivable department to send out invoices. If this is the case, the investigator asks the business officer:

- How and when does the service submit billing information to the central accounting office?
- What elements should be included on these submissions?
- Should the information be submitted in small batches throughout the month, or all at once by a certain date?
- What assurance is there that the billing will, in fact, be made if the information reaches the accounting office by the deadline?
- Can any of the submissions be made electronically?
- How reliable is electronic billing submission?
- How can staff check that the electronic transmission was completed accurately?
- What kind of input can the manager have about what information identifying each transaction appears on the invoice?
- What kinds of reports will the manager receive to show invoices entered, payments received, delinquent accounts, or income over expenses?

The investigator asks the business officer how the institution credits a department. The Technical Information Service is fortunate in that Purdue University credits its account with the income as soon as it submits billing information for a client. The university assumes that it will collect the money in a timely manner. Of course, we experience a small amount of bad debt, but the university does not debit our account for these bad debts until they are over a year past due.

Other fee-based information services are not so lucky; their institutions do not credit their accounts until the clients' checks clear the bank. If some clients are slow- or non-payers, then the service faces not only the burden of monitoring all past due accounts but also the dilemma of deciding when to suspend service and how to do this without jeopardizing a potentially lucrative long-term business relationship. The time involved in tracking which of hundreds of client companies billed each month have accounts 90 days or more overdue can be significant. Some high-volume clients work in companies that for one reason or another do not pay their bills promptly. The client may represent thousands of dollars a year in income, but the manager, seeing the unpaid balance creep upwards, wonders where to draw the line. Suspending service may mean losing the client. Not suspending service may mean that the fee-based information service will have to cover a hefty unpaid balance out of its own reserves.

How does the institution pay its bills? Ideally, invoices such as those from document suppliers and courier services should be sent directly to the fee-based information service so staff can quickly match them with their internal records for items ordered or services received, and then approve them for payment. The investigator finds out:

- Can the service pay its own bills directly with an institutional checking account?
- If so, can the service pay all of them, or must those above a certain amount be approved by someone else?
- What recordkeeping is required?
- Who is ultimately liable?
- If another office actually pays the bills after the service's staff have reviewed and approved them, what assurance does the manager have that the bills will be paid accurately and in a timely manner?

Legal Considerations

In the business plan, the investigator need only identify those few legal issues that the manager will later have to address in more detail. One issue, the matter of possible sales tax liability, has already been mentioned.

Copyright. A major legal issue for fee-based information services is that of copyright. Can a fee-based information service make copies under the fair use provisions of the U.S. copyright law (Section 107) and/or under the provisions of copying for libraries (Section 108)? Is the service exempt from paying royalties for one or both of these reasons? Or should it pay royalties? If royalties are due, will the service follow the CONTU guidelines (National Commission 1978) or pay royalties on everything except U.S. government publications, pre-1920 imprints, and possibly copies of technical reports or other publications issued by its own institution?

Review the literature, especially for any recent changes, during the implementation stage and base the final decisions on a more thorough understanding of the law as it affects fee-based information services than can be provided in this book.

Determining fair use is based on a combination of weighing the following four factors:

1. The purpose and character of the use;
2. The nature of the copyrighted work;
3. The amount copied; and
4. The effect of the use on the potential market for the copyrighted work.

Exemption for copying by libraries requires following the law as it pertains to:

1. No commercial advantage:
2. Open collections;
3. Notice of copyright;
4. Articles and small excerpts; and
5. Multiple or systematic copying.

Several authors agreed that in a non-profit fee-based information service, staff should in most cases be able to make copies for clients under the fair use provisions of law (Bunting 1994, pp. 183-184; Carter and Pagel 1984, p. 257; Gasaway and Wiant 1994, pp. 55-56; Heller 1986). The non-profit service, acting "as an agent of the requester may be able to make copies that the requester could make [under the fair use provisions]" (Gasaway and Wiant 1994, p. 55).

Alison Bunting explained that the issue hinges on "whether a fee-based document delivery service provides an institution or library with direct or indirect commercial advantage. Most library fee-based document services, especially in non-profit institutions, are not making a profit but are recovering costs. Under these conditions, most libraries agree there is no commercial advantage" (Bunting 1994, p. 183). Carter and Pagel believed that their library's "duplicating services do not raise the same questions as information brokerage" and thus interpreted the fair use section of the copyright law to mean that as library employees staff could make copies (within other copyright guidelines) for anyone who requested them (Carter and Pagel 1984, p. 257).

Bunting mentioned, however, that many publishers do not hold this opinion and view library fee-based services as "indistinguishable in purpose and effect from [the activities] of commercial document suppliers" (Bunting 1994, p. 184). Gasaway and Wiant countered the publishers' position by stating that "this issue is not cost recovery but whether the library makes a profit on the sale of copies" (Gasaway and Wiant 1994, p. 56).

The investigator notes that many corporate clients rely on the service to pay any copyright fees due since they interpret the law to mean that any copied documents they acquire are excluded from the fair use provisions. These clients are willing to pay premium rates for documents because, among other things, having the service handle copyright payments relieves them of the tedious necessity of recording and paying royalties directly.

Some managers in non-profit fee-based information services, along with their administrators and legal counsel, advise paying copyright fees. The financial consequences of not doing so might be enormous if the service were later found to have violated the law. James C. Thompson advised that "it would be wise to be conservative until the laws are clarified, or, better, replaced" (Thompson 1983, p. 64).

The time involved in maintaining records proving fair use according to the CONTU guidelines is considerable. Some managers prefer to pay copyright on everything rather than manage an additional set of records for thousands of annual copying transactions, some of which will require copyright payments anyway.

Services operating with the intention of making a profit almost certainly do not qualify for any exemptions from paying copyright royalties. These services have declared that they exist with the purpose of commercial gain.

No one may be absolutely certain which interpretation of the copyright law is the correct one as regards library fee-based information services until there is a court decision. Since a court decision will only occur following a lawsuit, this is an event that managers fervently hope will never happen, or will, at least, happen to someone else!

The investigator, implementer, and manager stay aware of copyright decisions and interpretations that affect fee-based copying. The whole question seems a very murky legal issue, and new cases or decisions may change affect fee-based services.

At this point in the business plan, I suggest that the investigator assume that the proposed fee-based information service will indeed pay copyright on virtually every document it copies or orders to be copied on its clients' behalf. This decision can be changed on the advice of the university's legal counsel during the implementation process. The only remaining question at this point, then, is whether the document pricing structure will include copyright fees up to a certain limit, or whether all copyright fees will be an add-on cost to the base price.

Liability. Another legal consideration to include in the business plan is that of liability. For example, who is responsible if a client makes a decision based on information provided by the service, and then, apparently as a result of that decision, someone is injured or the company loses money or some other calamity occurs? Respondents to Anne Mintz' survey listed these examples of information malpractice:

> misrepresenting oneself in obtaining information, industrial espionage, misrepresenting the work one can perform, presenting "half-baked" products, breaches of client or source confidentiality, doing something illegal, purposely giving false information, and sloppy research (Mintz 1984, p. 21).

In an effort to protect themselves against possible legal action, some services require that before staff undertake any research, the clients sign a statement agreeing that they will not bring suit against the staff, the service, or the university in the case of any kind of loss. A slightly less drastic measure involves including a statement with the search results pointing out that the information specialist cannot be held accountable for information gathered from secondary sources, and that clients should use caution when interpreting the results.

In my opinion, neither of these approaches is palatable. In essence, with these statements the service conveys the impression that although the client is paying several hundred dollars for a search conducted by an experienced information professional, the results may be inaccurate, incomplete, misleading, or all three. This approach will hardly inspire confidence in a new client to whom $300 represents a sizeable portion of the research budget. In nearly 10 years of operation, TIS has encountered a few cases of clients who were less than satisfied with search results for various reasons, but none of them has ever hinted or threatened that their unhappiness might lead to a lawsuit. Avoid potential misunderstandings by advising the information specialists to include in the initial phone reference interview a short explanation of both the benefits and the limitations of database or manual searches for each client's specific project.

Confidentiality. Confidentiality is another issue. Most clients assume that the service will respect their confidentiality by not divulging their research interests to anyone. In fact, some clients specifically ask fee-based services to make various inquiries on their behalf so as not to reveal their interest on a particular topic by calling other companies, agencies, or organizations themselves.

A few very nervous clients may ask a staff member to sign a confidentiality agreement. This situation can be tricky. Considerations include:

- Can the specialist, as a university employee, sign a legally binding confidentiality agreement?
- If clients present their companies' confidentiality agreements, should the specialist ask university counsel to review the document in advance? How much time will this review take?
- Who is ultimately liable if the specialist signs an agreement, but client confidentiality is later compromised in some way?

- Even with a signed confidentiality agreement, can the service legally refuse to release files if faced with a subpoena?
- What is the state law for confidentiality of library records?
- What provision does the university make for liability coverage for its employees?

Fortunately, these situations are extremely rare. Most clients do not require such positive assurance, and the staff can always choose to decline those few projects for which clients insist on signed confidentiality statements.

Licensing Restrictions. Will the service purchase licensed products, such as reference works on CD-ROM? Might staff consider using locally mounted databases or CD-ROMs that the library has already purchased or leased? If so, review these products' licensing agreements before purchase or use by service staff. Many of the products are sold with the understanding that portions of them will not be repackaged for third parties or that the academic prices preclude use by non-primary users. Some databases accessible through bibliographic utilities such as Dialog also carry similar restrictions. Negotiate with the CD-ROM or database producers to revise the standard contracts with wording that sanctions the uses to which the service will put the product.

The Service's Name. Establishing the service's name presents other legal considerations. The investigator suggests several names, and the library administration may propose others. The service's name is very important. It reflects what it is or does, yet is also both distinctive and easily remembered. It should not be easily confused with another similarly named service on campus; TIS gets a few calls a year intended for the library's Technical Services department. The investigator checks the *Burwell World Directory of Information Brokers* (Burwell 1995) to be sure that the proposed name is not being used by another organization, either a broker or an academic fee-based information service. Some years ago, one service received a letter from a software company's attorney pointing out that the service was using the same name as one of the company's products. This service changed its name to avoid further legal entanglements, a move resulting both in expensive reprinting of everything with its name on it and also in efforts to imprint its new identity on its clients. So the investigator checks trademark and business sources to be sure that the proposed name will not cause potential headaches later.

Sometimes it is advantageous to include the institution's name as part of the service's name. The institution's name provides immediate recognition and a sense of excellence by association to at least the local segment of the potential client base. However, the institution's name may do little to enhance the service's image in the minds of more distant clients.

Avoid using a name so generic that it lacks any distinctive elements. Try not to use library jargon, such as "document delivery" in the name. In fact, avoid using any version or derivative of the word "library" in the name.

One service went so far as to trademark its name to prevent anyone else from using it. This process is relatively inexpensive but generally not essential.

Check the proposed name for acronyms. It may be advantageous for the service's name to have a catchy acronym or initialism, but do not overlook a potentially embarrassing or undesirable one. The initialism for the Technical Information Service is TIS, but some people choose the acronym and pronounce it by hissing the much less attractive "tisssss."

Strengths and Weaknesses

It is easy to be enthusiastic about pointing out the proposed service's strengths but more difficult to be honest about its weaknesses. There will almost always be at least a few weaknesses, and the astute investigator lists them rather than waiting for the library administrators to point them out later. The plan then proposes solutions to these weak points.

For example, if a medium-sized university proposes a service, the library collection will not have the depth of its cousins at major research institutions. A proposed solution would be to develop superlative document special order capabilities. Or, if the institution is located in a relatively rural area with a small local industry base, the plan explains how the staff will market services to businesses in the region's larger cities.

Performance Evaluation

How will the manager and administrators determine that the service is meeting its objectives? The proposal includes suggestions for measuring the service's performance. One possibility is determining that the service has billed (and collected) a particular dollar amount after six or twelve months of operation. Another is that a certain number of clients from the target market segment have responded by placing orders. Other measures include the level of repeat business or the percentage increase in orders over a certain time period.

The business plan suggests both short- and long-term evaluation measures to ascertain if the service has met specific goals. Include a timetable for making these assessments.

Implementation Time Frame

Library administrators will find a section outlining a suggested implementation time frame helpful. Based on the research, the investigator suggests two or three scenarios for making the service operational. Each scenario briefly describes the major steps needed to turn an empty space into an operating fee-based information service, pointing out that many of the steps would occur simultaneously. The personnel officer can assist in advertising for a manager, for example, at the same time that the office walls are being painted and the furniture ordered.

The investigator recommends one of the scenarios as the optimal one, based on a combination of factors such as the time it will take to accomplish the major steps, the amount and duration of initial funding, and the speed with which the administrators hope to establish the service. It may be easier to refer to the number the months after administrative approval, rather than to specific dates. The investigator has probably worked the academic environment long enough to know that projects that progress on schedule are usually the exception rather than the rule. If the investigator hopes that the administrators will approve the business plan in January and thus bases all projections from that date, needless revisions or confusion may result if the approval comes in March. A better solution is to label particular implementation activities as occurring in Month Three after approval, for example.

MOVING TO THE NEXT PHASE

By the time the investigator reaches the point of recommending an implementation time frame, the basic research has ended. During the research phase, the investigator focused on the major issues to propose answers to the questions the administrators will ask. Solving many of the details of operating a fee-based information service must wait until the start-up phase, partly because too much emphasis on details at this stage will rob valuable time from investigating the major points, and partly because workable solutions to minor problems will be easier to handle during implementation.

The investigator also realizes that the research phase can be virtually infinite. There will always be another potential client base, another possible marketing avenue, and another helpful piece of equipment or software. The savvy investigator knows when to stop. When the majority of the research has been completed, the investigator sits down with the notes and organizes the final report.

CITED REFERENCES

Broadbent, H.E. 1981. "Pricing Information Products and Services." *Drexel Library Quarterly* 17(2): 99-107.
Bunting, A. 1994. "Legal Considerations for Document Delivery Services." *Bulletin of the Medical Library Association* 82(2): 183-187.
Burrows, S., and A. LaRocca. 1983. "Fees for Automated Reference Services in Academic Health Science Libraries: No Free Lunches." *Medical Reference Services Quarterly* 2(2): 1-15.
Burwell, H.P., ed. 1995. *The Burwell World Directory of Information Brokers.* 12th edition. Houston, TX: Burwell Enterprises.

Cady, S.A., and B.G. Richards. 1982. "The One-Thousand-Dollar Alternative: How One University Structures a Fee-Based Information Service for Local Industry." *American Libraries* 14(3): 175-176.

Caren, L., and A. Somerville. 1988. "Issues Facing Private Academic Libraries Considering Fee-Based Programs." *The Reference Librarian* (22): 37-49.

Carter, N.C., and S.B. Pagel. 1984. "Fees for Service: The Golden Gate University Law Library Membership Plan." *Law Library Journal* 77(2): 243-274.

Downing, A. 1990. "The Consequences of Offering Fee-Based Services in a Medical Library." *Bulletin of the Medical Library Association* 78(1): 57-63.

Felicetti, B.W. 1982. "Information Brokering: What Is It, Why It Is, and How It Is Done." Pp. 2-19 in *So You Want to Be an Information Broker?*, edited by K. Warnken and B. Felicetti. Chicago, IL: Information Alternative.

Finnigan, G. 1995. "The Rise of Value-Added Document Delivery Services." Pp. 13-30 in *Document Delivery in an Electronic Age*, edited by D. Kaser. Philadelphia, PA: National Federation of Abstracting and Information Services.

Gasaway, L.N., and S.K. Wiant. 1994. *Libraries and Copyright: A Guide to Copyright Law in the 1990s*. Washington, DC: Special Libraries Association.

Grant, M.M., and D. Ungarelli. 1987. "Fee-Based Business Research in an Academic Library." *The Reference Librarian* (19): 239-255.

Green, T.C. 1993. "Competencies for Entry-Level Independent Information Professionals: An Assessment by Practitioners." *Journal of Education for Library and Information Science* 34(2): 165-168.

Heller, J.S. 1986. "Copyright and Fee-Based Copying Services." *College and Research Libraries* 47(1): 28-37.

Herman, L. 1990. "Costing, Charging, and Pricing: Related but Different Decisions." *The Bottom Line* 4(2): 26-29.

Josephine, H.B. 1992. "University Libraries and Information Services for the Business Community." Pp. 321-329 in *The Marketing of Library and Information Services*, Volume 2, edited by B. Cronin. London: Aslib.

Kibirige, H.M. 1983. *The Information Dilemma: A Critical Analysis of Information Pricing and the Fees Controversy*. Westport, CT: Greenwood Press.

Marvin, S. 1988. "ExeLS: Executive Library Services." *The Reference Librarian* (22): 145-160.

Mintz, A.P. 1984. "Information Practice and Malpractice: Do We Need Malpractice Insurance?" *Online* 8(4): 20-26.

National Commission on New Technological Uses of Copyrighted Works (CONTU). 1978. *Final Report of the National Commission on New Technological Uses of Copyrighted Works*. Washington, DC: National Commission on New Technological Uses of Copyrighted Works.

Olaisen, J.L. 1989. "Pricing Strategies for Library and Information Services." *Libri* 39(4): 253-274.

Roeder, C.S. 1987. "Access Fees in a Hospital Library: A Program for Pharmaceutical Company Representatives." *Bulletin of the Medical Library Association* 75(2): 171-173.

Thompson, J.C. 1983. "Regional Information and Communication Exchange: A Case Study." Pp. 55-76 in *Conference on Fee Based Research in College and University Libraries*. Greenvale, NY: Long Island University Center for Business Research.

Warner, A.S. 1990a. "Charging Back, Charging Out, Charging Fees." *The Bottom Line* 4(3): 32-35.

Williams, S.F. 1987. "To Charge or Not to Charge: No Longer a Question?" *The Reference Librarian* 19: 125-136.

Williams, T.L., H.L. Lemkau, and S. Burrows. 1988. "The Economics of Academic Health Science Libraries: Cost Recovery in the Era of Big Science." *Bulletin of the Medical Library Association* 76(4): 317-322.

Wood, F.K. 1987. "When Do Dollars for Information Service Make Sense? The Wisconsin ISD Experience." *The Bottom Line* 1(4): 25-27.

72 / *Fee-Based Information Services*

Zais, H.W. 1977. "Economic Modeling: An Aid to the Pricing of Information Services." *Journal of the American Society for Information Science* 28(2): 89-95.

FURTHER READING

American Library Association. 1997. *Internet-Plus Directory of Express Library Services: Research and Document Delivery for Hire.* Chicago, IL: American Library Association.

Balachandran, S., and V. Witte. 1987. "The Off-Campus On-Line Computerized Literature Search Service." Pp. 24-36 in *The Off-Campus Library Services Conference Proceedings*, edited by B.M. Lessin. Mount Pleasant, MI: Central Michigan University Press.

Casorso, T.M., and S.J. Rogers. 1987. "Targeting Your Market." Pp. 1-9 in *Fee-Based Services: Issues and Answers*, compiled by A.K. Beaubien. Ann Arbor, MI: Michigan Information Transfer Source, University of Michigan Libraries.

du Toit, A.S.A. 1994. "Developing a Price Strategy for Information Products." *South African Journal of Library and Information Science* 62(December): 162-167.

Franks, J.A., and K.K. Montgomery. 1991. "LINE: The Fee-Based Service at the University of Central Florida Library." *Mississippi Libraries* 55(Spring): 15-17.

George, L.A. 1994. "Taxes and TQM: Taxation of Fee-Based Services in the U.S." *Fee for Service* 1(3): 43-45.

George, L.A. 1996. "The Price is Right: Analyzing Costs in a Fee-Based Information Service." *Fee for Service* 3(2): 7-10.

Hill, S. 1991. "Charging for Information Services: Is There a Best Way for Internal and External Cost Recoveries? *New Zealand Libraries* 49(9): 14-16.

Lunden, E. 1983. "Marketing the R.I.C.E. Operation." Pp. 113-127 in *Conference on Fee Based Research in College and University Libraries.* Greenvale, NY: Long Island University Center for Business Research.

Meader, R. 1991. *Guidelines for Preparing Proposals.* 2nd edition. Chelsea, MI: Lewis Publishers.

Siegel, E.S., B.R. Ford, and J.M. Bornstein. 1993. *The Ernst & Young Business Plan Guide.* 2nd edition. New York. Wiley.

Smith, P.K. 1980. "Marketing Online Services," Part 1. *Online* 4(1): 60-62.

Smith, P.K. 1980. "Marketing Online Services," Part 2. *Online* 4(2): 68-69.

Talaga, J.A. 1991. "Concept of Price in a Library Context." *Journal of Library Administration* 14(4): 87-101.

Warner, A.S. 1987. *Mind Your Own Business: A Guide for the Information Entrepreneur.* New York: Neal Schuman.

Warner, A.S. 1987. "Selling the Service." Pp. 11-17 in *Fee-Based Services: Issues and Answers*, compiled by A.K. Beaubien. Ann Arbor, MI: Michigan Information Transfer Source, University of Michigan Libraries.

Whitmell, V. 1996. "Staffing the Fee-Based Library Service." *Fee for Service* 3(1): 6-12.

Wood, E.J. 1983. "Strategic Planning and the Marketing Process: Library Applications." *Journal of Academic Librarianship* 9(1): 15-20.

Chapter 4

Presenting, Defending, and Revising the Business Plan

THE FINAL REPORT

As with any piece of writing, the investigator aims the report at its audience, the library administrators and any other interested parties, such as a potential funding agency. The report anticipates this audience's major questions, and answers them clearly and completely. Including every detail learned during the investigation is both unnecessary and inadvisable. The report's organization is critical; readers should be able to follow a logical sequence from one point to the next one. If parts of the audience are not librarians, the report explains any jargon or acronyms.

As with most kinds of business writing, use strong action verbs in the active voice. Break up the text with figures or with numbered or bulleted points, if appropriate. Avoid the use of negative words whenever possible. Give specific examples rather than vague generalities. End the report with a section that clearly and positively recommends a course of action and that also requests administrative approval.

Before submitting the final business plan to the library administration, set it aside for a week and then read it again with fresh eyes.

The Last Check

- Are all the points clear?
- Do they progress in a logical order?
- Is the report divided into sections and subsections?
- Could a reader unfamiliar with the concept of fee-based information services quickly grasp the main points of the business plan?
- Has something been omitted?
- Are all the calculations accurate?

- Are the budget and other recommendations realistic?
- Run the text through the spell checker one last time.
- Are the pages numbered?
- Is there a title page?
- Is the report so long that it would benefit from a brief table of contents?
- What does the report look like: adequate margins, clearly readable font, logical headings, text broken appropriately with graphs or tables, pages numbered, accurate references to appendices or figures?
- Would the report look more professional in a cover?

Then ask at least one other person, preferably a colleague who has not worked on the project, to review the draft and jot down notes. Were there any unclear points, jargon, awkward transitions, missing words, spelling or grammatical errors, or blind references? If the investigator worked on the plan at the request of a mentor such as a department head or assistant director, ask that person to review the draft as well. The mentor has a stake in a clear and accurate business plan, and should be willing to comment on it before it lands on the director's desk.

The Executive Summary

Once the investigator is satisfied both with the report's appearance and content, write the executive summary. The executive summary captures the essence of the document in a few well-written paragraphs that clearly define the project. It appears first in the report after the title page and the table of contents, if any. No more than two or three pages long, the executive summary presents the highlights of the report, briefly touching on the major points:

- Definition;
- The rationale for starting a fee-based information service;
- The mission;
- The services;
- The expected client base;
- Requirements for staff, equipment, and space;
- Marketing suggestions;
- Budget;
- Funding;
- Implementation time line;
- Anticipated future growth; and
- Benefits to the library and the institution.

Conclude the executive summary with a strong paragraph recommending that the library approve the business plan and move toward implementation. Write the summary so that it can stand on its own. The library director may use the summary alone to acquaint university administrators with the proposal, so be sure it is clear, positive, persuasive, and free of library jargon.

Report Submission

When the investigator and the mentor are satisfied with the business plan, submit it to the administration with a brief cover letter reminding the administrators of their initial interest in the proposal, pointing out that any deadlines for turning in the plan have been met, reiterating the recommendation to establish a fee-based information service, and indicating willingness and availability to discuss the report or answer any questions about it.

Defending the Business Plan

Susan Tertell pointed out that a fee-based information service "can never be successful without the full and continued support of [the] library administration. Because so many rules must be bent, so many new procedures established, and so many accepted ways of doing things overturned, a firm belief in the importance of such a service must be held by all involved" (Tertell 1983, p. 51). A solid proposal helps build the administration's support for the service.

Although it is possible that the library administrators will approve the first draft of the business plan exactly as it is written, such wholesale enthusiasm is unlikely. The investigator stands ready to answer questions about the plan, especially ones related to costs. The administrators will be cautious about allocating thousands of dollars in start-up funds without a clear understanding about how the funds will be repaid, if required, and how the service will generate enough revenue to cover expected ongoing expenses. They will also be particularly interested in the benefits to both the library and to the institution of operating a fee-based information service.

The administrators may ask for an oral presentation and summary of the report or they may call a meeting to discuss their questions and concerns. The investigator welcomes the opportunity rather than immediately fearing the worst. Defending the proposal does not mean taking a defensive stance; it means being ready and willing to listen to the administrators' comments, concerns, and questions. Since the idea of a local fee-based information service may be a new or hazy concept for them, the investigator's role is to answer their questions demonstrating the depth and thoroughness of the background research, yet acknowledging that the project does represent some risk. The investigator's job is to point out that the potential and expected benefits far outweigh the initial risks. The investigator should also feel comfortable occasionally answering a tough question by saying: "I don't know the answer to that question, but I will find out and let you know." Then do it.

Compromising

Few investigators will be lucky enough to have even the most enthusiastically supportive library administration approve the first draft of the business plan without suggesting some alterations. At least some of the recommendations, most likely concerning the budget, pricing, space, equipment, and staff, will almost certainly be negotiated into compromises.

The investigator prepares for these negotiations. By following the outline in Chapter 3, the business plan recommended the optimal configuration for the new fee-based information service, but the investigator also learned which features could be scaled down or eliminated, at least during the implementation phase.

The investigator and the mentor should also be prepared to make reasonable compromises to gain the administrators' approval. Reducing the marketing budget by 20 percent, delaying the purchase of a second fax machine, or starting with a half-time instead of a full-time billing clerk will probably not cripple the start-up effort. However, the investigator also understands the difference between reasonable compromise and agreeing to conditions that would severely jeopardize the service's chances of success. Both sides must be realistic and flexible.

Navigating the Pilot Project Suggestion

Administrators reluctant to commit the resources necessary to launch a fee-based information service may suggest that the library start in a small way on an experimental basis. They argue that the library should first determine if the local market for information services truly exists and if people will really pay for services. Surely a pilot project is a sensible way to test the waters. Then, with the income from the project and with proof of a solid client base, the library can develop a full-fledged service.

This argument sounds perfectly reasonable, especially in situations where the options are a trial run or no service at all. Before agreeing to a pilot project, the investigator and the mentor insist on the following points:

- Hire special staff for the project; do NOT add tasks to the duties of existing staff, with the possible exception of the project administrator, who will have regular duties reduced proportionally to the involvement in the project. Be sure that the new staff clearly understand the risks of working on a limited duration project that may not be renewed.
- Provide project staff with their own space and equipment. They should not have to struggle for access to equipment used for serving primary users.
- Establish quantifiable measures of the project's success in advance. For example, the project might have to show that it recovered a certain dollar amount or filled a certain number of document requests. Near the end of

the project, measure the project's success and decide whether to legitimize the service as a permanent unit made based on the results of those measurements.

- Define marketing activities.
- Set prices at or close to the prices calculated for cost-recovery. Setting prices artificially low for a trial period not only results in inaccurate conclusions drawn from any measurements but also makes the later transition to a higher priced, true cost-recovery, permanent service unnecessarily more difficult.
- Establish a budget for the project.
- Set a realistic duration for the pilot project, with one year being the minimum. An experimental program running for only a few months does not allow enough time to market the service adequately or to cultivate repeat clients. People will also hesitate to accept temporary jobs of less than a year's duration; the success of the. project may be jeopardized by staff constantly seeking permanent employment elsewhere.

Most libraries that have tried the pilot project approach did so by adding tasks for serving non-primary users on a fee basis to the existing staff's workload. In my opinion, this practice is highly inadvisable and so full of pitfalls as to seriously jeopardize the project's success. Although such an approach worked to some degree in their library, Caren and Somerville cited a number of problems, many of them related to staffing:

- Overburdened staff did not welcome the imposition of demands from non-primary users;
- Staff had trouble prioritizing client requests above requests from campus users;
- Staff with expertise in certain subject areas handled a heavier work load from external clients;
- To meet demand, some staff handled projects after regular working hours or at home;
- The program was not actively promoted;
- Program expenses were difficult to differentiate from normal library expenditures;
- Some client requests were turned down because of lack of staff time;
- The program made a profit, but the librarians realized that the profit was not a fair test of the fee-based information service concept because the library heavily subsidized costs such as salaries, telephone calls, and equipment (Caren and Somerville 1988, pp. 40-44).

A trial run like this would probably be even more difficult to implement in a decentralized library system with many branches. In addition, the proliferation of "do-it-yourself" electronic sources in most libraries over the last decade has vastly reduced the need for librarians to perform mediated database searches for the academic community. Thus, many librarians' online searching skills are a bit rusty these days.

James Thompson has recommended that a new fee-based service:

> be a separate administrative unit. It will be easier to justify its creation, and in later years its continuation, if it can be shown that or to what extent it is a cost-recovery operation. In addition, work will be easier to control if it's concentrated in a single department. Otherwise, two problems may occur. First, requests, forms, and documents will pile up in desk drawers all around the library, and whoever coordinates the outside requests will spend too much time tracking them down, answering status requests, and so forth. Second, different departments will assign different and inconsistent priorities to various client groups (Thompson 1983, p. 69).

Elizabeth Lunden summarized the danger of trying to introduce a new service with current resources by writing that "the resulting breakdown in service is difficult if not impossible to overcome" (Lunden 1983, p. 119). After conducting site visits to 11 libraries, Douglas Ernest observed that "librarians felt themselves stretched to meet the needs of their primary clientele and dared not embark on outreach programs [using existing staff] that might have promised more than they could deliver" (Ernest 1993, p. 399). Jerome Lom reported "staff confusion and uncertainty as to where reference service ends and a fee-based transaction begins" (Lom 1986, p. 297). Kathy McGuire pointed out that "marketing and promoting the service is a full time job" (McGuire 1993, p. 125). Vicki Whitmell wrote that "the question of loyalty will arise as there will be conflicting demands from paying clients who expect priority service" (Whitmell 1996, p. 6).

Staff at one specialized business library that integrated its services to primary and non-primary users recognized several difficulties.

> Switching roles from a low key directing mode, then to a teaching mode and finally to that of providing a professional fee-based service to sophisticated business and industry clients with specific deadlines requires a very specific combination of personality, professional expertise, planning and versatility. For many librarians, the ability to perform a triple role on a daily basis ... is difficult" (Grant and Ungarelli 1987, p. 249).

Over time, this library hired librarians with skills and personal characteristics compatible with its needs. It is highly unlikely, however, that a library embarking on an experimental project will be fortunate enough to have the right mix of people already on board.

Another library encountered a host of difficulties in offering a corporate membership program with services handled by a variety of staff who also had other duties working with the primary clientele. These difficulties included:

- Subconscious efforts to build a collection that more closely matched the needs of the paying clients than the needs of the primary users;

- Significant use of staff time, leaving less time available to assist local patrons;
- Unexpectedly high expenses such as computer time; designing, printing and distributing brochures; developing billing procedures; mailings; and other incidental costs;
- In an effort to control demand, photocopy requests were limited to three per day per client;
- Uneven quality of the services provided since different staff members had different perceptions of the program's importance (Carter and Pagel 1984).

A late, low quality, or unfilled document order may lose more than the few dollars that the service would have billed; clients who might potentially place several hundred or several thousand dollars' worth of orders might decide to take their business elsewhere. There are plenty of competitors who can meet those deadlines. To the average businessperson, universities do not project an image of an organization able to respond quickly. The fee-based service staff works hard every day to counteract that image of ivory tower slow motion by proving that they can supply information and documents quickly and accurately. In today's business environment, clients will not tolerate more than one or two mistakes or delays before they switch to another provider that better meets their deadlines. Reliability is extremely difficult to achieve in a trial situation when services are provided by staff trying to squeeze a few projects into already over- or fully committed schedules.

Would the concept of a fee-based information service really be given a fair chance in a piecemeal trial approach fraught with difficulties ranging from staff resentment to the absence of a marketing plan? Probably not. In short, it is much better, both from the viewpoint of the staff and of the clients, to make the commitment and start a fee-based service in a small way as an independent unit, rather than trying to test the concept with current staff, or even as a small experimental pilot project.

USING CONSULTANTS

After a few discussions, the administrators may feel comfortable and confident enough to commit the start-up funds, possibly pending minor revisions of the business plan and its budget and implementation schedule. Complete the revision promptly and resubmit it for final approval.

However, in some cases the administrators will indicate that they would feel more comfortable with an independent assurance that the plan is feasible, that the client base exists and can be reached, and that a cost-recovery fee-based information service would be both valuable and viable in the local environment. At this point, the investigator suggests hiring a consultant.

The American Library Association's Fee-Based Information Services in Academic Libraries (FISCAL) discussion group maintains a list of those of its members who are willing to consult on the subject of new fee-based information services. These consultants charge for their work, either officially as a research project assigned to their own fee-based services or personally as free-lance consultants. In either case, a consultation will cost at least several thousand dollars.

Hiring a Consultant

The fees generally include an hourly rate, plus reimbursement for travel, lodging, meals, and other incidentals. The consultant reviews the business plan and then visits the site for one or two days to talk with the investigator, the business officer, the personnel officer, the mentor, and possibly others in the library administration, to get a good idea of the local situation. Then, combining personal experience as a manager of an established fee-based information service, the specialized knowledge of the information industry, and the information gathered from the business plan and the visit, the consultant prepares a report.

The investigator should not feel that calling in a consultant indicates that the work on the business plan was necessarily incomplete or inaccurate. The administration has indicated its continuing interest, and provided funds to obtain a second opinion from someone already experienced in managing fee-based information service operations, someone who will view the local situation with a fresh perspective. If the work on the business plan is solid, the consultant will confirm its findings and recommendations. On the other hand, if it contains a few flaws, oversights, or oversimplifications, the consultant points them out and recommends corrections and improvements.

Selecting a Consultant

The investigator prepares a written description of the work the library wants the consultant to do, the consultation's goals and objectives, the general time frame, and a clear indication of what final product, such as a report or presentation, the library requires. Next, the investigator interviews several potential consultants by phone before recommending one to handle the assignment. The best way to approach the phone interview is to call each candidate, briefly describe the project, and ask to schedule a time for a longer conversation about it if the consultant is interested. If the consultant is not interested in the project, ask for referrals to colleagues.

During the second, longer phone interview, the investigator asks a number of questions to assess the candidate's ability to complete the project in a timely, professional, and cost-effective manner. Points to cover include:

- References or other evidence of having completed a similar project before;

- Number of years' experience in managing a fee-based service;
- Involvement in another service's start-up phases;
- Involvement with preparing the established service's annual budget and other financial reports;
- Professional credentials;
- Similarity of the proposed consultant's service to the one planned at the local institution in terms of institution type, library collection size, subject emphasis, and/or client base;
- Hourly rate for the project, and an estimation of how many hours it would take to complete the assignment, including travel, the site visit, and writing the report;
- Resume; and
- Samples of professional writing.

Pay equal attention to the questions that the consultant asks the investigator. Rate the interviewee for:

- Clear expression of thought;
- Listening skills;
- Asking what written material will be sent in advance for review;
- Asking for a copy of the written project description and the business plan;
- Indicating how soon after the campus visit the consulting report would be completed;
- Willingness to provide a written cost estimate or bid for the project;
- Availability for a visit to campus; and
- Genuine interest in the project.

Check in advance to be sure that the local institution will accept an invoice from the consultant personally or if the invoice must come from the consultant's home institution. For a variety of reasons, a prospective consultant may prefer to bill the work personally rather than as an employee of his or her own university.

Working with a Consultant

Based on the answers to the interview questions, the bids, and the investigator's opinions about each candidate based on the phone conversations, the library hires a consultant. For the best possible outcome, the investigator should send the consultant copies of all relevant documentation a few weeks before the visit. The packet should contain the latest draft of the business plan as well as any supporting material such as the availability of grants or loans, description of the collection, information about the anticipated client base, and so on. The more information the consultant learns in advance of the visit, the more productive the time spent on campus.

The investigator's preparations for the consultant's visit are as carefully arranged as they would be for a job applicant's:

- Coordinate lodging accommodations with the consultant's arrival time;
- Provide information about airport shuttles or other local transportation;
- Prepare an itinerary for the length of the visit, listing in a logical order the people the consultant will meet and allowing plenty of time at the end of the visit for a wrap-up session;
- Arrange for the consultant to be escorted from one office to the next;
- Plan breaks and meals;
- Distribute the itinerary in advance to both the consultant and the staff involved in the visit;
- Make sure the local staff understand the purpose of the visit and will assist the consultant;
- Confirm all arrangements a few days before the visit; and
- Double check that all the relevant background material reaches the consultant in enough time for thorough review before arriving on campus.

The Consultant's Visit

During the visit, the investigator makes every effort to see that the consultant moves smoothly and promptly from one office to the next. The breaks and meals, while providing some relaxation, are also opportunities for the investigator, staff, and consultant to speak informally and to clarify or raise points from earlier discussions or from the material sent to the consultant in advance. The investigator notes any further information the consultant indicates is needed, and makes sure it is sent as soon as possible. After the visit, the investigator sends a brief note:

- Thanking the consultant;
- Encouraging phone calls if questions arise while the consultant prepares the recommendation; and
- Reiterating the date by which the library expects to receive the final report or presentation.

Ideally, the consultant's final report will confirm the investigator's original recommendation that the institution establish a fee-based information service. The best reports add a new dimension or polish based on the consultant's experience managing a successful service. The consultant will almost certainly point out a few areas where the investigator's original report would benefit from some improvement. These notes do not necessarily reflect negatively on the investigator; a practitioner usually has a better understanding than the most diligent researcher.

Also ideally, the consultant's report allays the library administrators' lingering misgivings and confirms that a fee-based information service would indeed be an asset to the library and to the institution. However, the administrators may also choose not to accept the consultant's recommendations, either in whole or in part, no matter how positive they may be. There may be broader institutional, financial, or other concerns that suggest that this is not the best time to open a fee-based information service. However, the chances are very strong that if the administrators agreed to hire a consultant in the first place, they are probably close enough to approval that the consultant's positive report will provide the final confirmation. And in at least one case, an institution later hired its consultant as the manager of its new fee-based information service.

REVISING THE BUSINESS PLAN

The investigator reviews the consultant's report and incorporates its suggestions and conclusions into the revised business plan. Point out the major areas where the consultant agreed with the original business plan. However, if the investigator does not agree with some of the consultant's findings or recommendations, these issues should be identified as needing further discussion with the library administrators.

Submit the revised plan to the administration, with the consultant's report appended as an attachment. The approval process begins again for, it is hoped, the final round. After the library administration approves the business plan, the implementation stage is next.

CITED REFERENCES

Caren, L., and A. Somerville. 1988. "Issues Facing Private Academic Libraries Considering Fee-Based Programs." *The Reference Librarian* (22): 37-49.

Carter, N.C., and S.B. Pagel. 1984. "Fees for Service: The Golden Gate University Law Library Membership Plan." *Law Library Journal* 77(2): 243-274.

Ernest, D.J. 1993. "Academic Libraries, Fee-Based Information Services, and the Business Community." *RQ* 32(3): 393-402.

Grant, M.M., and D. Ungarelli. 1987. "Fee-Based Business Research in an Academic Library." *The Reference Librarian* (19): 239-255.

Lom, J.A. 1986. "Fee-Based Reference Service: A Reevaluation." *RQ* 25(3): 295-299.

Lunden, E. 1983. "Marketing the R.I.C.E. Operation." Pp. 113-127 in *Conference on Fee Based Research in College and University Libraries*. Greenvale, NY: Long Island University Center for Business Research.

McGuire, K. 1993. "Information Direct: Birmingham Library Services' Fee-Based Business Service." *Law Librarian* 24(September): 125-126.

Tertell, S.M. 1983. "Fee-Based Services to Business: Implementation in a Public Library." *Drexel Library Quarterly* 19(4): 37-53.

Thompson, J.C. 1983. "Regional Information and Communication Exchange: A Case Study." Pp. 55-76 in *Conference on Fee Based Research in College and University Libraries*. Greenvale, NY: Long Island University Center for Business Research.

Whitmell, V. 1996. "Staffing the Fee-Based Library Service." *Fee for Service* 3(1): 6-12.

FURTHER READING

Finer, R. 1986. "The Consulting Process." Pp. 131-158 in *Information Consultants in Action*, edited by J.S. Parker. London: Mansell.

Chapter 5

Implementing the Business Plan

THE IMPLEMENTER

The implementation phase begins once the library administration approves the business plan, in either its original or its revised form, and indicates which of the several proposed implementation schedules best meets its expectations. The key person at this stage is the implementer.

The implementer may be the same person as the investigator, or may be someone else on the library staff, or the administration may recommend that the manager implement the plan. If the manager is to be hired from outside the organization, or if appointing an internal candidate is a lengthy process, most implementation tasks will in this case wait until the manager is in place. However, even if the administrators anticipate a delay in beginning the implementation phase, they should delegate someone to initiate any major time-consuming or long-term tasks, such as significant renovations of the office space, especially if these tasks depend on the schedules of other university units.

As with the investigator, clearly define the implementer's role from the outset, especially if the administrators do not anticipate that this person will join the service's permanent staff. The implementation stage will be time-consuming, so if the implementer is not the manager, arrange some release time from usual duties. The implementer asks the administration for a clear indication of when the responsibilities will be relinquished; if not on a specific date, then when certain specific tasks, such as office renovations or the arrival of the manager, have been accomplished. If the implementer will eventually join the service staff full-time, but works on the implementation phase on a part-time basis, the administration decides what percentage of the salary will come from the library budget and what percentage from the service's budget.

If the office space is unavailable, or not yet at least minimally furnished and equipped when the implementer arrives, assign adequate space and equipment on a temporary basis elsewhere.

SETTING THE LAUNCH DATE

Setting a launch date gives the implementer a goal and a deadline around which to plan the implementation tasks. Choose a realistic date: not so soon that that a single setback would throw the whole project off schedule, but also not so distant that it seems it will never be reached. The implementer and the library administration should come to a clear agreement, based on the recommendations presented in the plan, about the launch date.

As with any large undertaking requiring the coordination of dozens of tasks, some things will inevitably go wrong. The printer may order the wrong paper stock for the brochures; the phone company may be delayed in installing new lines; someone may overlook an equipment order; the implementer may be unexpectedly called away from the office for two weeks for family reasons; or the first round of interviews for a billing clerk may not identify a satisfactory candidate.

Although some of the implementation tasks must be handled sequentially (there may be little point hiring the staff until the furniture has arrived and the microcomputers have been installed, for example), many others can be undertaken simultaneously. This chapter identifies the tasks, but the order in which they are done is usually not critical, as long as the implementer keeps track of all the tasks to ensure that they will all be completed satisfactorily and in a logical order by the launch date.

IMPLEMENTATION BUDGET

In approving the business plan, the administration made a commitment to the implementation budget, either as a separate budget or as part of the first year's budget. If all the service's start-up funding comes from a grant or loan or other fund, the library's business officer usually designates a separate account number against which expenses will be drawn. However, if the library funds the implementation phase in whole or in part, assigning charges to the correct account may be confusing in the early days, especially if the implementer is a current staff member working on the implementation part-time while also incurring other expenses related to other responsibilities. To avoid potential confusion, one of the first things the implementer does is to ask the business officer to explain clearly what funds or account numbers are to be used for costs associated with starting the fee-based service. Other financial considerations will be addressed later in this chapter.

NAMING THE SERVICE

If it has not already been decided, settle on a name for the service. A name gives the project a sense of reality and begins to build identity within the library and the institution. Decide if it is important for the name to be trademarked. Obtaining a trademark is relatively straightforward and inexpensive.

GETTING ADVICE

After settling the essential preliminary issues such as the new service's name and launch date, the implementer may feel overwhelmed at the amount of work and the seemingly endless details ahead. Hundreds of questions arise, many of which seem only answerable by trial and error—or, perhaps, by current practitioners.

Established Services

Managers of other fee-based information services have written job descriptions, bought software, designed invoices, printed brochures, organized files, reported copyright, selected document suppliers and database vendors, prospected for clients, compiled statistics, and hired staff. What better people to ask for guidance and support?

The implementer is right to seek advice, of course, but exercises both wisdom and restraint in tapping this resource. Fee-based information service managers are extremely busy people. According to their service's fee schedules, their professional time is worth $60 to $80 an hour. Most of them will respond graciously to the occasional phone call asking a specific question such as "Approximately what percentage of your document delivery orders require rush handling?" or "We're getting ready to print our brochure for the first time, and we plan to mail out 5,000 to our target client base within the first three months. Based on your experience, do you think this is advisable?"

However, asking five managers what brand of fax machine they use may result in nothing more than four or five different answers, leaving the implementer no closer to a decision that should have been made based on some questions to the local office equipment store, the university purchasing department, and the interlibrary loan office.

Conducting Surveys

Questionnaires have their place in library research, but 10-page surveys sent out by managers of fledgling fee-based services is not one of them. I have found most of the ones sent to me to be inadvertently both irritating and impertinent. Most of these surveys have been clearly sent to dozens of services, often with very little apparent effort to match the size and type of institution as closely as possible with that of the survey implementer's. How can it possibly help an implementer from a community college (or even from another comparably sized research institution, for that matter) to know that after 10 years of operation, Purdue's Technical Information Service has nine full-time staff, two offices, 150 hours a week of student assistant time, four laser printers and three fax machines of various brands, and a postage scale that can weigh packages up to 10 pounds? Little of this information is of much use to a new service. (And I have wished for years that we had initially invested in a scale that weighed packages up to 25 pounds!)

Impertinent questions include those that ask for details about cost-recovery income, successful marketing techniques, staff salaries and fringes, funding, and so on. Even when invited to check a box indicating that the answer falls within a range of dollar amounts, I usually decline to complete these sections.

Practicing managers will be less inclined to answer questionnaires that inquire for page after page about the brand names of their equipment, the number of document requests their service filled each year for the past decade, their client percentage breakdown by SIC code, and the names of their top 10 document suppliers. Quite apart from the time needed to answer these questionnaires, most managers will be reluctant to provide such detailed information to someone who is, after all, a competitor. In addition, every service operates under different institutional constraints with different definitions of even such basic terms as "cost recovery" and "client."

Operating a fee-based information service is *not* an academic exercise, even if it functions on a nonprofit basis within an academic institution. It is very close to running a business. The people who manage these businesses are usually congenial and collegial, but only to the point where their answers do not jeopardize their own service's success and competitive edge. They are not being uncooperative or unfriendly; they are just thinking like the businesspeople they need to be ensure their own services' continued success. The implementers and managers of new services often simply have not been in the business long enough to start thinking like businesspeople, too.

Many implementers seek advice from their more experienced colleagues more for the reassurance value than because they are unable to develop their own solutions. Implementers should realize, however, that most decisions will not be fatal to the program's success if they turn out to be wrong, or even simply misguided. After all, TIS can always buy a new postage scale.

Hiring Consultants

Several other solutions are possible for obtaining advice. If the library called in a consultant at the investigation stage, the implementer may make arrangements to retain the consultant on an hourly basis to answer occasional questions or to review drafts of the proposed marketing materials. If the library did not use a consultant's services, the implementer can approach an experienced manager who may have been especially helpful during the investigation phase and ask if this person would act as a sounding board at that service's advertised research rates. The manager may be willing to answer occasional questions as a professional courtesy. However, the implementer offers to pay for the expertise and does not feel offended if the adviser declines to answer some questions.

Site Visits

Another way to get some help and advice is to arrange to visit a nearby service, if this option is geographically feasible. Call well in advance and clearly indicate the visit's purpose (e.g., learn about document delivery work flow, billing software, staffing patterns). If the visit lasts more than half a day, the implementer offers to pay for the manager's consulting time at the service's published hourly rate. Do not expect (or ask) colleagues to part with any trade secrets, such as how much revenue the service generated last year or which European document suppliers they use. Pay for a meal to which the manager and senior staff are invited. Follow up the visit with a personal thank you note, even if the institution will also send a check for the consulting services.

STAFF

In most cases, the implementer begins work without first having to hire any support staff. One of the tasks, however, will be to work with the library personnel office to write job descriptions in anticipation of hiring the initial complement of support staff a month or two before the service's launch date. If the implementer is not familiar with the institution's hiring and personnel policies, learn basic procedures for identifying, interviewing, hiring, training, and evaluating new staff.

Appendix B contains job descriptions for several positions in Purdue's Technical Information Service. Remember that these descriptions are for staff in a service that has grown to the point where a number of job functions have become specialized. In a new service, many of these functions would be combined into fewer positions. Vicki Whitmell's article includes a sample job description for an information specialist (Whitmell 1996, p. 11).

Hiring the Professional Staff

If the implementer is also responsible for coordinating the selection process for professional staff, such as the manager, or the manager and an information specialist, choose this work as one of the first to set in motion. Besides coordinating a selection advisory committee, the implementer may also be responsible for drafting the job descriptions and for securing the necessary university approval for advertising new positions. Advertising regionally or nationally usually requires writing a job ad and learning the university procedures for placing it. The library personnel office assists in some of these tasks, but the implementer's responsibility is to see that tasks are handled in a timely manner. Even if the university is located in a large urban area from which it is expected that a pool of strong candidates will be quickly identified, the interview and hiring process may be lengthy, and the successful candidate may require four to eight weeks from the acceptance date before beginning the new job. Unless the institution has a proven track record of approving new professional positions and identifying and hiring librarians very quickly, allow six to nine months before the first newly hired professional reports to work.

While writing the job description, give some thought to the professionals' titles. It is unfortunately a fact that the title "librarian" does not always conjure up in the general public's mind the image of a skilled information professional. Consider other titles such as "information specialist" or "information researcher" (Wilkins 1992, p. 26).

Also allow a few weeks for the new professional to visit at least the major campus libraries, to learn how to use the office equipment and software, and to get any supplementary training needed to become familiar with selected commercial databases.

Finding qualified professional staff for fee-based information services, especially start-up operations, often takes longer than anticipated. Many traditional academic librarians feel uncomfortable with the concept of charging for services and soliciting clients. Some corporate librarians have salary requirements well beyond the range that a university offers. Other experienced and highly qualified corporate librarians do not have MLS degrees, which may be a requirement for the job, at least for the manager's position. In addition, many potential candidates are understandably nervous about the risk of accepting a position in an as-yet-unproved service that, if it does not show unmistakable signs of success within a year or two, may leave them unemployed.

Attributes of a Successful Manager

The literature describes several attributes of a successful manager for a fee-based information service. Grant and Ungarelli emphasized that the manager be "people oriented" and continued to explain:

> No matter how technologically advanced our profession becomes, there is no substitute for that rare ability to treat our patron/clients' information problems as if they were our own. The manager of the department should be a manager of people, problems, and goals. To maintain a facility for training and education of staff, clientele, and prospective clientele, and for marketing, requires exceptional verbal and writing abilities (Grant and Ungarelli 1987, pp. 249-250).

Grund commented that the "ability to work with corporate clients, to speak the language of business rather than academe, and to grasp the immediacy of client needs is essential" (Grund 1992, p. 116).

The search committee looks for candidates who embody as many as possible of the following attributes:

- Sets the tone and standards for excellence in customer service;
- Acts as an advocate for the service to the library and university administrations;
- Guides policy and procedure;
- Develops effective marketing and public relations strategies;
- Hires the right staff;
- Acts as an experienced resource person to the other professional staff for complex research projects;
- Has a high personal drive for excellence, achievement, and organization;
- Fosters a drive for excellence in others;
- Provides rewards for staff in an environment in which the rewards are usually demands for ever more service delivered ever more quickly;
- Accepts responsibility;
- Has a strong profit orientation (even in a nonprofit environment, the bottom line is important) and good business sense;
- Accepts small failures and learns from them;
- Communicates and listens effectively;
- Resolves conflicts equitably;
- Has solid research skills and is able to synthesize and repackage information;
- Supervises and administers in a flexible and adaptable manner;
- Solves problems, makes decisions, sets goals, and evaluates situations quickly, intuitively, and creatively;
- Fosters cooperation and team spirit;
- Works hard; and
- Takes pride in high quality work.

Support Staff

In selecting support staff, I have found that prior experience in customer service, especially in a busy commercial or retail environment, is far more important than previous library experience. Previous computer experience is helpful but not essential. Unless the manager is lucky enough to interview a dynamic person with experience in a corporate library's interlibrary loan unit, almost any new hire will have to be trained for the fee-based service's specialized job duties.

Staff Personality Traits

During the interviews and reference checks for all the permanent staff, look for evidence of work with attention to detail, the ability both to make appropriate independent decisions and to work as part of a team, an appealing phone personality, a genuine commitment to customer service, and the energy to keep up with an often hectic pace. Without these traits, the most experienced database searcher or clerical assistant will become a liability rather than an asset. "The pressures of deadlines to be met, confidentiality to be maintained, and the highest professional standard of work, suit some people and not others. Anyone who likes an ordered, planned existence is never going to survive in an environment where priorities may change not only every day, but every hour" (White 1981, p. 65).

Student Assistants

Student assistants will be assigned most of the document retrieval work. Usually hiring student assistants is an easy process, but ask about the procedure in advance:

- If the launch date does not fall near the beginning of a school term, how difficult will it be to find students in the middle of semester?
- What is the hiring pay range?
- How can the service reward students with a pay increase after several months or semesters of satisfactory work?
- What are the rules about hiring and scheduling work-study or international students?
- If a student's work performance or attendance record are not satisfactory, what are the options and procedures for termination?
- Is there an evaluation procedure for students?

SPACE

When they approved the business plan, the library administrators also approved the space designated for the new fee-based service. Preparing this space is one of the first things the implementer will coordinate. Questions include:

- Are there current occupants who will move out?
- If so, when will their new quarters be ready?
- Will they take all the current fixtures with them, or will arrangements have to be made for removing abandoned furniture if the new service does not plan to use it?
- What renovations, if any, should be scheduled?
- What is the time frame for completing renovations?
- If the office needs painting or re-carpeting, complete these activities before the furniture and equipment arrive.
- If the painting is delayed, where can the new furniture be stored on a temporary basis?
- When can the phone company come to install the telecommunication lines?
- Should the walls be painted before or after the lines are installed?

A hundred other questions related to the particular space in question occur to the implementer. As with several other tasks in the implementation phase, office preparation may take more time than anticipated. Most large academic libraries have someone whose job includes facilities planning; this person can provide invaluable help in navigating through the local work order maze.

EQUIPMENT AND SUPPLIES

The business plan specified the equipment needed for the start-up. Now the implementer's job is to identify the best models within the budget limitations. A new employee will also benefit from a crash course in the institution's purchasing procedures, although there is usually someone in the business office who acts as a liaison between the library and the institution's purchasing department or standard suppliers. Ordering standard office supplies like wastepaper baskets and staplers will probably be very easy; ordering major pieces of equipment like laser printers and fax machines often requires special review and approval.

The implementer finds out who assembles and installs large pieces of furniture and equipment. Discuss any equipment or supplies related to the office computer network with the department that will provide ongoing support for it. Arrange in advance for somewhere to store large pieces or large orders if the new office space will not be ready when they arrive.

COMPUTING SUPPORT

Establishing a good working relationship with the library's systems, automation, or information technology department is essential. Someone from that department should have already provided the investigator with general information about the computer equipment, software, and network needs for the new office, but now the implementer requires ongoing support to help select, order, install, test, modify, customize, troubleshoot, and maintain the computer equipment essential for running the operation.

The business plan should have specified the need for a PC on every staff member's desk and the need for a local area network (LAN). In order to work quickly and efficiently in as automated an environment as possible, every staff member needs a computer. Scheduling a two-hour daily block to run searches on a shared machine is not practical in an operation where the workload and deadlines fluctuate radically from one hour to the next. A network and a relational database are also essential; everyone on staff needs immediate access to current client addresses, billing files, and document order information.

However, a fee-based information service is not interlibrary loan or circulation; although it performs some of these functions for external clients, its mission and its needs are different. The interlibrary loan management software used locally may adapt perfectly well in the fee-based environment, but there may also be a better solution. The implementer weighs several factors. Choosing software that is already locally supported is usually wise, but only if that software performs, or can be easily adapted to perform, the necessary tasks. The service may need specialized software. The information technology (IT) department staff can assess these needs and recommend other packages. Many software companies will send demonstration disks to let the implementer and the IT staff evaluate their potential usefulness. Paying a programmer to develop specialized software is another option, but one that should reserved for an established service that already has experience with managing files or databases for client addresses, billing, and document tracking. The implementer considers options and opportunities for staff training for whatever software is selected. And finally, if in practice the program turns out not to be as effective as hoped, the manager can always choose another one later. Data from most programs can be exported from the old software to the new, so that changes can be accomplished with minimal re-keying.

Established services may find that they need a microcomputer support student on staff 12 to 20 hours a week to maintain and improve current systems, equipment, and network access, as well as to work under the staff's direction to investigate new equipment and software. A position like this may not be necessary during a new service's implementation stage, however, if the library administration assigns sufficient microcomputer support to the project on a temporary basis while it is being established. The implementer establishes a clear understanding about the service's priority. Assurance of assistance "when needed" may turn out to be an inadequate few hours each week of different students' time when they are not scheduled for other tasks.

PRICING

Review the business plan's pricing strategy. Make any changes now, before obtaining official university approval and before printing the promotional materials. Revisit the copyright question. Does university counsel agree or not that the fee-based service's document delivery activities fall under the fair use provisions of the U.S. copyright law? If not, how will the service add copyright charges to the base document fee?

The implementer sets in motion any special requests needed for formal university approval of the fee schedule.

MARKETING

During the implementation phase, one of the most challenging and rewarding aspects of fee-based information service management begins: marketing. Although a few people will stumble across the service without having seen one of its promotional pieces, the majority of clients first learn of the service through its marketing efforts.

Some promotional efforts are expensive; others cost little more than time. Rather than relying on a single marketing method, the implementer combines several in order to reach the widest possible potential client base within the target audience already identified. Relying too heavily on no- or low-cost options may build the client base too slowly to reach cost-recovery goals, yet it may be equally unwise to print and distribute thousands of expensive color brochures as the sole marketing activity.

A wise implementer also reviews the target audience to be sure that the marketing effort is not being directed towards one or two narrow segments or geographical regions to the exclusion of all others. While a marketing campaign that is too broad is equally inadvisable, the implementer strives to select a target audience that is varied enough in its base that the service will not founder if one or two industries or regions experience economic downturns.

In addition, the implementer keeps in mind that all marketing efforts "emphasize solutions and benefits, not the process" (Warner 1983, p. 97), the collection, (McGuire 1993, p. 125) or other library resources. Potential clients are usually not interested in how many volumes the library owns or which databases the staff search. They are interested only in the direct benefits of hiring the service to find the answers they need.

The implementer reviews the list of possible marketing pieces and ideas in the business plan and also the promotional materials from other services that the investigator gathered earlier. Keeping the marketing budget firmly in mind, the implementer chooses the three or four options most likely to reach and attract the target audience.

The Brochure

The brochure is the most important piece, the marketing effort's cornerstone. It establishes the service's name, logo or other identifying graphics, tone, and philosophy. It clearly identifies the target audience, the scope of the services, and the price list. Although it should be professionally designed and produced, a piece that is too sophisticated and glossy may detract from its message. A too-slick piece may also raise awkward questions about the wise use of start-up funds or the taxpayers' money, or whether too large a percentage of cost-recovery income will be plowed back into the promotional budget. Slick production also does not compensate for a wordy or unclear message.

As the investigator did with the business plan, so should the implementer get second and third opinions on the brochure's draft before approving it for printing. Give the library administrator to whom the investigator reports a chance for input. Another good idea is to schedule half an hour with one of the marketing professors from the business school for a fresh, experienced opinion.

Working with a Graphic Designer

At most universities, there is a graphic design department, often attached to the printing operation. The implementer spends some time with the graphic designer assigned to the project. Review pieces that the department, and that designer in particular, have recently produced. A good designer has answers to all the questions about lead time, printing time, the bid process if the project requires one, revisions, reprintings, paper stock, inks, foil stamping, and so on. During this early stage, the plan may be to print just the brochure, but if related pieces, such as a folder or special envelopes or a newsletter, are planned in the future, the implementer mentions them so the designer can think ahead to see how these other pieces will relate to the brochure in terms of paper stock, colors, and logos.

A good designer takes the implementer's draft and prepares a mock-up of the brochure, using elements such as graphics, spacing, colors, and fonts to produce a professional look. The designer advises the implementer about the use of photographs in the brochure, and outlines the procedure for having photos taken. The implementer is the customer, however; if any of the elements is unsuitable or unappealing, ask for alternative suggestions. Add the month and year of printing in small type in an unobtrusive spot. Over the years, the brochure will go though several reprintings with or without minor revisions, and the staff need to be able to tell one version from another at a glance.

When the final design is approved, the designer produces a proof of the brochure. The implementer reviews it very carefully (reading it backwards as well as forwards is one technique), and asks at least one other person who has never seen the text before to review it as well. A typographical error or forgotten word overlooked at this stage will be immortalized on thousands of brochures; such oversights will not inspire confidence in potential customers.

Mailing Lists

The business plan suggests several avenues for obtaining mailing lists of potential clients. The implementer chooses the best target groups, and makes arrangements to buy the mailing lists, which usually arrive on disk. Avoid the mistake of buying all the lists at once. Time the first one to arrive very close to the launch date.

Although all the addresses may be printed at once to save time, mail the promotional pieces in batches over several weeks. Once the wave of inquiries from the first mailing list subsides, the staff will send out pieces to the names on the next list. This second list should have only just arrived from the issuing organization; the implementer avoids holding lists. too long, since then the benefits of address corrections will be lost.

Many list suppliers, such as trade associations, sell their lists with the understanding that they will be used for single, not multiple, mailings. The implementer should not abuse this understanding; most lists include a few addresses used to check that each mailing occurs only once per purchase.

Mailing the Brochures

Although the brochures will not be mailed until just before or at the launch date, the implementer makes a number of decisions.

- How many of the brochures will be mailed?
- Were the brochures designed to take an address label and be dropped in the mail, or will they be sealed in envelopes? With or without a covering letter?
- Will the campus printing office handle these mass stuffing and mailing operations, or will they be done from the fee-based information service's office?
- Does the printing office prefer addresses on labels or on disk? What are the preferred specifications for either?
- What is the minimum number for any special mailing rates? Bulk mail is less expensive, but recipients pay less attention to it.
- How many pieces should be mailed at a time? It will probably be cheaper per piece to send out 1,000 all at once rather than 200 a week, but if 10 percent of the recipients call for more information, can the staff handle 100 inquiries in one week?
- How should the cover letter's wording vary depending on the target audience?
- Should a second mailing to the same list follow several weeks or months after the first one?

Advertisements in Print Media

Purdue's Technical Information Service used advertising during its early growth stage to expand its client base, rather than during its implementation phase. One reason was that since advertising is an expensive marketing option, we waited until we were adequately staffed and confident of our abilities to meet customer needs. With an established revenue stream, we also felt more confident in paying relatively high advertising rates. We had also learned by then that while it is easy for a potential client to grasp the concept of rapid document delivery, it is much more difficult to explain the benefits of a database search in 20 words or less of print. Almost all potential clients have at least once in their professional careers floundered about trying to obtain some kind of publication, and our ad speaks solely about meeting this need. A document is tangible; a research project seems less so.

However, if the investigator or administrators recommended that print advertising coinciding with the launch date will be beneficial, the implementer plans an ad campaign. Where will the ad appear? What will it say and what will it look like?

After reviewing the suggestions in the business plan, the implementer pays another visit to the graphic designer. While the designer drafts sample ads, the implementer calls the advertising offices of the various local, regional, or trade publications identified as being ones read by the target audience and asks for current advertising rates and reader profile statistics. The manager approves the final ad layout and makes arrangements for the ads to appear soon after the launch date.

Other Marketing Techniques

Many other effective marketing techniques, such as selected speaking engagements and appearances at trade fairs, are best left until the service has an established track record. It is much more convincing to speak of real-life examples of research projects and types of clients than to explain what the service is going to do when it opens next month. In addition, it is wiser to embark on this type of promotion when there is a full staff back at the office to explain further and to perform the work being extolled.

CLIENTS

Keeping track of clients is a critical, although time-consuming, task. At first, it will be relatively easy to build a client list by adding names as orders arrive. As time goes on, however, client list maintenance becomes increasingly important as client information requires updating: clients or their companies change their names, addresses, area codes, and phone or fax numbers. Department names, building numbers, and mail stop codes sometimes change. Some clients change jobs and continue using the service at a new address. Others stop using the service. Current and correct information is imperative so that orders, invoices, and promotional mailings reach clients quickly.

The implementer develops the client database with these facts in mind. Choose software that allows global changes, the easy addition of new fields, quick sorting, and fast generation of lists and mailing labels. Consider establishing company codes as well as individual user codes to identify records. A client list integrated into the billing database facilitates document tracking. Choose a system that allows all staff immediate access into the client database, since printed lists become obsolete quickly. Consider password protection to ensure confidentiality.

Draft procedures for making changes to existing client records. Are all staff authorized to do so, or only selected ones?

RESEARCH SERVICES

Most fee-based information services include research as one of the major services offered to clients. The implementer makes arrangements well before the launch date to prepare the staff for handling research projects.

Negotiating with Clients

Landing a research project assignment in a fee-based information service is generally more complex than the traditional situation of a patron approaching a reference librarian. Since money is at stake, the client may cooperate through the reference interview and then decide not to assign the project based on a combination of several factors such as cost, turnaround time, perceived value of the results, personal response to the information specialist's confidence and professionalism, or perceived understanding of the nature of the search results. The specialist's first job is to assure the client that the service can efficiently and cost-effectively find the information and present it in a clear, organized fashion, within a reasonable amount of time and within the client's budget. This negotiation usually takes place by phone, so an articulate, business-like, positive phone manner is every bit as important as advanced searching skills. An information specialist who sounds hesitant, inflexible, or negative over the phone will seldom convince prospective clients to part with several hundred dollars for a research project.

> Good communication skills are essential in this negotiation process, since many of our clients have never had computer literature searches done before and have no idea what to expect in terms of flexibility of retrieval, turnaround time, output, cost, etc. Conveying realistic expectations of retrieval, and of expense, is vital to achieving client satisfaction (Hornbeck 1983, p. 33).

The implementer recommends hiring candidates who exhibit these skills, and plans a training program around the vital necessity of convincing prospective clients that the service will meet their information needs.

Use of Local Resources

Academic library colleagues have seen the demand for traditional mediated database searching dwindle over the past decade with the introduction of CD-ROMs, locally mounted databases, and the Internet. However, information specialists in fee-based information services continue to search databases through connections to the major vendors as the primary means of completing most client research projects. These specialists find that the licensing agreements between their institutions and the CD-ROM or locally mounted database providers usually limit use to the institution's staff and students. The negotiated price often prohibits access, even by a staff member, for resale to a third party, especially when that third party works for a company. Searchers also find that they cannot search the local databases and CD-ROMs in as flexible a manner as they can the commercially available databases. They may not be able to combine terms as well, or limit by language, or search 20 years of the file at once. Traveling to other campus library locations to use CD-ROMs takes time, and there is no guarantee that the workstation will be free when the searcher arrives. Even if the search results can be captured electronically, post-processing time to make the results look clean and professional takes longer. Finally, the range of databases available on campus is often much more limited than those available commercially.

A small percentage of research projects requires manual searching through the library's print collection, either as a supplement to an online search or as the entire search. Most librarians who are good online searchers are equally adept at quickly extracting information from print sources as well.

Search Results

The implementer makes suggestions about how final search results are presented to the client. For database searches, the format of one full record with abstract per page is both an attractive and a handy one. It allows the searcher to remove easily any false hits (my favorite example is a search about mobile restaurants which turned up a number of records about restaurants in Mobile, Alabama). This format also lets the recipient arrange the citations in whatever order is most appropriate, and facilitates document delivery when the client faxes back copies of selected records. Of course, citation-only or title-only results are best printed with several per page, but it is worth taking the extra time to process the file so that the pages break between records, not within them.

Give some thought to the "boilerplate" text for the search cover letter. The searcher customizes a few sentences to refer to the particular search and search strategy, but there are usually several standard paragraphs that apply to most projects.

Database Documentation and Training

The implementer selects one or two major database vendors and applies for passwords. It is a mistaken economy to make searchers share a single password for a major vendor to save the relatively modest annual membership fees for each additional account. In the long run, it is more cost-effective for each professional to have a personal account so that the specialists can search simultaneously.

The implementer obtains basic training materials and database documentation from each vendor. Purchase advanced database documentation selectively; the specialists order other titles later as they gain experience with the types of questions clients ask and the kinds of files needed to answer those questions. The implementer also identifies and obtains major database-specific thesauri and search aids. If the new service focuses on providing engineering and technical information, for example, a copy of the *Ei Thesaurus* is essential.

If the service hires the professional staff before the launch date, the implementer arranges for them to attend training sessions with the selected database vendors. Newly hired searchers' experience is not always a perfect match for the service's subject focus. A brush-up workshop or advanced seminar develops sharper searching skills.

Back-up Research Assistance

The implementer also identifies potential back-up searchers within the library system. If the service starts with only one or two professionals, there will almost certainly be times when a combination of illness, vacation, sudden demand, or marketing commitments leaves the office understaffed. The back-up professionals should be experienced searchers in the appropriate subject files offered by the primary database vendor, and also attuned to the service's philosophy, mission, and goals. The library administrators make the official assignment for back-up searchers based on the implementer's recommendation. The implementer's responsibility is to provide basic orientation for the back-up searchers. These searchers may complete the entire search from reference interview to search post-processing and preparing a client report letter. In other cases, the back-up searchers send a diskette or electronic file with the search results back to the fee-based service office for the staff there to format and print. In either case, the final results should reflect the standard office style.

The fee-based information service staff realize that these searchers provide back-up only in emergencies (e.g., staff illness) or in short-term pre-arranged situations (e.g., staff vacations). These librarians have other responsibilities, and while willing to help occasionally, may feel overloaded if called upon to complete too many searches. Due to prior obligations, they may also be unable to work on projects as quickly as the service and the clients might like or expect. While the library administrators may agree to a few hours of the back-up searchers' time being spent meeting the service's obligations on an emergency basis, they will expect the development of a mechanism to reimburse the library for any database charges racked up on the back-up searcher's regular account. In some institutions, administrators may also suggest an arrangement whereby the service reimburses the library for the searchers' time as well. After all, the service will bill the clients for both the amount of time spent on the search as well as for the database fees incurred.

The implementer also considers possible solutions for tapping colleagues' expertise in subjects for which the fee-based information service staff have little training or experience. Is it possible to ask the chemistry librarian to run an occasional search if none of the service staff have a chemical background? Or would it be better to refer these questions to another fee-based information service staffed with searchers who have these specialized skills?

Office Reference Works

Besides database documentation, the implementer also purchases essential office reference tools. This step is an easy one to overlook. After all, the service is located in a library system filled with both general and specialized reference works of every description. However, at least a few titles are indispensable and will save the staff the time of making endless trips across campus to look up one or two addresses or phone numbers. Consider obtaining:

- Local phone book;
- Campus phone book;
- Directory of federal agencies;
- Directory of state agencies;
- Directory of city agencies;
- Publishers' directory;
- Periodical abbreviations book and/or comprehensive acronyms book;
- *Statistical Abstract;*
- *The Burwell World Directory of Information Brokers;*
- *Ulrich's International Periodicals Directory;*
- Index to the *Code of Federal Regulations;*
- *Encyclopedia of Associations;* and
- Technical reports series codes book.

A service focused on meeting specialized subject requests substitutes or adds other standard titles. Staff later add to the list as they learn what titles best help them meet clients' requests quickly.

Deciding which titles to obtain also depends to some extent on the library in which the service is located; if the business library's reference room is a few steps away, for example, the service may be able to leave the *Encyclopedia of Associations* off its list. The implementer compares prices of titles available in CD-ROM, database, and print formats. Are the office computers networked with a CD-ROM player, for example?

DOCUMENT DELIVERY

Preparing for document delivery involves making decisions about the most effective and customer-centered ways to handle a number of issues, while at the same time responding to colleagues' concerns about the use of the library collection. The implementer addresses the issues and makes decisions that seem both simple and logical. Remember, however, that there is a difference between theory and practice. A procedure that seems very straightforward on paper may prove cumbersome in practice; expect that changes after the launch date will be the rule rather than the exception.

The first step in preparing for document delivery is to define what services will be provided. Most services in medium- to large-sized academic libraries find that they can supply from the local collection well over half the document requests they receive. Is everything eligible for supply, with the obvious exceptions of reference works, reserve material, and items in special collections? The implementer requests clear directives from the library administration before the service begins, to avoid any misunderstandings with colleagues from whose libraries the service fills the orders.

Forms

Although the implementer's goal is to automate as many processes as possible, there is no escape from the paperwork that develops around document delivery.

Document Order Forms. As the implementer develops office forms for various functions, one question will be whether to prepare document order forms for clients to use. While it is certainly true that the staff will be able to process requests more easily if they are submitted in a standard format, clients usually prefer submitting their requests in whatever format is most convenient for them. After all, they pay a premium rate for fast document fulfillment and expect that the service will handle their requests in whatever way they choose to submit them.

The Technical Information Service accepts document orders however the client prefers to send them. We receive purchase order forms, database search results, bibliographies, handwritten notes on company stationery, in-house order sheets, and printouts from in-house document order systems. In fact, staff prefer to see citations in their original form rather than in rewritten or retyped versions into which errors are likely to creep. We draw the line at taking phone orders for several reasons: the possibility of a hearing or transcription error, the extra time involved, and the fact that we then have no proof that the order was both legitimate and authorized.

Several years ago, a new fee-based information service developed a document order form that they required their clients to use. TIS immediately stopped sending document orders to that service, because it was not cost-effective for us to prepare the service's special forms and then to duplicate everything in our standard format. Our only current exception to this practice is a European document supplier that requires that requests be submitted on a special form. Because this supplier is sometimes the only possible source for certain types of specialized documents, we converted their paper form to an electronic template and simply "fill in the blanks," print and fax the form, and then edit the electronic version into our standard paperwork. Another service encourages clients to use its internal processing form by rewarding them with a dollar discount for each request submitted on the form, a much more reasonable solution than forcing clients to send requests in a certain format.

Internal Processing Forms. No matter how clients submit orders, staff almost always print the requests first for easy and flexible sorting and processing.

The service's staff generate at least one other piece of paper to serve as a means of identifying, retrieving, shipping, billing, and filing each order. Over time, TIS staff learned that taking the time to print separate retrieval copies paid off in better control over timely order fulfillment. Most services also generate a separate cover sheet or packing slip for each item or for each shipment. The billing process produces at least two pieces of paper: one for internal records and one for the client.

The implementer experiments with the office software to design paper forms and to suggest the procedure for producing and handling them. The forms will evolve over time as staff learn from actual practice the best ways to enter and arrange various elements.

Document Delivery from the Local Collection: Loans

A few services decline to lend any books; another lends books except for conference proceedings. TIS lends industry standards for one week; other services do not lend these specialized items at all. We photocopy Purdue theses but honor Purdue's agreement with University Microfilms International (UMI) not to photocopy Purdue dissertations. How will retrievers check out books? The best solution is to arrange for a special card for each staff member and each student retriever, so that any overdue items are clearly the responsibility of the fee-based service, not of the individual employee.

Establish a uniform loan period, preferably one that allows the client two or three weeks' use but that requests the materials' return at least a few days in advance of the actual due date. How will staff track overdue books and quickly retrieve the corresponding paperwork if the client requests a renewal? It is also important to note the date the material is returned, in case there is a later question about this event.

Overdues. Plan a process to flag overdue books to remind clients of the due dates. Because loans are usually such a small percentage of total document delivery, it may not be worth the trouble of setting up electronic files to track due dates. TIS keeps the paperwork for loans in a box; once a week a clerk thumbs through the forms to identify overdue material and then prepares a form letter for each client. The special TIS library cards allow student retrievers to check books out for eight weeks, but we lend them to clients for three weeks. The library itself does not consider the material overdue until five weeks after TIS does. By that time, the client has received at least two overdue notices.

TIS does not charge clients overdue fines; our main interest is in the timely return of loaned items. In practice, clients return the vast majority of items within a few days of the due date. Very few of them need more than one overdue reminder to return other items.

Renewals. The Technical Information Service renews books at no additional charge. A few other services add a modest renewal charge to the bill. Some services do not bill for loans until the item is returned, in case it is either renewed for a fee, or lost and billed for replacement. This practice may save a little work in these relatively infrequent cases, but some clients (especially other fee-based services) prefer faster billing so they can turn around and invoice *their* clients.

In my opinion, renewal fees are nuisance fees. Not many clients ask for renewals, and it is a simple process on our end. To save a return phone call, we tell clients we will call them within a day if the item *cannot* be renewed; otherwise the book is due three weeks from today.

Once in a great while a Purdue patron places a hold or recall on one of the books we loaned. Usually a quick phone to the client is all it takes to receive most items back promptly.

Lost Books. It is inevitable that a few books a year will be irretrievably lost. Some incidents are accidents; a few may be intentional. At TIS, if we have not received a book back after two overdue notices, we send a polite but firmly worded letter that the client is jeopardizing further loan privileges, and that if we have not received the book back within 10 days from the date of the letter, we will bill the replacement cost plus a nonrefundable $100 processing fee. Almost all of the "lost" books arrive shortly thereafter.

If the warning letter does not produce the material, we bill as promised. Our next step is to purchase a new copy of the lost item, if it is still in print, and send it to the appropriate campus librarian with a note explaining that it is a replacement copy for the one our client lost. If the item is no longer in print, we offer the librarian a choice of a transfer of funds for the estimated replacement cost or of our services to purchase quickly a similar book of similar price to add to the collection. On average, fewer than half a dozen books loaned to TIS clients each year are irretrievably lost.

Document Delivery from the Local Collection: Copies

Providing photocopies sounds like a straightforward proposition, until the implementer looks more closely at copyright laws and guidelines. How much is too much copied from a single publication? Two articles? Three chapters? What if a single article comprises half the issue? What about three chapters from a reference book? Many of these questions will have already been answered by the institution's Interlibrary Loan department. While the fee-based information service may decide not to follow every guideline the same way, the ILL policy or practice is a useful, institutionally approved starting place. The implementer writes general guidelines for new staff and student assistants. Some instances may have to be decided on a case-by-case basis when the service starts, but staff need to be educated to know when a case warrants review.

In actual practice, policy exceptions will often be possible. TIS staff occasionally arrange with colleagues for one week emergency loans to clients of selected bound periodical volumes or of lesser-used reference or reserve titles. The library staff always have the final say, of course. For the implementation stage, however, try to keep the guidelines as simple as possible.

Document Delivery from Outside Sources

If the decision has been made to offer document special orders (items not available locally) starting on the launch date, first consider how staff will identify potential suppliers for specific orders. Commercial suppliers alone will be insufficient; although their journal holdings are generally extensive, they usually do not have strong holdings for books, conferences, technical reports, and other specialized documents. Besides obtaining commercial suppliers' printed or electronic holdings lists, access to and training for OCLC and/or RLIN will be essential. Since most established services draw on at least several dozen other libraries' collections, connecting to these libraries' online catalogs individually presents an enormous investment of time better spent elsewhere.

Using OCLC's Worldcat through local access to FirstSearch is not a viable alternative either. For one thing, the searching and browsing options are not nearly as powerful as the features in the full OCLC database. Second, using Worldcat through the institution's academic licensing arrangement may be prohibited by the licensing agreement. However, rather than setting up separate accounts with the appropriate bibliographic utilities, the service may be able to piggyback onto accounts that the library has already established. Most fee-based information services need access to these utilities' bibliographic databases only; document ordering is generally handled separately from standard interlibrary loan practice.

Based on the ways the staff identify sources holding the documents needed, the implementer reviews the list of fee-based information services and commercial document delivery firms identified in the business plan. The planning files probably already include brochures, price lists, and catalogs from selected document suppliers. With which ones will it be essential to have accounts in place by the launch date or by the approximate day on which special orders will be offered? Are there any other suppliers who should be considered?

Special Order Procedures. After identifying a good mix of potential document suppliers, the implementer designs an ordering mechanism. Even if the new fee-based information service is so closely related to the institution's ILL department that staff have training and access to OCLC, I advise against ordering documents using the OCLC ILL subsystem. Lending libraries will not always notice or distinguish the difference between a borrowing institution's ILL department and its fee-based service. Taking advantage of lower (or nonexistent) fees from a lending partner for items destined for paying customers raises ethical concerns.

Most commercial suppliers offer one, if not several, methods of automated ordering. While these methods may be convenient, it may be advisable, at least at first, for the service to develop standardized internal system for faxing orders to suppliers. For one reason, maintaining a paper trail is important for financial and legal reasons even in this electronic age. Secondly, suppliers have so many different ordering systems, and fee-based information services need so many suppliers, that both the learning curve and the time needed to place orders on multiple systems will be high.

At TIS, we search OCLC on a PC, capture the record electronically, print the holdings, and then build a document request form around the record. After faxing the request to the selected document suppler, we reformat the record to conform to our standard document form. We place a few orders using the Dialorder feature on Dialog, use the phone occasionally when contacting commercial publishers or trade associations, but fax the vast majority of orders. In a new service, the manager will work out the details later, but the implementer puts some initial thought into the general process of placing and tracking special orders.

Some document delivery sources can be used as needed, with documents arriving promptly and invoices either included with the shipment or following on a monthly billing cycle. Other document suppliers are much easier to use with a deposit account. However the library business office may balk at setting up more than a few deposit accounts, even at minimal funding levels.

Document Delivery Work Flow

Managing document delivery work flow sensibly and efficiently is challenging. For one thing, the document delivery volume will almost certainly be higher than the research project work flow. For another, everyone in the office, from the manager down to the student assistants, at least occasionally works on some of aspect of document delivery. The work flow is also unpredictable; some days will be very heavy, others much lighter. There are few predictable slow times, except over the holidays in December, since corporate clients do not operate their businesses on an academic schedule.

The implementer sketches out two document work flow diagrams, one for items filled locally and one for items obtained as special orders, to help staff understand the order in which different tasks are handled. These diagrams will be refined over time as the document delivery operation becomes more complex.

In general, the flow for items filled locally is as follows:

1. If the client is new, add to the client list.
2. Give each document request a unique tracking number.

3. In the case of client orders with several items per page, organize the order so that there is a separate sheet for each request.
4. Search the local online catalog on a PC.
5. Capture online records, being sure to include the ISSN or ISBN numbers and the local holdings information.
6. Edit the captured records to show vital identification and retrieval information.
7. Include both the in-house document numbers and any order numbers the client provided.
8. Add client address information, including separate "bill to" and "ship to" addresses, if required.
9. Indicate any special handling instructions, such as RUSH or FAX or COPY AND BIND.
10. Print forms, at minimum an internal processing/retrieval form and a document cover sheet.
11. Add basic information about the order to the document tracking database.
12. Assign the retrieval form to a student assistant.
13. When the item has been retrieved, review the order for completeness, accuracy, and neatness.
14. Ship the item with the document cover sheet, complying with any special shipping instructions.
15. Using the retrieval form, check if copyright is owed on any photocopied items, and complete appropriate logs.
16. Price the retrieval forms.
17. Prepare billing from the priced forms.
18. Update document tracking database.
19. File paperwork.

Of course, there are many possible variations to this procedure. Rubens and Wulff's article includes a table indicating the major tasks, decisions, and options at each stage of handling document requests for locally owned material (Rubens and Wulff 1988, p. 175)

Staff handle items that are either checked out or not on the shelf differently. Other types of items, such as patents or industry standards, are part of uncataloged collections and so need not be checked first in the online catalog. Citation verification may be necessary, but the fact that a request is a bad cite may not be evident until the retriever returns with a photocopied table of contents to prove that the article does not appear as cited.

The flow for items obtained as special orders is similar:

1. If the client is new, add to the client list.
2. Give each document request a unique tracking number.
3. In the case of client orders with several items per page, organize the order so that there is a separate sheet for each request.

4. Having determined that the item is not held locally, search OCLC or RLIN on a PC.
5. Capture online records, being sure to include the title, the ISSN or ISBN numbers, the publisher's name, series name, and the holdings list.
6. Edit the captured records.
7. Select a document supplier.
8. Edit the captured OCLC or RLIN record into a document order form.
9. Print the order form and fax it.
10. Edit the order form into the standard document format.
11. Include both the in-house document numbers and any order numbers the client provided.
12. Add client address information, including separate "bill to" and "ship to" addresses, if required.
13. Indicate any special handling instructions, such as RUSH or FAX or COPY AND BIND.
14. Print forms. Be sure that the in-house paperwork clearly indicates that this item is a special order and notes the supplier's name.
15. Add basic information about the order to the document tracking database, including the supplier's name.
16. When the item arrives, review the order for completeness, accuracy, and neatness.
17. Ship the item with the document cover sheet, complying with any special shipping instructions.
18. Check if copyright is owed on any photocopied items, and complete appropriate logs.
19A. If an invoice was sent with the item, or if the item was prepaid by check or credit card, or if the item was free, price the order.
19B. If the invoice or deposit account statement will arrive later, file the paperwork and price it later when the invoice or statement arrives.
20. Prepare billing from the priced forms.
21. Update document tracking database.
22. File paperwork.

Special orders require more decisions and steps than most in-house orders. Staff learn the general prices charged by other services and choose suppliers based on a combination of factors such as price, reliability, and promptness in replying with information about delays or cancellations. Some suppliers are better or faster than others at shipping items directly to a third party. Others bill sooner or in a better invoice format.

The implementer further contemplates how the staff will handle the following inevitable occurrences:

- A document is ordered, but never arrives;
- An order arrives, but the supplier never sends a bill;

- Billing errors (e.g., billed twice, wrong amount);
- Shipping errors (e.g., a rush orders shipped as a regular request, wrong item sent, mistakes with third party shipping); and
- Poor quality document received.

Cancelling Document Orders

Some cancellations are inevitable. Sometimes a citation is hopelessly scrambled or sketchy, and the client cannot provide further clarification. In other cases, the item is too old or too obscure for a supplying source to be identified. Or a supplier may be identified, such as a university laboratory or an association, but the piece is no longer available. Sometimes the client's deadline is so short that obtaining the item in time is impossible. Often, the staff identify a source but the client decides that the final cost will be too high.

Other clients only want items that can be supplied locally; they approach other suppliers on their own if the service cannot fill their order. Occasionally copyright restrictions or unusually high copyright fees dictate cancelling an order. For those clients who place requests over OCLC, unfilled orders become automatic cancellations.

Whenever possible, staff make every effort to suggest alternatives to the client before cancelling an order. Can the deadline be extended or the maximum cost be increased? If the book is checked out locally, is the client willing to wait a few weeks or to pay a little more to get the item sooner as a special order? The service is legally prohibited from copying an entire journal issue, nor can it lend it, but since the issue is still in print, would the client like to purchase a copy?

Be sure to count cancellations as well as filled orders so that the service's statistics accurately reflect the staff's work load. TIS finds that of all document requests submitted each month, about 80 percent are eventually filled. This percentage has remained steady for years.

Recording Copyright

The implementer registers with the Copyright Clearance Center (CCC). The next decision is whether the service will record copyright transactions manually on the CCC forms using the CCC's *Titles and Fees* printed list, or whether staff will enter the transactions using the CCC's Web site.

Another major choice involves deciding when in the document delivery flow to check and record copyright payments. If staff refrain from shipping items until the copyright has been checked, some orders might be delayed at times when staffing is low and/or document volume is high. However, if staff check copyright after the items have been faxed or mailed, they may encounter unpleasant surprises of copyright payments of $20, $40, or sometimes as much as $100 for single articles.

Finally, the implementer recommends a procedure for handling cases in which a publisher's titles are not registered with the CCC.

Other Document Delivery Considerations

How should the staff be trained to recognize orders for items in major uncataloged collections that the library owns. Examples might be NTIS microfiche, industry standards, NASA reports, or government documents. Staff also need to learn to recognize items such as these that the library does not own and that are either held uncataloged elsewhere or easily obtained from specialized document suppliers.

How will the service handle bad citations? At TIS, an information specialist checks appropriate database files after the documents clerk has checked the online catalog and OCLC. How will charges for bibliographic verification be handled?

The implementer need not definitively answer these questions, but being aware of them will shape how the document delivery component of the service is organized.

Relationship with the Interlibrary Loan Department

Now is the time to formalize the arrangements with the Interlibrary Loan department about how the fee-based information service staff will handle requests submitted by for-profit organizations after the launch date. The ILL supervisor may have concerns about scheduling time on the OCLC terminals. Setting up a standard time each day is the best arrangement. Other concerns may include the possible loss of revenue for the ILL department when the fee-based service starts handling requests for which ILL currently assesses a fee. This issue should have been identified earlier in the planning process; now is the time to implement the solution.

DELIVERY OPTIONS

Most services offer at least two levels of service for both document delivery and research projects: standard and rush. Some services also offer super rush turnaround, at least for document delivery.

Delivery options include a growing array of standard and overnight couriers, the U.S. Postal Service, fax, Ariel, and electronic file transfers. Take time to determine the "standard" methods and then decide how much to charge extra for each type of non-standard delivery. Naturally the client pays for the actual cost of an expedited package, but how much will the service add as a rush handling fee? How will staff respond to the client who says, "Treat this as a regular order, but fax it to me when you've copied the article?" Is this a rush order or not? What about instances when an urban service's client sends round a bicycle courier to pick up a package? Does the client get a discount because the service incurred no shipping charges?

Resolving shipping and distribution questions in advance prevents many headaches during the service's first weeks and months.

FINANCIAL CONSIDERATIONS

The implementation phase generates some financial activity. While this activity is still fairly low, it is a good time to work with the library business office to develop ways in which both the manager and the business officer can keep current on the income and the expenditures of the service's budget.

Budget

The implementer works with the library business officer to revise the budget from the plan into an actual management tool. Find out how the library expects the manager to monitor the service's budget. Ask questions such as:

- Does the manager have to know and record the exact cost of the pens, staples, and notepads the staff orders from Stores?
- Does a mechanism have to be created so the manager is informed of, and keeps track of, expenses that normally might not be reported to a library unit head, such as the monthly phone bill or the annual copier maintenance agreement?
- Which invoices should be sent directly to the service's office for pre-approval, and which go straight to the library business office?
- How will the pre-approval process work?
- Who processes payment for the invoices?
- Who bills the clients?
- Who answers clients' questions about apparent discrepancies or inaccuracies on their bills?
- Who approves changes and who makes corrections?

Not all of these questions can be definitively answered before the service actually begins handling orders for clients. The implementer meets frequently with the business officer during this phase, however, to discuss these issues and to reach tentative agreements about how these different situations will be handled. Once again, actual practice will probably require some procedural fine-tuning later, so both parties should be prepared for at least some changes during the first few months after the launch date. However, if the implementer, and later the manager, have consistently and positively involved the business office staff with the service's goals and objectives, the confusion can be kept to a minimum.

Monthly Activity Statements

Work with the business officer to develop a monthly activity statement. The manager will use these monthly reports to keep an eye on income and expenses. Many potentially hazardous financial problems can be avoided or minimized if the manager reviews the monthly report carefully. Monthly, quarterly, and/or annual summaries or compilations will also be presented to the library administration.

These reports from the business office are in addition to any internal statistical, activity, or planning reports that the manager chooses to compile and distribute.

Billing

If the service works with a few clients before the official launch date, the staff have a chance to try out the accounting functions of the office software and to work with the library's business office staff to be sure that the billing submissions are correct and complete. If there are no pre-launch bills, however, the staff would be wise to create a few dozen sample entries and work though the whole process of preparing billing records. It is much easier to identify and correct problems in a low volume or test environment. Testing the billing mechanism is a critical step, especially if the institution requires that the service forward invoice information to other departments for the actual billing and collection. Billing is often the one aspect of running a fee-based information service over which the service staff has the least control.

Payments

Even if the institution allows a variety of payment options, I recommend that the new service choose the bare minimum at first. There will be so many new procedures to test that also juggling payments by invoice, by several different credit cards, and by deposit account may lead to confusion. While different options please clients who can now choose a preferred billing method, they can cause difficulties even for experienced staff in established services. Inevitably, a few documents that were supposed to be charged against a client's deposit account are invoiced separately. One client at a firm prefers to make credit card payment; a co-worker wants invoices. Someone who is not authorized to use his company's deposit account places an order. Someone else wants to close a deposit account. Yet another client exhausts a deposit account balance but keeps ordering. Accepting credit card orders usually involves additional bank fees that may not have been calculated into the break-even formula; these will be incidental on a $300 research project, but more significant on a single $15 document order. Keeping track of these details and correcting errors are time-consuming tasks better left until the service has experienced staff, full-time accounting support, and at least the second generation of its document tracking/billing software.

The institution may in fact prefer to stick with an established invoice method until the service has proved that its revenue stream warrants offering several other options for accepting payments. The manager can later decide not to advertise the fact that the service accepts alternative payment methods, but to offer deposit accounts, for example, to selected clients with established track records as high-volume users.

Some services both send invoices and process payments. If the institution allows this option, an experienced accounting clerk is essential. The service establishes virtually fail-safe methods for approving invoices and for processing payments, and follows to the letter the institution's procedures for handling payments. One advantage of this arrangement is that the service will be quickly aware of clients who do not pay their bills promptly. If the service does not process its own payments, the implementer arranges with the business officer for monthly printouts listing any seriously delinquent clients.

CLIENTS

Although the official launch date may be weeks or months away, at what point can the service begin to offer at least limited services? These potential early clients may be businesspeople who call the reference desk needing extensive assistance or expedited document delivery. They may be people contacting the interlibrary loan office for premium services that that office does not offer. In those institutions where setting up a fee-based information service is intended in part to formalize and expand services already being offered on an ad hoc basis to a few clients, there will already be a small built-in client base to whom the service can be advertised early.

There are several advantages for accepting early some projects and document orders. The psychological boost to the implementer and other new staff is enormous; even before the marketing effort has officially begun, there is evidence of clients ready and willing to pay for services. Handling these early requests helps the staff test and evaluate office procedures, work flow, software programs, forms, billing and accounting procedures, filing methods, shipping, and so on in real situations. The early trickle of income will also please the business officer and the library administrators.

As with any new service, there is a danger in promising too much before the staff can actually delivery it promptly, accurately, and cost-effectively (Marvin 1988, p. 157). The implementer might arrange to provide document delivery from the local collection, for example, but decide not to try handling special orders until the office staff is fully hired, equipped, and trained. In order to be responsive to clients' requests for services that cannot be supplied yet, the implementer can outsource work to another fee-based service.

Outsourcing means that the local staff will broker the requests with established fee-based information services. For example, if the local collection does not own a document, the staff send the request to another service to be filled from that service's collection or from other sources if necessary. The established service sends the document to the emerging service, and staff there forward it to the client. The disadvantages are a longer fulfillment time and a higher cost; the advantages are that the new service both fills the client's needs and also does not risk losing the client altogether to the established service, as might happen with a referral. In addition, the new service begins networking with established services and learns how established services handle and present their work. Outsourcing works better for documents than for research projects, since at least some detail is generally lost if a searcher does not speak directly with the project's end user. The implementer balances the need to assist a client with a research project beyond the service's present capabilities with the danger that if referred, the client may never return.

RECORDKEEPING

Tracking information such as the number of new clients attracted each month, the total number of document orders filled, or the average number of hours needed to answer a research question can be tedious and time-consuming. Staff generally do not list keeping and compiling statistics among their favorite activities. However, keeping track of these numbers, or being able to produce them easily, is critical at all stages in a fee-based information service's life cycle. Administrators and grant agencies regard hard numbers as evidence that a service is meeting its objectives.

Try to determine in advance which groups of people will require what kinds of statistics and how often they will need them. What does the manager need in order to make informed decisions? The library administrators? Granting agency staff? Other interested library colleagues or university administrators? Clients? What information do these groups need on a regular (monthly, quarterly, or annual) basis?

In some cases, the same statistical report will satisfy more than one group. In other cases, prepare customized reports. When the manager proposes a new clerical position, for example, the request will be more favorably received if accompanied by appropriate figures proving that document delivery has increased by an impressive percentage over the past 18 months.

As the implementer proposes procedures and customizes software, think about the types of statistics and reports that might be needed. It is much faster and easier to capture the data at the point of action than to reconstruct it months or years later. Think beyond the minimum statistical information that will satisfy requesters. For example, library administrators may be satisfied with the total number of document orders filled each month, but a more informative report might include breakdowns by each campus library from which the documents were retrieved. The resulting statistical report will then be of interest not only to the administrators, but to colleagues heading the campus libraries.

Anticipate other occasional requests for specialized statistics. Is the internal tracking database configured so that staff can answer questions such as:

- What percent of all clients who ordered documents last year have in-state addresses?
- What percent of revenue is derived from document delivery and what percent from research projects?
- On average, how many document orders are not filled?
- How many of the clients added in the last six months are from target industry groups?

Addressing and solving, or at least proposing solutions to, most of the issues raised in this chapter smooth the transition from a bare office space to a functioning fee-based information service.

CITED REFERENCES

Grant, M.M., and D. Ungarelli. 1987. "Fee-Based Business Research in an Academic Library." *The Reference Librarian* 19: 239-255.

Grund, D. 1992. "Fee-Based Information Services: Serving Business/Strengthening the LRC." Pp. 113-121 in *Community College Reference Services*, edited by B. Katz. Metuchen, NJ: Scarecrow Press.

Hornbeck, J.W. 1983. "An Academic Library's Experience with Fee-Based Services." *Drexel Library Quarterly* 19(4): 23-26.

Marvin, S. 1988. "ExeLS: Executive Library Services." *The Reference Librarian* 22: 145-160.

McGuire, K. 1993. "Information Direct: Birmingham Library Services' Fee-Based Business Service." *Law Librarian* 24(September): 125-126.

Rubens, D., and J. Wulff. 1989. "Nuts & Bolts Guide to Fee-based Document Supply in the United States." *Infomediary* 2(3/4): 193-195.

Warner, A.S. 1983. "Selling Consulting Services, Buying Consulting Services." Pp. 95-105 in *Managing the Electronic Library*, edited by M. Koenig. New York: Special Libraries Association.

White, M.S. 1981. *Profit from Information: A Guide to the Establishment, Operation and Use of an Information Consultancy*. London: Andre Deutsch.

Whitmell, V. 1996. "Staffing the Fee-Based Library Service." *Fee for Service* 3(1): 6-12.

Wilkins, A. 1992. "The For-Profit Syndrome: Will Libraries Be Next?" *North Carolina Libraries* 50(Special Edition): 24-26.

FURTHER READING

Kotler, P., and R.A. Connor, Jr. 1977. "Marketing Professional Services." *Journal of Marketing* 41(1): 71-76.

Levitt, T. 1981. "Marketing Intangible Products and Product Intangibles." *Harvard Business Review* 81(May/June): 94-102.

McGrath, K. 1996. *Trademark: How to Name Your Business & Product*, 2nd edition. Berkeley, CA: Nolo Press.

Mitchell, E., and S.A. Walters. 1995. *Document Delivery Services: Issues and Answers*. Medford, NJ: Learned Information.

United States Department of Commerce. Patent and Trademark Office. Annual. *Basic Facts About Registering a Trademark*. Washington, DC: U.S. Department of Commerce, Patent and Trademark Office.

Warner, A.S. 1987. *Mind Your Own Business: A Guide for the Information Entrepreneur*. New York: Neal Schuman.

Chapter 6

Launching the Service

The launch date arrives. Despite the inevitable frustrations and delays during the implementation phase, everything finally comes together. The manager looks at the staff sitting on new chairs at new computers in a freshly painted office and staring at boxes of brochures. The capability to provide services is in place, and possibly also pretested to some extent. Now the challenge is to find clients who make the phone ring and the fax buzz.

MARKETING

Marketing is not just the new brochures and speaking at the local entrepreneurs' club luncheons. Marketing is also the way the clerk answers the phone, and the way the students copy and staple the articles, and the way the address labels are typed. Marketing is the way the information specialist handles the phone reference interview, presents the price quote, runs the search, prints the results and writes the cover letter. Marketing is finishing projects on time, billing them accurately, and filing the paperwork so it is quickly retrievable if the client calls with a follow-up question. Virtually everything the staff do has an impact on the way clients perceive the service. Slick brochures and clever advertising will not counteract the perception of sloppy work that a crooked photocopy, inaccurate invoice, or a correction fluid dotted address label presents.

Part of marketing is also selling. Many librarians are not entirely comfortable with the notion of selling, but for the service to succeed, the staff must understand that their jobs involve, and in fact depend on, selling practically every minute of the day.

During the first months after the launch date, staff in a new service should expect to spend a large percentage of their time, often as high as 50 to 70 percent, involved in formal marketing efforts. There is a wide assortment of possible marketing avenues, including mass mailings, advertisements, and personal appearances from which the wise manager will select a combination best suited to reaching the service's target audience.

119

While using only one marketing method is probably not enough, employing too many of them simultaneously is an equally disastrous decision. Eager to demonstrate the service's viability, the temptation is to try to reach thousands of potential clients as soon as possible. Resist the temptation and stick with the marketing strategy developed in the business plan and fleshed out by the implementer. Stay alert to new opportunities, however. Do not let a good marketing chance slip by simply because it is not mentioned in the business plan.

Although response rates are generally relatively low for any single type of marketing for a fee-based information service, the manager starts slowly at first. If the first mailing of 1,000 brochures should be fortunate enough to yield 100 phone calls the next week, can the staff handle the load in an efficient and timely manner? Even if only 10 of the 100 calls actually result in orders, the staff must still reply to 100 people, send out follow-up mailings, add names to the client database, prepare the next wave of scheduled mailings, and handle, ship, and bill the 10 orders. All this may occur at the same time that the manager is away on a two-day marketing trip, the senior clerk is training new student assistants, and the recently hired billing clerk is still learning the accounting software. At the beginning, it is much better to complete a few transactions well and cultivate repeat clients than to struggle filling too many orders haphazardly, thus presenting a less than professional image that will not inspire many clients to submit more orders. Everything will take longer at first as the staff develop, learn, and modify procedures. The payoff is a core of loyal, repeat customers and a sensible, efficient office routine.

Mailing Lists

Based on the recommendations in the plan, and building on the implementer's work of obtaining contact names and price quotes, the manager obtains mailing lists and supervises distributing brochures to the target audience.

Mailing brochures can be a very simple procedure of sticking them in envelopes, running them through a postage meter, and shipping them out in the thousands. Simple? Yes. Effective? Probably not very. To be successful, the piece must at least attract the recipient (or the secretary) enough to open it and then to glance at its contents (or pass it along to the boss). Even better, it should entice the recipient to read the contents, and possibly to file it. Better still, the recipient picks up the phone and calls for more information.

Direct mail marketing books guide the manager through the maze of possible ways to nudge the recipient through these stages. Using first class postage stamps, especially appropriate commemorative stamps (not the latest LOVE stamp), has been proven to provide better response than a bulk rate postage meter. A short, one page cover letter briefly describing the service is a plus. A letter addressed to the recipient personally, rather than to "Dear Medical Professional" is even better. A signed letter improves the response rate; the manager or information specialists need not personally sign thousands of letters, but assign the task to student assistants or others on staff with good handwriting. Use blue ink, not black, so that the signature cannot be mistaken for a mechanical one.

Another way to improve the response rate is to include a separate or tear-off prepaid postcard for the recipient to drop in the mail. Purdue's Technical Information Service has used this technique beginning with the first version of its brochure. The postcard includes boxes for the client to check for a phone call or for additional brochures. It is important to be committed to responding to the postcards within a week of receiving them. The postcards' arrival is evidence that the potential clients' first impression of the service was favorable; the second impression should be of a prompt call from a positive, articulate staff member. The employee should be prepared for the fact that the respondent may not in fact have an immediate information need, but may only want a little more information about the service. Keep in mind that a short, friendly, and helpful conversation now may yield actual business later.

After the call, the staff send a follow-up mailing. This letter can be a "boilerplate" note, but personalized with an allusion to the recent phone conversation. For even better future results, the envelope contains something else. Over the years, TIS developed a packet for new clients that includes several promotional pieces and article reprints written by the senior staff. A new service will not have assembled all these inserts yet, but it should have at least one other piece on hand to send to new prospects. One relatively inexpensive possibility is tabbed Rolodex cards (in both sizes) with the service's name, address, phone, and fax numbers. Another option is a small calendar with monthly tear-off sheets, suitably emblazoned at the top with the service's name and phone number, that the client can stick (possibly literally) on a desk or in-basket.

One manager reported that mailing brochures to companies, special libraries, public libraries, and economic development agencies did not yield a satisfactory response (Richards 1991, p. 16). In my experience, carefully choosing appropriate mailing lists increases the likelihood of attracting new clients. Staff must be patient, though. In many cases new clients call TIS months or even years after receiving a brochure; they filed the brochure against the day when an information need would arise.

A third possibility might be a coupon offering the user a half-price or free document, but I urge caution with this approach. TIS tried this once as promotional offer for attendees at a conference at which we exhibited. We printed the coupons on lime green paper, and requested that clients mail in the forms rather than fax them, so we could make certain the coupons would not be endlessly reproduced. We found that very few people took us up on our offer, and those who did ordered odd and unusual documents that we could not fill from the Purdue Libraries collection, a prerequisite for the free offer. We agreed to waive our handling fee if the clients wanted to place special orders on the items, but our overall experience of the coupon approach was not positive. The conference was one attended mainly by special librarians, however; the general professional public might be less likely to order esoteric documents. Remember to print an expiration date on the coupon.

Use the return postcards as a way to begin building the client database. Building the client database directly from the purchased mailing lists is ethically questionable at best and possibly illegal at worst if the manager bought the list on the understanding that it would be used only once. It is also an inefficient use of staff time and of the marketing budget for future mailings. The database should contain the names of people who, if they have not yet actually placed an order, are at least potentially likely to do so in the future based on some indication of interest.

Advertisements

Advertising is often easier than managing mailings, but it is also more expensive and, in my experience, less likely to yield enough results to warrant the expense. If advertising is one of the new service's marketing options, the implementer should have already prepared at least a professionally drafted version of the ad for insertion in selected publications. The manager need only approve the final design, and make arrangements with the newspapers or journals for buying advertising space. The publication's advertising sales staff will explain how to submit the ad.

Space the ads wisely. Especially at first, choose one publication rather than several, and then place the ad in it several times over a year's time. When callers mention having seen the ad, the staff need not guess or ask which magazine is meant, and will be better able the gauge the ad's effectiveness in that publication. It is usually less expensive per insertion to pay for space in multiple issues, but usually the ads need not appear in consecutive issues. In fact, many trade magazines and regional business newspapers have special issues devoted to different topics, so it may be possible to select the most appropriate special issues in which to place the ad. As an added feature, many trade journals print a number or code in each ad and invite readers to circle the corresponding codes on a special mail-in card for the ads that interest them. The publisher then sends the names and addresses of these readers to the appropriate advertisers, so they can follow up with more detailed mailings.

Do not overlook advertising in annual membership or other directories. A directory's effective life span is much longer than that of a single periodical issue. A regular advertiser in the major publication is often eligible for reduced advertising rates in the directory issue.

If many trade associations hold conventions or exhibits locally, the manager identifies likely targets from the convention bureau's listings and calls for advertising information for the program or exhibit publications.

There are other types of advertising besides magazine and newspaper ads. Radio spots might draw a satisfactory response for services located in or near large cities. However, while it is appropriate to include the service's listing in the phone book's white pages under the institution's library section, one fee-based service dropped its advertising in the yellow pages after becoming involved in legal action with an independent information broker claiming unfair competition because the service was nonprofit (Josephine and Reneker 1989; Josephine 1989, pp. 215-217). Some other forms of advertising, such as billboards and bus cards, are probably not appropriate.

Press Releases

Press releases provide an avenue for free advertising. Review a few books on public relations or marketing for small businesses or nonprofit organizations to find suggestions for, and samples of, press releases. Some standard word processing software includes press release templates. Keep the press release short; two double spaced pages should be the maximum. Write a snappy title, and open with an eye-catching or thought-provoking statement. Include a few quotes about how the service helps businesspeople find information. Use quotes from clients (with permission) if there has been some written feedback already, or from the manager if not. Be sure to add the service's full name and phone number.

Send the press release to local daily newspapers, regional business newspapers, and appropriate trade magazines. Be sure to vary the focus slightly if necessary for each of the intended audiences. Not all the publications will run the piece, but enough of them will to bring in a few queries. Send press releases to the same publications about once a year, being careful to rewrite them with a different twist for each annual submission. If a truly phenomenal event suggests a real news story ("White House Staff Contact Local Information Service") send out a press release at once—with the client's permission, of course.

An added advantage of using press releases is that sometimes a newspaper staff writer picks up a release and calls for background information to write a longer story for the business section. A news story is free advertising at its best. However, the manager expects that at least some comments from the interview will be mildly but unintentionally distorted. Although this is irritating, a few minor errors do not warrant a blistering letter to the editor. A newspaper writer working under deadline, with a hundred other things clamoring for attention, will probably not synthesize everything the manager mentioned into a totally accurate article. The piece will make a good impression on the library administrators to whom the manager sends copies, and will prompt a few phone calls from potential clients. If the article is especially good, get permission from the publisher for reprints to include in the service's promotional packet.

Business Cards

Order a good supply of business cards for all the professionals. Exchanging and distributing cards is an established way of doing business; prospective clients and other contacts expect the service's professional staff to have a pocketful at any business gathering. The institution probably has a standard business card format, but the format rules may be flexible enough to allow the service's name and the staff's specialized title. "Library" and "librarian" are not as effective on a card as the name of the service and a title such as "information specialist."

Most established fee-based information services use professionally printed folders for holding research results or for mailing customized marketing packets. These folders usually have slits on one of the inside pockets to display the information specialist's business card.

Personal Appearances: Off-Campus

On the surface, personal appearances at business club luncheons and other professional groups' monthly meetings seem another inexpensive marketing avenue. The professional, rather than the support, staff handle these appearances, which usually mean four to eight hours away from the office, possibly including a free meal. The information specialist meets a group of professionals at their meeting, socializes for awhile, and then makes a speech or other presentation describing the fee-based information service and how it can help meet the listeners' information needs.

For this method to work effectively, several things must come together. The information specialist must be comfortable and effective speaking to groups, and must inspire confidence by conveying the image of a competent researcher as well as of an effective speaker. Solicit or accept invitations from groups composed of people who are likely to have information needs and who are also in a position in their companies to make the decision to use the service. Keep the presentation relatively brief to hold the listeners' attention, tailor talks to the professional interests of each group, and include a short question and answer period.

Remember that the talk should not be just a sales pitch. At the end of the presentation, the listeners should know a few more things about finding or using information in their field than they knew before. The speaker's job is to show, without any "hard sell" tactics, that the information service can obtain or compile relevant information quickly, efficiently, and cost-effectively.

Presentations usually include appropriate graphics, but keep it simple. Take back-up graphics as insurance. Transparencies and an operational overhead projector are more effective than flashy computer images on a laptop that refuses to cooperate. Remember to distribute or display brochures and business cards as well.

The cost per person contacted is higher for personal appearances than for any other marketing option. The manager or information specialist not only spends time arranging, confirming, and preparing for the meeting, but also spends time traveling to and attending the function. Marketing textbooks call this the "opportunity cost;" while the manager is away from the office, other tasks that result in billable hours, such as phoning clients or running database searches, are delayed. The hope, of course, is that the cost of the manager's absence for a day will be more than amply recovered by future requests submitted by at least a few people in each audience.

So the manager balances the high opportunity cost of personally explaining services to a relatively small group with the much lower cost of handling regular office duties while supervising a clerk mailing several hundred brochures. Choose speaking engagements carefully, based on a combination of factors such as distance, the likely number of attendees, and the types of attendees, taking into consideration both their professional affiliation and job titles. Another consideration in scheduling these meetings is to be sure there are enough staff left in the office to meet clients' needs. In the early, critical days, the service cannot afford to lose potential clients who after two or three calls perceive that they can never get through to an information specialist for a cost quote on their projects.

Another key in making personal appearances successful in generating business is to double check with the meeting organizer about the talk's focus. Does the planner want the speaker to talk mainly about the fee-based information service, or is a mini-workshop on Medline searching tips or how to identify industry standards expected? Talk with the organizer to find out how long the talk should be, how many people are expected to attend, and what equipment, if any, will be needed or available for the presentation. How early should the speaker arrive? Is there anything special the speaker should know about parking, the meal, the attendees, the conference hall? To avoid potential misunderstandings, check in advance that the organizer understands that the manager does not expect any monetary compensation for the appearance.

Personal Appearances: On Campus

Do not overlook meetings and appointments on campus. A first contact in person is much more effective than just a phone call or a mailing. The list below suggests the types of departments to contact. If the directors and staff of these departments understand what the fee-based service does, they will be more likely to make appropriate referrals. Conversely, the manager who understands these other programs' objectives, and communicates them to the fee-based information service staff, also assists clients better by making helpful referrals. Make a note to touch base with these people or their successors at least once a year, even if the follow-up contact is by phone. Add their names to the service's campus mailing list.

- Meet or revisit the directors of campus offices that offer complementary services to the business community.
- Contact the central university switchboard, and explain the service. Many callers needing copies of the institution's own publications phone here first.

- Visit the university news service department.
- Meet the director of the campus visitor's center and leave a stack of brochures.
- Contact the department that organizes conferences on campus.
- Find out which departments print directories of university services, and be sure that the fee-based information service is listed in the appropriate ones.

Finally, remember to keep in touch with library colleagues. A new manager finds time to visit the heads of the campus libraries and to explain the service's mission. When necessary or appropriate, include brief updates about the service on staff meeting agendas. Send short news pieces to the staff newsletter when the service achieves significant milestones. Send brochures to the professional library staff. "The goals and objectives of any library activity must be thoroughly defined and communicated to all individuals even remotely involved, if the program is to succeed" (Lom 1986, p. 297).

Conferences and Exhibits

Attending conferences and exhibits is in some ways similar to making personal appearances in that a professional staff member will be away from the office, usually for several days. In addition, exhibiting usually also involves additional costs, such as renting a booth, overnight lodging, and meals, besides transportation. Sometimes renting a booth costs less if the service has also advertised in the conference bulletin or exhibit guide. If only one staff member attends, the long day on the exhibit floor will be exhausting. If more than one goes, the office may be seriously understaffed.

In addition, it is much more difficult to describe, demonstrate, and sell a relatively invisible service, as opposed to a tangible product that passersby can see and touch. A pile of brochures is not enough; find something else eye-catching. For example, invite attendees to drop their business cards into a bowl for a chance at winning a desirable giveaway item, such as a trade directory, that has some relation both to information and to the conference's theme. See if the directory's publisher will donate the volume or provide it at a deep discount in exchange for the publicity it will get.

Choose conference appearances selectively. The attendees should be a close match for the target audience the service identified in its mission. They should also hold positions in their companies that are both likely to require at least occasional information services and senior enough to have the authority to order services.

A new service limits these appearances to at most once or twice annually during its start-up years. TIS has averaged one conference appearance per year, mostly at very specialized or regional library conferences. Realize that there may be a long time lag between the exhibit dates and the time that new customers call with requests. In the meantime, add their names (from the business cards collected for the giveaway item) to the service's mailing list and keep them informed of the types of projects and documents the service successfully completed for other clients.

For more details, read the section on exhibiting in Alice Sizer Warner's book *Mind Your Own Business* (Warner 1987, pp. 113-116).

Articles

There is no need to wait until the local media call for a story about the new service. The manager can write an article and submit it to regional trade or business magazines or to the business editor for the local newspaper. Remember, however, that an article is different from an advertisement or a press release. Approach the subject from a general point of view. For example, point out how frustrating or time-consuming it can be for a businessperson to gather specialized information. Offer the reader several choices for easing this frustration, one of which is, of course, calling the fee-based information service. Or focus on one type of specialized information, such as patents or finding information about international companies; write generally about finding these kinds of information, and then mention ways the reader can hire someone else to do the research.

When the article appears, ask the editor for permission to make multiple copies (newspaper articles) or for reprints (magazine articles). Several hundred reprints on glossy paper provide another item to add to information packets sent to new clients. The manager understands the importance of forwarding copies to the library administration.

Networking

Networking is a kind of marketing. In the fee-based information service environment there are three kinds of networking: to the local institution's own staff, to colleagues in other fee-based services, and to colleagues in other libraries.

The concept of a fee-based information service will probably be a foreign one to most of the local library staff, despite the initial efforts of the investigator who spoke with several key department heads while making notes for the business plan. The manager makes both formal and informal efforts to keep the staff informed about the service's progress. The staff newsletter may be one forum, as may brief announcements at staff meetings or casual conversations with colleagues over lunch or coffee. The manager may be unable to answer some questions about situations that have not yet occurred, such as overdue or lost books, until the service is actually operating. Be candid about this inability. Mailing copies of promotional items to local professional staff is also an easy and effective way to keep staff aware of the service. Colleagues who understand the service's goals will be supportive and will be more likely to make appropriate referrals to the service.

By the launch date, the investigator, the implementer, and the manager will have made several informal contacts with managers in established fee-based information services. These people, and their counterparts in other services, are one of the first groups to receive the new brochure, along with a customized letter announcing when the new service will be operational. The letter suggests the benefits of mutual document delivery activity, mentions any special local collection strengths, and asks for a recent brochure and price list in return.

Most established services with strong document delivery components keep an eye out for new suppliers, and many are also willing to send some business to a newcomer. The manager must be sure, however, that the service is ready to accommodate document delivery requests from the pros. A corporate client unfamiliar with document delivery services may overlook a few blunders while a new service struggles to establish its procedures; another fee-based information service may not be so forgiving if the book it asked to be overnighted directly to its customer turns up on its own doorstep the next morning.

The new service also draws on the resources and expertise of the established services, and learns which ones best meet its own clients' needs. Ordering documents is also an unobtrusive way to find out what other services' packing lists, envelopes, mailing labels, and invoices look like. In addition, the manager makes every effort to attend the American Library Association's FISCAL (Fee-Based Information Service Centers in Academic Libraries) discussion group at their two meetings at both the ALA mid-winter and annual conferences. The group provides a helpful informal network of colleagues from all types of libraries and from all stages of starting and managing services.

Contacting colleagues in other libraries is the third major networking strategy. It may be most profitably used after the new service has established its procedures and its reputation. Purdue's Technical Information Service staff have found that many Indiana public librarians frequently encounter business patrons who want quick delivery of material the library does not own or who want the library staff to do their research for them. Many of these librarians have enthusiastically greeted the knowledge that TIS can fill both these needs for their patrons. TIS staff diplomatically approach the topic by stressing that our services are a supplement to, not a substitute for, public library services. We place an ad in the Indiana Library Federation's annual conference program and in its membership directory. We also send periodic letters to our colleagues in public libraries around the state. A small but steady stream of new clients comes to us each year referred by these librarians.

Client Visits

In a classic business situation, the consultant visits the company to meet senior staff and learn their requirements and expectations for the project under discussion. This scenario is certainly appropriate for a major consulting project running to five or six figures, but is generally a wasteful use of the service's professional staff's time for projects of a few hundred dollars. Since most clients understand the difference between a relatively short information-gathering project and the in-depth analysis for which they would hire a consultant, most conversations take place by phone.

If a client mentions a visit, the information specialist can usually sidestep the issue by pointing out that most clients have found that their projects can be discussed by phone, thus saving the client the time of taking a meeting. But sometimes a client insists. Purdue's Technical Information Service has not encountered this situation very often, largely because the largest client concentration is 60 miles away. A client who wants to speak with an information specialist in person is usually someone starting a small business who feels more comfortable making face-to-face contact before committing personal funds for research or before revealing the details of what may be a patentable process or device.

If it proves impossible to dissuade politely some clients from making a personal visit, invite them to the office, and add the time spent on the interview to the total project time. In most cases, the personal interview will not be necessary from an information handling point of view, and will also be more time-consuming than a phone interview. But also in almost every case, the client will assign the project, so it is possible to recover the cost of the time spent.

However, it is almost never necessary that the client actually be present when the specialist runs the search. When the specialist makes arrangements for the visit the client insists on, learn enough about the project during the preliminary phone call so that sample database records can be prepared in advance. During the visit, show the client the samples, but resist the urge to log on to demonstrate.

A service operating in a large urban area may find that its staff spend more time in personal reference interviews simply because so many more of its clients are local. In some cases, a site visit to the client's office is mandatory. If, for example, the service offers to organize a corporate library for a client, a site visit is essential. The potential income from such a project also makes it worthwhile to spend half a day away from the office to see the site and discuss the project.

Cold Calling

I do not recommend cold calling as a useful marketing technique for fee-based information services. Most busy professionals regard cold calls as a nuisance at best. They will not be disposed to listen favorably to what is essentially a sales spiel when they have two calls waiting, three people in the outer office, and a meeting in five minutes. Use staff time and the marketing budget for other, more effective, marketing efforts.

However, follow-up calls to people who have responded to initial mailings are appropriate, as are quick conversations with clients to whom search results have recently been mailed.

World Wide Web

The Web can be an effective place to post information about the service, but a new fee-based information service uses it cautiously. A good first step would be a short description of the service linked the local library's home page. The description invites readers to call or to fax messages to the service. The staff want to avoid a lot of extraneous messages from people who are not seriously interested in paying for research or documents. Replying to these messages is time-consuming. In addition, the staff may not wish to take a chance on filling orders coming over the Web or via electronic mail without having first contacted the client to be sure that the request is legitimate and that the client understands that there is a fee for services. An initial "real time" contact also establishes details such as the speed with which the client needs the item, the complete address, and a phone number.

Resist the urge to explore and implement World Wide Web marketing techniques until after the service is well established and staff are thoroughly familiar with the work flow and issues such as shipping to other countries.

Talking about Money

Marks pointed out that "librarians as a group tend to be uncomfortable when it comes to dealing with money. ... The discomfort is associated with attaching a value to the work we do and the services we deliver to our clientele. Perhaps one of the reasons that libraries are not valued is due to our inability to establish a value for our own activities" (Marks 1992, p. 21).

New staff with most or all of their previous work experience in a traditional library environment may find it very difficult at first to talk with clients about money. I know that at first I sounded very hesitant and apologetic about discussing charges after Purdue University's Technical Information Service implemented its fee schedule. This feeling vanished after a few weeks. Business clients expect to pay a fee for service, and they expect that special services, such as rush handling or special orders, will cost more. They understand that some services, like document delivery, have relatively fixed prices, while others, such as research projects, are variable with in a preestablished range.

The manager helps staff realize that successful marketing also includes sounding confident and businesslike when discussing fees, bills, payment options, and other financial topics with clients.

Staff Attitude

Finally, the best marketing tool of all is a friendly, helpful, pleasant, customer-oriented staff. For most clients, the only direct personal contact they have with the service is by phone. Voice tone is crucial. A person who feels surly, irritated, tired, or otherwise less than cheerful will convey these feelings by tone, even if the words do not express it.

The manager encourages all staff to present a positive manner on the phone. Require all staff to read at least one book on business phone etiquette. Lisa Collier Cool's book is a good example (Cool 1988).

DAILY OPERATIONS

With the service launch comes establishing a general office routine. The staff test the work flow and learn what methods work best. The manager should not be surprised at the number of details that looked perfectly reasonable on paper during the implementation stage, but that need additional refinements in practice.

Learning to handle priorities is a difficult skill. The first priority is always to fill customers' requests, but even this can be challenging with hourly judgment calls about which orders to process first. Also vying with the staff's attention are internal demands for statistics compilation, timely billing or filing operations, clients calling for status reports on previous orders, suppliers cancelling special orders, supplier invoices requiring reconciliation, mailings, budget estimates, meetings, housekeeping tasks such as ordering supplies or backing up computer files, preparing reports, hiring student assistants, staff training, and a dozen other distractions.

The smaller the staff, the more likely it is that everyone will be juggling several different tasks at once, not all of them directly related to client orders, but all of them vital if the service is to survive. Having hired staff with strong organizational skills and the ability to prioritize tasks pays off at this stage.

MEETING CLIENTS' NEEDS

After all the months of preparation, nothing matches the thrill of receiving the first orders. Every new order represents potential income, every satisfactorily filled request means a happy client, and a happy client may become a repeat client. Repeat clients in sufficient numbers and with sufficient volume ensure the service's future.

Staff always remember that every first-time caller may represent potential future income of thousands of dollars. Certainly, some new clients place one-time orders. The majority submit a relatively modest number of requests each year. But a critical minority annually channel hundreds of document orders for their organizations. At the point of that first phone contact, of course, the service's staff will not know into what category the caller falls. Treat all callers as if they are the next potential high-volume client.

What do clients look for in an information service?

- Speed;
- Flexibility and convenience;

- Accurate and high quality products;
- Multiple delivery options;
- Fast and equitable resolution of occasional errors;
- Prompt notification of cancellations or delays;
- Neat presentation of the filled order;
- Courteous and friendly staff;
- Timely, accurate, and easy-to-read invoices;
- Quick status reports; and
- Reasonable prices.

If performance in most areas is consistently superior, most clients tolerate less than stellar performance in certain areas (e.g., invoice format, something the service may have no control over). But most clients who experience more than occasional difficulties with missed deadlines, incorrect or incomplete orders, or staff unresponsiveness will take their business elsewhere. Even heavy users, who are more likely than other clients to exhibit supplier loyalty, will look for another information provider if service responsiveness drops off noticeably. Unlike undergraduate library users, business clients are not a captive audience. They can choose among a growing array of information providers vying for their business.

A dangerous trap that can ensnare staff at nonprofit fee-based information services at any stage in their development is the drive to generate revenue. In moderation, this is certainly a healthy attitude, since without sufficient income generation, the service cannot survive. The bottom line also provides a tangible indication of the service's success. However, do not lose sight of the fact that the primary mission is to meet the clients' information needs reliably and professionally. If the focus shifts too heavily toward cranking out invoices, customer service may suffer.

Part of the reason many clients like dealing with fee-based information services is that these services, almost by definition, cannot grow so large that clients are reduced to account numbers. These clients appreciate the customized attention their orders receive. They prefer to stick with a friendly and responsive fee-based service rather than to switch to a generally less personal commercial service. If the information service degenerates into an impersonal numbers-based assembly line, it risks losing clients.

Research

Searching databases is the usual method of answering clients' questions. Appendix C provides examples of the wide range of questions that clients have asked Purdue's Technical Information Service. Information specialists formulate a search strategy based on the reference interview with the client, execute it in one or more files, download the results the next day, edit the results into a standard format, print them, review them, write a cover letter, and ship the results to the client.

However, information specialists quickly learn that not all jobs can be completed comfortably in the office with a database search. Many projects require manual searching through library materials, either as a supplement to the online search or as the search itself. Other projects call for extensive phone calls to government agencies, trade associations, or other experts. Some clients ask the service to acquire product samples or to make phone calls on their behalf.

The answers to a few questions simply cannot be answered through conventional sources. For example, one TIS client wanted to know the number of medical gloves bought annually by police and fire departments in major U.S. cities. After some preliminary checking, it became clear that the only way to obtain this information was to call each fire and police department and ask. The client also wanted to know the ratio of the number of gloves to each city's population. *Statistical Abstract* yielded recent population figures, and the information specialist prepared a table to show the ratios.

In rare instances, although an information source can be identified, it cannot be obtained. In the example above of the medical gloves, the information specialist identified the top five manufacturers of medical gloves but, for obvious and legitimate reasons, the companies declined to divulge the names of their customers. Officials at one city's fire department also refused to reveal how many gloves they purchased.

In a few cases the information specialist is unable to find an answer to a client's question. Some answers are either virtually impossible or prohibitively expensive to find. An example of this type of question is: "How much did all branches and locations of the federal government spend on software last year?"

Other questions seem straightforward, but finding information about them proves difficult. For example, the first time I was unable to identify any patents for a particular device, I was certain that I must have overlooked a vital element in the search strategy. I was astonished at the client's delight at my lack of success. The fact that no relevant records existed encouraged her to apply for a patent that she was eventually granted.

It is important, however, that clients understand that the service bills for a lack of results, even if that very lack is the anticipated outcome. It takes time and other resources to determine that there are, in fact, no answers or no results.

Most clients' questions are complex enough to require at least a few hours' work. Handling ready reference queries depends on a number of factors, including who the client is, the information specialist's workload, and just how "ready" the question really is. Billing a client for the few minutes it takes to look up a company phone number or a trade association address is not efficient. Handling the question as a courtesy for an established client builds good public relations.

However, answering too many "freebies," especially for new clients, both devalues the service and takes up the specialists' billable time. The caller usually expects the equivalent of rush service because the question is not difficult. Some quick look-up questions sound deceptively easy and then turn into time-devour-ing monsters. Reneging on the promise of a free answer reflects badly on the service. Since most TIS clients work at least 60 miles from campus, we often point out that in these cases, contacting their local public library's reference desk will be much more cost-efficient.

Each service develops a standard, although flexible, policy for handling ready reference questions. The only cardinal sin would be to refer the off-campus client to the home library's reference desk, unless there is a clear understanding that the reference staff expect to answer quick questions for non-primary users.

Limits

Librarians are trained to meet the patron's needs, but within reasonable limits. For instance, academic librarians show students how to use various reference tools effectively, but draw the line at actually doing the research. In a fee-based information service, the definition of reasonable limits becomes much more elastic. After all, the client is paying for premium service and expects premium work. In addition, staff at a new service are so eager to attract clients that they may be startled at the notion of turning away some business. The limits are mainly ones of time, scope, ethics, policy, and institutional constraints. Sometimes the clients themselves impose limits, such as of time or price, that the service is unable to accommodate.

Time Limits. In terms of time, the limits are reality and resources. For example, staff are very occasionally able to fax an article within 15 minutes of receiving an order, if the item is housed in the same building, is actually on the shelf, and if someone is available to drop everything and literally run off to handle the order immediately. However, even large, established fee-based information services are unable to fill more than a few orders a day so quickly. In some cases, no matter how much the client is willing to pay, it is physically impossible to get from the office to the appropriate library location and back within 15 minutes on foot. In dire emergencies, staff can ask their colleagues at a branch library to copy and fax an article to a client, but this arrangement should not be abused. In addition, raising client expectations to think that rush orders can routinely be filled so quickly may set a dangerous precedent.

Time may be a limiting factor for research projects as well. Information specialists juggle their workload to some extent to accommodate rush requests, but sometimes it simply is not possible to drop everything else and squeeze in another search. The specialist may have made prior commitments to other clients to finish their searches that day, or the search may be too complex handle in a single block of time or the results may be too lengthy to make it cost-effective to print on demand, rather than waiting to download the next day. The searcher may also simply be swamped and unable to accommodate a rush search that day and still maintain any reasonable hope of working on or finishing other projects.

Scope Limits.   A second limiting factor is scope. An order may be too large or too complex for the service to handle. Could the service handle a request for 200 documents to be shipped out by the next day? Can an information specialist reasonably hope to fill a request for "everything" about a complex subject, even if the client has a generous research budget?

Staff should feel comfortable suggesting alternative deadlines or alternative avenues in a positive manner. If the client insists that the deadline cannot be lengthened or the project description reduced or segmented, staff realize that the best thing to do is to decline the order. There is no rule that says the service must accept every order. Even a doable request may have to be declined if staff absences or current heavy workload preclude accepting a large new order. Consider outsourcing or referring these requests to other fee-based information services.

Another issue concerning scope is that no fee-based information service can efficiently and cost-effectively handle every type of request. Some requests fall outside the staff's areas of expertise or require access to databases to which the service does not subscribe. Other projects are so massive or so specialized that the information specialist's best response is to suggest that the client contact a market research firm or other industry expert.

Ethical Limits.   Ethical considerations present a third possible limitation. Different managers' comfort levels about these situations differ. Chapter 9 explores some of these issues further, but here are a few examples:

- Conducting Internet searches for clients who do not want Web site producers to learn of their companies' interest in these files.
- Accepting an assignment to find information that the searcher suspects may be used for illegal purposes.
- Taking advantage of a publisher's university discount program to obtain a book that will be sent to a corporate client.

Would doing these things be unethical? Each fee-based information service decides these issues for itself and sets limits accordingly.

Policy Limits.   The service might also set limits based on internal or library policy. Obviously, these should be as few as possible, especially since the service's goal is to expedite the flow of information, often by "de-emphasizing formal library protocols" (George 1993, p. 43). Clients who hear too many reasons about why the staff are unable to fill their requests will look for a service better able to meet their information needs. However, reasonable formal limitations may be an unwillingness to make book loans outside North America, or to make any loans of conference proceedings. Common sense limitations include declining to lend more books to a client with a history of losing loans, or refusing to handle any more orders from a client whose account is seriously in arrears.

At TIS, we arrange for book loans to be sent from our U.S. document suppliers directly to North American clients, but we decided not to accept the responsibility of acting as an agent for obtaining loans from interlibrary loan departments and then shipping those to our clients. If a client wants a loan of an item not held by any of our partner fee-based information services, we offer the purchase the book on the client's behalf if it is in print or suggest that the client obtain a copy through the ILL unit at a local public library. One service in an urban area arranged for loans of other libraries' books if local clients were willing to visit the office and use them there (Marvin 1988, p. 148).

Another type of limitation might be those imposed by the institution. For example, there might be no mechanism by which the fee-based information service can accommodate credit card sales, or the procedure might be so cumbersome and time-consuming that in the long run it is better to decline a few orders if this is the only way some clients claim they can pay for services.

Clients' Limits. Client-imposed limits are relatively rare. The most frequent one, other than impossibly tight deadlines, is that a client's budget is not large enough for the searcher to be able to retrieve much relevant information. Staff politely decline projects in these cases, and suggest a few alternatives for the client to complete the research personally.

A few clients insist that their projects be handled in a certain manner. For example, one client insisted that I conduct a patent search using key words only, no matter how hard I explained that using the classification codes would result in much more precise and comprehensive results. Another will not hear of using the descriptors in Compendex, but demands that his searches be limited to key words in the title field. Each service must decide if it feels comfortable with producing less than satisfactory results at a client's insistence.

SURVIVING THE FIRST MONTHS

At least some of these scenarios may be ones that a fledgling service can hardly imagine happening, at least in the immediate future. In their excitement at receiving requests for document delivery and for research, staff may eagerly promise anything, hoping that somehow they will successfully find the material, meet the deadline, or formulate the search. The manager helps staff learn to distinguish between those requests that are new and unusual, but possible to accomplish, and those that are impossible or inadvisable. False promises damage a service's reputation far more than polite cancellations, refusals, or referrals. Staff rehearse ways to cancel, delay, or refer queries in a positive manner. Compare a client's likely reaction to these two responses:

A. "Gee, I don't know if we can find stuff like that. Well, why don't you fax it in anyway, and when my boss gets back, I'll have her take a look at it."

B. "Our library collection doesn't include German standards, but we use a reliable supplier for international standards. The prices can vary a lot depending on the length of each standard, so please fax in your request. I'll get a price quote for it and call you back by the end of the day."

In the second response, the clerk offered the client a real option and clearly indicated what would be done with the request and how long it would take. Remind staff periodically that the same message can be conveyed in several different ways, some of them unintentionally negative and off-putting. I once called another service to speak with a colleague and was flatly told: "She can't talk with you right now. She's busy." How much better it would have sounded to hear: "She's on another line just now. May I take a message and ask her to call you back?" I shared this experience with my staff as a classic example of how not to answer the phone.

A new, small service will probably initially experience a low volume of requests, but even this low volume may be too much if staff absences or other setbacks occur. Staff should be prepared to negotiate with clients pleasantly and positively. Try to offer an option whenever possible. If every effort to verify a citation has failed, offer to try again if the client can supply a copy of the original reference. If there is not enough time to copy and fax an article today, would receipt by 10:00 a.m. the following morning be a satisfactory alternative? Fifty articles are too many to ship by tomorrow; if most of them arrived within four days, would that be satisfactory? If the only searcher is at a training workshop today, when will the client be available tomorrow for a return call to discuss the project?

If the client cannot wait, it is far better to decline the order or make a referral rather than to make delivery promises that cannot be met. In the same vein, if an information specialist accepts a request that later turns out to be beyond the service's present ability to complete, call the client as soon as possible, offer several alternatives as referrals, and do not charge the client for any time or other expenses.

As the service grows and as staff gain confidence and experience, they will remember with amazement how long it once took to handle requests that they now consider routine orders. In these early days, the staff learn everything from scratch (who supplies military standards?) and develop or refine procedures (at what point in the order fulfillment process should we check copyright?) as they go. Although I hope this book will help managers and staff at new fee-based information services avoid some major pitfalls, there is no substitute for the insights gained through actual trial and error experience during a service's first few months of operation.

CITED REFERENCES

Cool, L.C. 1988. *How to Give Good Phone: Telephone Techniques to Increase Your Power, Profits, and Performance.* New York: D.I. Fine.

George, L.A. 1993. "Fee-Based Information Services and Document Delivery." *Wilson Library Bulletin* 67(February): 41-44, 112.

Josephine, H.B. 1989. "Fee-Based Information Services in Academic Libraries: Competitors in the Private Sector?" Pp. 213-218 in *National Online Meeting Proceedings*, compiled by C. Nixon and L. Padgett. Medford, NJ: Learned Information.

Josephine, H.B., and M.H. Reneker. 1989. "In Defense of FIRST and Freedom of Access to Information." *College and Research Libraries News* 50(5): 377-379.

Lom, J.A. 1986. "Fee-Based Reference Service: A Reevaluation." *RQ* 25(3): 295-299.

Marks, K. 1992. "Libraries: No Longer Free or Fee." *North Carolina Libraries* 50(Special Edition): 20-23.

Marvin, S. 1988. "ExeLS: Executive Library Services." *The Reference Librarian* (22): 145-160.

Richards, D. 1991. "Starting a Fee-Based Service in a Rural Area." *The Bottom Line* 5(1): 14-17.

Warner, A.S. 1987. *Mind Your Own Business: A Guide for the Information Entrepreneur.* New York: Neal Schuman.

FURTHER READING

Machovec, G.S. 1994. "Criteria for Selecting Document Delivery Suppliers." *Information Intelligence, Online Libraries, and Microcomputers* 12(5): 1-5.

Ward, S.M. 1990a. "Client Prospecting: Techniques for Fee-Based Services." *MLS: Marketing Library Services* 4(6): 4-6.

Chapter 7

The Established Service: Growth and Maturity

An established service is one that has successfully survived its first few critical years. It has attracted, trained, kept, and perhaps slightly expanded a staff dedicated to customer service. Its marketing program has developed a client base generating enough new and repeat business that the manager's heart no longer palpitates each time the monthly budget summary arrives. The library administration expresses its approval with the service, and colleagues understand its objectives. Funding and income seem relatively secure and predictable.

The manager knows, however, that the service cannot rest on its laurels. The continued success of a fee-based information service depends on a number of factors, including continued institutional support, the regional and national economy, trends among the major industries represented by its client base, and the continued dedication of its staff. The information industry is among the most rapidly changing. A service whose products met client needs last year may not survive next year if the staff neglect to keep up with new trends, changing information resources, and clients' shifting needs and expectations.

While staff constantly fine-tune procedures to provide ever more efficient and responsive service, the manager is also responsible for looking at the larger picture to spot trends and opportunities. "Fee-based services need to be future oriented, anticipating needs, perceiving trends in the information gathering industry and responding to the anticipated demands of the service" (Marvin 1988, p. 157).

EVALUATION

To some extent, a responsive, empowered staff constantly evaluate the services they provide and look for ways to improve them. Observing internal processes and striving to improve them work well up to a point. However, customer feedback is also an essential part of understanding what the clients like about a service, and what they would prefer to see offered or improved.

139

The results of an evaluation tell the manager of a healthy service what the staff do well to attract and keep customers. If the service has encountered a decline in orders or revenue, evaluation results may help pinpoint problems. Survey results also suggest possible improvements in some of the other issues discussed in this chapter, such as marketing, financial considerations, and the service mix.

The results of formal evaluation are also sometimes the best or only way to get institutional attention or approval. The manager constantly seeks tangible evidence of the service's success, not only to point out the service's continued value to its customers and the positive reflection it makes on the institution but also to support requests for additional space, staff, funding, or equipment.

Review both the library and the business literature for more details about selecting, designing, implementing, and analyzing different customer evaluation instruments.

Feedback

Client feedback is vital to the health of any service. Feedback may be inferred, informal, or formal. It is the staff's responsibility to notice inferred feedback. One example of inferred feedback is noticing that a certain segment of the target audience responds to the initial marketing letter and brochure more strongly than other segments. Staff might conclude several things from this observation:

- More clients will be gained by concentrating on marketing to this segment;
- Revise the current marketing letter to make it more effective when sent to target audiences in other segments; or
- The information needs of the strongly responding segment most closely match the service's resources for meeting those needs.

Another example might be noticing an increase in the number of billing questions from clients the week after the invoices go out; some calls are inevitable, but too many of them may indicate an unacceptably high error rate creeping into the billing process or an inherently confusing invoice layout.

Informal feedback includes the pleasant comments a client makes on the phone or scribbles at the bottom of a new order ("Thanks for your help finding that Russian conference paper last week. Here's another impossible citation!") During the December holidays, the office receives several dozen greeting cards and, in the best corporate tradition, a few boxes of chocolates or mixed nuts from a few especially grateful clients. Repeat business and prompt invoice payment also fall under the heading of informal feedback. But, except for the occasional letter or note praising the completion of an especially critical search or the procurement of an unusually obscure document, the manager cannot put these instances of informal feedback on the boss' desk as concrete evidence of client satisfaction.

In an academic environment, librarians are used to lots of feedback. Patrons (usually) say "thank you." Colleagues and supervisors indicate agreement and approval. Formal and informal evaluation procedures help staff judge their achievements both in relation to their peers and to their own potential. The corporate world does not always operate this way. From the clients' perspective and experience, they place an order, they receive the product or service, they pay the bill, and if they are satisfied, they call again when another need arises. In the business environment, there is no greater praise than a repeat order. "Often the only way of knowing that a client has been satisfied with a search is if that client continues to use the service or refers other people to it" (Tertell 1983, p. 49).

I noticed a very peculiar phenomenon during the first years I worked in Purdue's Technical Information Service. For the first 18 months, when TIS was entirely funded by a state grant and services were provided at no charge, clients frequently expressed their appreciation in formal letters or notes. The moment TIS implemented the fee schedule, the notes and letters dwindled to a few a year. I found this sudden change very perplexing, since the staff were making every effort not only to maintain the same high level of service but also to improve it. Finally I understood that the early clients, who did not pay for services, expressed their appreciation for (and possibly also their surprise in) the quality of the work they received for free. When TIS started charging, clients expressed their appreciation by paying their bills and sending in more orders. The bottom line thus became the major indication of client satisfaction and service success.

However, I also discovered that a healthy balance sheet does not entirely fill the requirement for periodic formal investigations into customer satisfaction. Formal evaluation provides a chance to learn in the clients' words what they think about the service. Positive comments provide essential feedback to the staff and validation that the service is indeed meeting its objectives. Negative notes point out areas for improvement. Customers know what they want; they may suggest new service areas that had not yet occurred to the staff. Customers are often pleased to know that the service cares about their opinions. A strongly positive response may help support the manager's requests for additional staff, space, equipment, or other support to meet client needs (and thus increase revenue). Pointing to several clients' comments that they would welcome a certain feature, such as deposit accounts, may do far more towards making it possible than all the manager's protestations that this is indeed what the customers want. And finally, administrators sometimes need more than glowing income figures and the manager's intuition about what clients want or think.

Satisfaction Survey

Conducting a survey is one of the best ways to ascertain clients' views about the fee-based information service and how it meets their needs. The bibliography at the end of this chapter lists several excellent guides for conducting a useful, relatively inexpensive survey. It is possible to write and conduct a good survey, as well as to evaluate and report the results, without having a degree in statistics or hiring a consultant.

While a short section of this chapter cannot hope to address all the points admirably covered in the books recommended below, here are a few pointers:

- Survey clients no more often than once every two years. Clients may become irritated if asked to respond more frequently.
- Keep the survey as short as possible. Most clients will be too busy to fill out a long questionnaire.
- Keep the survey's objective firmly in mind. There may be a hundred things that would be nice to find out; what is essential to know?
- Consider sending the survey to a sample population, not to every client.
- Plan ways to assure client confidentiality.
- Follow up at least once to encourage nonrespondents to send in their surveys.
- Avoid open-ended questions whenever possible, but do allow room for the respondents to add a few personal comments at the end.
- Write and rewrite questions to remove possible ambiguity.
- Include a short cover letter explaining the survey's purpose.
- Be sure to include a self-addressed, stamped envelope.
- Set a reasonable deadline for responding. Most people will respond promptly or not at all.

Purdue's Technical Information Service has conducted two client satisfaction surveys, and plans a third for 1997. The first one, done in 1990 about a year after we started charging for our services, was a very crude effort (see Appendix D). At the time, however, this one-page questionnaire was extremely helpful in soliciting comments from over 200 clients who had contacted TIS for services during the previous year. The response rate was about 50 percent without any follow-up reminders, and almost all of the responses and comments were overwhelmingly positive.

The second survey, in 1992, was developed, conducted, and analyzed much more professionally with the assistance of a graduate assistant from Purdue's management school (see Appendix E). This second survey targeted Indiana clients only and achieved a 42 percent response rate.

The fewer the questions asked, the faster and easier it will be to compile the results. Using a spreadsheet program may be helpful, but if the questions are very few and very straightforward, as they were on the first TIS survey, counting hatchmarks on a scoring sheet may be adequate. Compilation may be as easy as making a few simple calculations to determine, for example, what percentage of respondents order documents, what percentage ask for research, and what percentage use both services. Other analyses, such as describing a typical client, are more complex.

Having gathered and compiled the results, the manager presents them to the library administration and to any other interested parties. With the 1990 TIS survey, I simply reported the results orally at several meetings. For the 1992 survey, the graduate assistant produced a 50-page report of her findings.

Draw conclusions from and act on the survey results cautiously. For example, suppose the results show that 75 percent of clients use document delivery services, 10 percent use research services, and 15 percent use both services. What do these results imply? Here are a few possible interpretations:

- Marketing efforts that promote document delivery have been successful.
- Clients in .the targeted industries need document delivery services more often than research services.
- Research service performance must be poor, overpriced, underpromoted, or all three, since so few clients request searches.
- Clients may not be fully aware of the kinds of research services available.
- Clients may have misperceptions about the value of research services.
- Many clients are corporate librarians who outsource their companies' document delivery but perform database searches themselves.

Some combination of these statements is probably close to the truth. Based on these results and possible interpretations, the manager might decide to expand marketing efforts for research services. An equally solid decision might be to increase marketing efforts for document delivery if, besides being the most heavily used service, it also produces a higher and more predictable income stream.

It may be difficult to quantify the answers to a few open-ended questions, but the comments are often enlightening. If more than a few clients mention the same issue, such as prices, invoices, or status reports, the manager reviews these seriously.

This section discussed conducting a relatively lengthy survey every few years. Another possibility involves sending selected clients, such as new clients or those requesting large projects, a much shorter survey to capture their reactions to the results of specific projects. Vicki Whitmell's article includes a copy of a good short survey (Whitmell 1996, pp. 10, 12).

SERVICES

Whether or not a fee-based information service conducts a user satisfaction survey, the manager periodically reviews the service mix.

- If some services are barely used, should they be dropped or should they be marketed more heavily?

- Would offering a new service fill a need that several clients have expressed?
- Has there been a significant increase or decrease in one of the services?

The manager calculates the costs and benefits of adding or dropping a service. For instance, if one client a year asks about hiring someone to complete an indexing project, the demand is probably not high enough to warrant training an information specialist to meet this occasional need. However, if many clients express an interest in learning to use the World Wide Web (or if staff perceive such an interest or need), it may be cost-effective to develop a seminar or workshop to teach this skill. An incidental benefit of advertising the workshop to a potential audience wider than the target industries is that many registrants will hear about the fee-based information service for the first time.

Although most services offer both document delivery and research, document delivery usually accounts for well over half of all revenue. Offering both of these complementary services meets the majority of customers' needs. However, several years ago one fee-based information service calculated that the income from a dwindling number of research projects barely paid the cost of keeping an information specialist on staff. This service solved the problem by referring all research projects to a local consortium of independent information brokers. Most projects were handled by a single broker, and all projects were shipped using the service's letterhead and billed by the service. To the client, the broker's involvement as an independent contractor was invisible. Without committing its own resources, the service continued to meet clients' occasional needs for research projects (George 1993).

In another case, a fee-based information service found that several years after it began, its clients predominantly requested research projects. Document delivery requests were relatively low. This service made the opposite decision; it outsourced almost all of its document delivery to another fee-based information service and concentrated on its strength of completing research projects.

Yet another service, located in an urban area, noticed that research requests dropped, partly as a result of a rate increase and partly because more clients visited the library to do their own research as the selection of CD-ROM databases increased. However, the demand for document delivery increased at the same time (Franks and Montgomery 1991, pp. 16-17).

Changing demands for different services necessitate changes in the staffing mix (professional and support staff) or in the marketing mix.

EXPANDING THE DOCUMENT SUPPLIER NETWORK

Since document delivery is usually the backbone of most fee-based information services, expanding the document supplier network is critical unless the service has made a conscious decision to supply local items only or to work with only a small, limited group of suppliers. A new service often starts out by placing special orders with other fee-based information services whose institutions hold particular items and by drawing on the resources of a handful of commercial suppliers. It will quickly become evident that while this mix satisfies a high percentage of document special orders, it will not satisfy all of them. The manager has three choices:

1. Cancel orders that the local collection and/or the approved list of suppliers cannot provide, or
2. Outsource these orders, or
3. Develop the expertise to fill them.

If the service fills a very high percentage of document orders from the local collection, possibly supplemented from a short list of suppliers, then cancelling a few difficult items should not damage its reputation. However, at least a few clients will ask for a referral to a supplier who will be able to fill the order. The dilemma then becomes one of making the referral and risking losing the client to a service with more flexible document delivery arrangements, or of risking losing the client by refusing to offer further assistance.

Outsourcing prevents these dangers. If the manager decides that the local service will not itself attempt to fill any, or certain kinds of, special orders, the staff may decide to outsource them. Outsourcing document delivery means passing the requests to another fee-based information service or document delivery provider. The pass-through provider obtains the items and ships them to the requesting fee-based information service, which then forwards them to its clients. The advantage of this procedure is that the clients' perception is that the service with whom they do business obtained the item. The downside is that, by acting simply as a go-between, the service loses some degree of control over both turnaround time and costs, both of which increase with this arrangement.

Outsourcing may be a good solution for a young service just starting to handle special orders. Staff can start by handling some of the more straightforward special orders themselves, outsourcing only the ones that stump them. As they gain expertise in identifying specialized suppliers, the need to outsource slowly disappears. Another advantage of this strategy is that during the transition, the service gains more satisfied clients.

Developing the expertise to handle special orders quickly and cost-effectively is a slow process. Asking the library's interlibrary loan staff for assistance is only marginally helpful since many ILL operations sacrifice speed in favor of lower costs. A fee-based service, on the other hand, meets its customers' needs by providing fast service; cost is generally not a major consideration. Each service learns for itself which suppliers are the most efficient and reliable. Efficiency and reliability include a host of variables, many of them subjective, such as:

- Turnaround time;
- Prompt notification of unfillable or delayed orders;
- Ability to meet deadlines and shipping requirements for rush requests;
- Clear and accurate invoices;
- Correct documents sent;
- Prompt and gracious corrections of occasional errors;
- Reasonable prices;
- Accuracy in filling orders to be shipped to a third-party; and
- High quality photocopies.

It is no accident that these points resemble the same list of attributes that clients require in a fee-based information service. After all, the fee-based service became someone else's client as soon as it began placing orders with other suppliers. The staff select their favorite suppliers based on the same criteria that clients apply.

The major difference is that a staff experienced with handling a wide range of document special orders deal with dozens of suppliers, not just one as most of their clients do. As a mature service, for example, Purdue's Technical Information Service uses several tiers of suppliers:

1. Six to eight suppliers at other fee-based information services that consistently meet the criteria above. We order dozens of documents per month from each of them.
2. Six to eight secondary suppliers at other fee-based information service. These are second choices for items unavailable from first-tier suppliers.
3. About 10 specialized suppliers. If we need an NTIS document, for example, we order it from NTIS. Or if we need a military specification, we use a commercial service that has proven consistently reliable and reasonably priced.
4. Document brokers with runners to major library collections. TIS works with a broker who sends retrievers to the Library of Congress, the National Library of Medicine, the National Agriculture Library, and other Washington, D.C., area locations. We call on the services of other brokers whose staff visit UCLA, Berkeley, Wayne State University, and Stanford, among others.
5. International suppliers. Through trial and error, we found reliable suppliers in countries like Australia, Canada, Japan, South Africa, and the United Kingdom. We found another one with a high success rate in supplying European documents.
6. All other types of suppliers. These include commercial publishers, trade associations, authors, university presses, government agencies (federal, state, and local), university departments, research foundations, and companies. We obtain hundreds of documents a year from these suppliers, but generally only one or two items from each one.

A newer service can start with the top tier and slowly build expertise on its way down the list. It need not develop expertise in all areas. For example, a manager might decide that the benefit of filling a few requests for esoteric international documents is not worth the additional costs of faxing orders overseas, handling payments in foreign currencies, paying high rates for shipping, and handling the higher incidence of status queries that, by their nature, these orders generate.

STAFF

The staff is the service's greatest resource. No matter how strong the collection or how new the equipment, a service's success rests largely with the interest, dedication, skills, and attitude of its staff. Providing information services and document delivery is very labor-intensive, customized work. It can also be very stressful when meeting the fast turnaround times many clients require. Staff constantly strive to provide quality in the midst of quantity. The relationship between the staff and the clients is every bit as important as the mechanical procedure of transforming a faxed request into an envelope containing the right set of photocopied pages.

Staff attitude is a critical component in attracting and keeping customers. Staff attitude starts with the initial phone contact, but continues through all stages of the service's work. A crooked label, a haphazardly stapled article, a smudged rubber stamp of the copyright notice, a missing page, the wrong book, an invoice sent four months after the transaction: all these are potentially symptoms of sloppy service and poor staff attitude. Providing excellent service is a team effort from the manager down to the student retrievers.

Empowering the Staff

After hiring the right people, two keys to keeping them involve satisfaction and empowerment. Filling dozens of article requests a day may not be inherently satisfying for the support staff after a few months or years. The manager promotes an environment that provides intrinsic satisfaction in the work. Techniques include:

- Providing positive feedback;
- Sharing clients' and administrators' positive comments with the staff;
- Encouraging independent action when appropriate;
- Compiling statistics showing growth or other achievements;
- Providing training and development opportunities;
- Inviting staff participation in decisions about office procedures;
- Holding regular staff meetings at which opinions are encouraged; and
- Making the process more efficient.

A major way to improve the staff's satisfaction is to empower them as much as possible. Within defined limits, empower experienced staff to handle the following tasks with minimal supervision:

- Plan their work flow;
- Set priorities;
- Make and keep promises to clients on issues such as turnaround time and document costs;
- Adjust document prices or credit accounts in response to a client's query or complaint;
- Select appropriate document suppliers;
- Call clients and suppliers to follow up on earlier queries;
- Make reasonable exceptions to customary practice or procedure; and
- Take advantage of training opportunities.

As a result of successful empowerment, the staff feel in control of their jobs, despite the inevitable repetitive nature of many tasks and despite the often frantic pace necessary to meet all the commitments. With empowerment, however, comes a greater emphasis on staff accountability. The manager helps the staff learn how to accept responsibility for occasional errors and oversights, correct them, and move on.

The professional staff enjoy the intrinsic satisfaction that handling clients' varied research projects and more challenging document requests provides. Because of the nature of their jobs and their advanced training and skills, the professional staff generally handle their work independently. However, they also should feel part of the team.

It is also important that the manager provide adequate professional development opportunities. The information industry changes quickly, and unless the professional staff receive timely training and education on new technologies, techniques, skills, and sources, they will no longer be able to fill clients' information needs as effectively. In Anne Mintz' opinion, "to engage in the practice of information without up-to-the-minute information or training is to engage in information malpractice" (Mintz 1984, p. 24).

These are very simplistic comments touching on only a few of the many dimensions of the supervisory and leadership skills that the manager offers the staff. However, it is important to realize that the fee-based information service staff may not receive some of the same kinds of immediate interaction and feedback as their counterparts elsewhere in the library system. In addition, institutional policy may prevent the manager from rewarding staff by recommending annual wage increases higher than the average received by other library staff, despite the fact that the service may enjoy an income level that would support attractive raises in acknowledgment of superior work.

Adding New Positions

Work levels increase as the volume of orders picks up with a service's continuing success in meeting the information needs of new and repeat clients. Up to a certain point, increased efficiency and economies of scale allow the existing staff to handle the higher volume readily. At some point, however, it will be clear that as the volume continues to increase at a relatively predictable rate, the current staffing level will be insufficient to meet demand. Since increased demand translates into increased revenue, the manager is in a stronger position than counterparts elsewhere in the library system to receive approval for adding staff. The manager follows the appropriate procedures for proposing new positions, being sure to include in the request supporting data about the service's increasing level of business. The manager addresses how the need for additional equipment and space for the new staff member will be met.

Task Specialization

As the staff grows, so will the specialization of tasks and expertise. This is a natural progression, but it presents some new dangers. It is probably not necessary for everyone on staff to know how to order a prepayment check in a foreign currency or where to obtain a military specification or how to ship an international package via Federal Express, for example. However, enough people should know how to do these things so that if one person is absent, others can fill in effectively.

The inevitability of vacancies is another reason for making sure that several people in the office know how to perform each of the more specialized tasks. Recruiting new staff, especially professional ones, can be a lengthy process. Vacancies can often be covered by some combination of temporary staff, overtime, occasional assistance by back-up searchers, and increased student assistant hours. In conjunction with the library personnel office, the manager recruits and hires new staff using the same procedures and criteria described earlier in the book. Training the new staff takes on a different flavor as the manager shows new hires how to perform the various tasks, rather than working with staff to develop the procedures from scratch, as is typical in a new service.

With specialization comes another potential danger. People naturally focus on their own work as being of paramount importance. A tendency to lose sight of the larger mission and goals develops. The manager fosters an environment in which the staff work as a team toward the common goal of meeting the clients' information needs. Bringing the staff together in short, regularly scheduled, and focused meetings provides one way to emphasize the importance of teamwork. The manager keeps the meetings brief and informal but uses the time to exchange information, solicit opinions, and encourage discussion.

The New Manager

A new manager coming into an established service faces additional challenges. A wise approach in entering any new department is to observe current practice thoroughly before making suggestions for changes and improvements. A fee-based information service is a complex operation. Changes in almost any process will have direct impact on other tasks.

CLIENT QUERIES AND COMPLAINTS

Nobody is perfect. It is inevitable that a few orders will be lost, or that Client A's order will be shipped to Client B, or that a rush order will be handled as a regular one. As the volume of business increases, the problems will inevitably increase, too. The manager's job is to see that the error rate percentage does not increase.

For example, if a new service handling 300 document orders during its fourth month of operation receives complaints about 10 items, the error rate is 3 percent. This is a very high error rate, but some allowances can be made for staff in a new service grappling with everything from training student assistants to marketing to invoice preparation. For a mature service receiving 2,000 document orders a month, a 1 percent error rate means that clients point out 20 mistakes on billing, shipping, or quality. The number of errors has increased, but the percentage rate is one that the manager accepts as reasonable. A 3 percent error rate on this volume of 2,000 orders would be an unacceptably high 60 mistakes.

The manager trains the staff how to handle customer queries, in part by providing guidelines for investigating the complaints. If the error was the service's fault, such as a page missing from an article, the wrong book sent out, or an incorrect amount billed, the staff member should be empowered to make the correction independently.

What will satisfy the client or, better yet, more than satisfy the customer? In the case of a missing page, the client will be satisfied if the staff faxes the page within a few hours. The client will be more than satisfied if, in addition to sending the missing page promptly, the service also reduces the charge for the document by 50 or 100 percent. If the error occurred for reasons at least partly out of the service's control, good customer relations suggest that the service offer to split the difference.

Allow the staff to make their own judgment calls in most situations, and then to follow through to be sure that the billing adjustment is made. Most clients, accustomed, like all of us in these types of situations, to listening to a string of excuses and/or talking to a seemingly endless chain of supervisors, will be very favorably impressed at the prompt, responsive, and courteous resolution of their complaints. Satisfied clients will overlook occasional mishaps if the staff maintain a helpful and responsive attitude.

Most clients will handle their complaints pleasantly, starting with the assumption than an honest mistake or oversight occurred. However, as in any customer service situation, there will always be a few unpleasant encounters. While remaining courteous, staff learn to handle these situations politely but firmly. Role-playing at staff meetings may be one way to learn how to respond appropriately. Staff also learn to tell when a client has become so angry or upset that the manager must step in to resolve the situation.

Another type of customer query requiring tactful handling is the "nuisance factor." Over the years, TIS has encountered clients who:

- Ask for an individual cost quote in advance on every document, despite the fact that almost all the requests fall into the same price range;
- Want staff to see if the item is on the shelf first before placing a firm order;
- Place a firm order and call to cancel several hours later;
- Tell inappropriate jokes or behave in a too-familiar manner;
- Ask for a status report on orders submitted only a few hours previously;
- Place a regular order, and call a few hours later to upgrade it to a rush;
- Send duplicate orders a few hours apart; or
- Try to wheedle a lower price or a free document.

With the exception of the jokesters, staff understand that once in a while someone needs an exact price quote in advance or must placate a boss desperate to find out how soon an article will appear in the fax machine. Clients who make a habit of these activities, however, become a nuisance. Fortunately, these instances are relatively rare.

The manager plays several roles in the area of customer queries and complaints. The manager handles those few instances of clients who react unpleasantly to something they perceive as the service's fault. The manager also resolves issues with those clients who believe in going "straight to the top" with any complaint, no matter how minor. On other occasions, the manager calls a "nuisance" client and explains, for instance, that while the staff make every effort to catch duplicate orders, there is no guarantee that all of them will be noticed, since several staff members work on document orders.

If a service has good quality control procedures in place, the number of complaints should be relatively low.

HIGH-VOLUME CUSTOMERS

As a fee-based information service gains a reputation for fast and efficient service, it will attract at least a few clients who place a large volume of orders, usually document delivery. These high-volume customers provide the "bread and butter" revenue stream for the service, so it is advantageous to provide outstanding service to these clients. The loss of one of these clients could cause the monthly document totals, not to mention the monthly income, to drop by 10 or 15 percent. One way to offer special services to these clients is to consider offering discounts to encourage even more order submissions.

Based on my 10 years of experience with Purdue's Technical Information Service, I have identified three types of high-volume document delivery clients. The first type is a company that places several hundred document orders each month. The orders come in relatively steadily all through the month. Sometimes these orders are coordinated by one or two company employees; in other cases, dozens of people submit orders. The types of order vary from regular to rush, from being locally owned to needing special ordering, and from clear citations on search printouts to hand-scribbled notes with abbreviated titles.

For a number of reasons, mostly related to the fact that these orders require almost as much handling as the handful a month coming in from each of dozens of other clients, TIS does not offer this type of high-volume client any discounts. Other services, especially those with more control in their own offices over billing, offer a flat discount of, for example, a dollar off each order if at least 50 documents a month are ordered.

The second type of high-volume client is characterized by a company, often a law firm, that usually submits a few dozen requests a month but that also periodically wants 200 to 400 orders filled within a week or less. TIS may offer a discount on these orders, negotiated separately on each occasion. A possible discount might be 15 percent off our standard document rate for an order in which at least 200 items could be supplied from the Purdue Libraries collection. We find that in large batched orders, there are some cost savings that can be passed on to the clients.

A third type of high-volume client is represented by a commercial document delivery firm looking for partner or supplier libraries able to fill large quantities of document orders with quick and reliable service. The manager usually negotiates a significantly lower per-document rate based on variables such as 500 or more orders per month, streamlined handling procedures, and the written assurance that the commercial firm will handle all copyright payments.

Volume discounts for research projects are more rare. First, most clients do not have an ongoing need for multiple searches each month. Secondly, there are few places to apply a discount. Database costs must be recovered, as well as the information specialists' time. TIS occasionally discounts projects on a case-by-case basis. Sometimes a project requires an extensive manual search, such as through pre-1970s volumes of an index, for example. An information specialist shows one of the clerks what to look for, and bills at a reduced hourly rate to cover the clerk's time, not the specialist's.

For maximum financial security, a mature service relies on about 75 percent of its business coming from repeat clients. The list of top 10 clients might account for as much as half of all business. However, the manager monitors these percentages occasionally. Having a single client company that accounts for 20 percent or more of business may lull staff into a sense of false security. In today's uncertain business world, the client may vanish overnight, leaving a serious gap in expected revenues. The company may suddenly fail, restructure, downsize, merge, or change its manufacturing focus and, thus, its information needs. Even a single personnel change, such as the retirement or hiring a corporate librarian, departmental secretary, head paralegal, or marketing manager, might drastically affect the volume of business.

The manager recognizes the danger of depending too much on a few heavy users. Cultivating a mix of heavy and moderate users keeps the service's bottom line healthy.

BUSINESS FROM INTERNATIONAL CLIENTS

Despite the extra time and handling required for filling requests from international addresses, staff at most fee-based information services enjoy the challenge of sending packages to Stockholm, Sydney, and Singapore. Unless the service has purposely sought international clients, most of these orders will trickle in slowly from people looking for copies of the local institution's dissertations, theses, technical reports, or other publications.

Over time, TIS has developed a procedure for replying to these requests by sending a cost quote, including shipping by a courier such as Federal Express or UPS, and requesting prepayment with a check in U.S. funds drawn on a U.S. bank or by credit card. Over half the time, the clients respond with a check or credit card information, and we ship the item. A small but growing number of these clients then continue to contact us, to obtain not only Purdue documents but also other items that they find difficult or impossible to obtain in their own countries.

TIS has developed ongoing business relationships with companies in countries such as Korea, the United Kingdom, Canada, Turkey, and the Ivory Coast. In most cases, our business relationship began with a single request for one or two Purdue items and has grown to filling a steady stream of requests. In at least two cases, the relationships have been mutually beneficial in that we have, in turn, occasionally asked our clients at these firms for help in finding difficult (to us, anyway) documents published in their countries. In exchange for their help, we provided a few of their document orders at no charge so that they would not have the trouble of billing us.

MARKETING

While most of the same principles and options discussed earlier in this book apply equally to continued marketing efforts by a growing or mature service, the manager considers other factors that influence marketing decisions. After several years' experience meeting the information needs of the business community, the manager defines what differentiates the local service from similar information providers. Is it the collection, special expertise in searching certain subjects, or innovative or unusual complementary services? How can the marketing plan capitalize on these unique strengths?

Word of Mouth

One new addition the marketing mix is word-of-mouth marketing. It is by far the most effective (and least expensive) marketing (Ernest 1993, p. 398; Freeman and O'Connell 1985, pp. 168-169; Maranjian and Boss 1980, pp. 41-42; Warner 1987, pp. 89-90), but it is also one that the staff cannot control, other than by providing such excellent service that clients continue to use the service and give glowing recommendations to their colleagues. Remember that negative word-of-mouth reports travel even faster and further than positive ones.

A second important new opportunity involves advertising on the Internet. This is called "cybermarketing," and it is discussed below.

Marketing Mix

The manager develops a marketing mix that experience has shown provides the best return, in terms of generating firm orders, for the expense. The results from a client satisfaction survey can help a manager pinpoint which types of clients use the service most, and thus suggest what audiences or industries to target. However, the manager keeps a close eye on trends suggested by the service's monthly statistics and by other indicators. For example, if the service is closely tied to a single industry or to a local economy currently experiencing serious downturns, the manager's task is to fine-tune the marketing effort to attract new clients in industries or regions less affected by these circumstances.

The marketing mix contains the same possibilities listed earlier, including various types of advertising, personal appearances, booths at trade fairs, and so on. Marketing plans are not static. The manager reviews the marketing plan and the marketing mix every few years (or more often if needed) and makes whatever changes are necessary to tailor the plan to the attract clients. Clients' needs change over time, and the service's marketing plan adapts to reflect these changes.

Law Firms and Corporate Librarians

Based on its funding sources and its initial mission, a new service may have concentrated on attracting practitioners in its target industries, such as pharmaceutical researchers or professional engineers. However, after a few years, a manager will in most cases notice that the service has attracted two types of clients who form a core of repeat users (Gaines and Huttner 1983, pp. 17-18).

The first type is law firms. Of course, if the fee-based information service has been set up in a law library, law firms will in fact be the target audience. But for general services, or for services specializing in medical, technical, or business areas, it may come as a surprise to find that a significant minority of clients are connected with legal services. Besides their obvious need for legal materials, law firms frequently need documents or information on environmental, technological, engineering, business, and other topics. Clients in law firms range from secretaries or paralegals in large firms to the attorneys themselves in smaller firms. These clients usually need immediate service, but cost (within reason) is usually not a problem. Depending on the way the manager sees current law firm clients using the service, it may be advantageous to develop a marketing strategy specifically targeting the legal community.

The second type of core clients are corporate librarians. Not only are corporate librarians responsible for obtaining documents for their users, but they also handle information research projects. They often struggle to meet increasing demand with stagnant or decreasing staffing levels. It makes economic sense for many of them to outsource document delivery. A responsive fee-based information service that offers reasonable prices, reliable turnaround times, special orders, bibliographic verification, rush services, and copyright compliance attracts these librarians. One corporate librarian wrote of her reliance on fee-based services in a letter to *Library Journal*:

> [Fee-based librarians'] technical expertise, reference techniques, [and] knowledge of their collections ... are immeasurably valuable. Fee-based librarians could provide a new vigor to the library field with their entrepreneurship, research skills, client relations, and managerial skills (Saunders 1993, p. 8).

By leaving most or all of their document requests in a service's hands, corporate librarians are then free to concentrate on research. Fee-based services "support and supplement the [corporate] librarian's resources when the occasion is appropriate" (Kingman and Vantine 1977, p. 320).

I was pleasantly surprised to find that after TIS gained many corporate librarians' trust with reliable document delivery, some of them also turned to us to handle occasional research projects as well (Ward 1991). The reasons vary:

- Handle overflow requests;
- Provide back-up coverage for vacations and illness;
- Search databases to which TIS has a subscription, but the company does not;
- Search files that the clients felt TIS information specialists could search more effectively, often in a subject area outside the client's area of expertise; and
- Coordinate time-consuming manual searches.

The manager may decide to develop a marketing strategy specifically designed to reach a specific audience of corporate librarians and/or law firms.

Current Clients

Although an established service seeks marketing opportunities to continue attracting new clients, it also has another group of people to remember in its marketing efforts: past and current clients. Marketing to clients is often overlooked. With a little reflection, however, the manager realizes that a client who ordered a few documents last month or last year is, in general, more likely to place another order than a similar person who has had no experience with the service. In addition, the cost of reaching these clients is lower, since the service already knows their names and addresses.

Developing Promotional Pieces

TIS developed a number of ways to keep clients aware that the service exists and stands ready to serve. We produce an eight-page annual report each year and distribute it to everyone on our mailing list (Ward 1991a). In addition, we print a short quarterly newsletter that highlights recent projects, success stories, milestones, and staff changes (Ward 1990). Finally, we send a card to all clients in December to thank them for their business during the past year and to offer our continued assistance in the new year. We also send these promotional pieces to those people on campus whom we wish to keep aware of our progress.

These items do double duty by not only providing ways to keep in touch with our current clients but also supplying us with professionally produced promotional pieces to send to prospective clients asking for information about TIS. Each year, the cost of designing and printing these pieces is included in the annual budget as part of the marketing initiative.

World Wide Web

Online marketing and cybermarketing are two terms used to describe advertising on the Internet using the World Wide Web. This chapter's bibliography lists several books that explore aspects of online marketing, although new editions and new titles will have appeared since this volume went to press.

In his book *Cybermarketing*, Len Keeler summarized the advantages of online marketing. While it supplements rather than replaces traditional methods, cybermarketing:

- Stretches the marketing budget;
- Saves time by eliminating steps from the traditional marketing process;
- Gives customers another way to place orders;

- Is information-rich and interactive;
- Reaches international audiences;
- Lowers barriers to market entry; and
- Is accessible 24 hours a day (Keeler 1995, pp. xiv-xv).

Before launching online ads, however, be sure to secure the institution's approval. The university, especially a public one, may perceive a clear line between a home page describing the library and a page soliciting document delivery orders. In addition, there are other issues, such as:

- Is the service's advertising acceptable to the network administrators?
- Should the service's page be developed in conjunction with those created for other library services? What links should be included?
- How can staff authenticate orders or other messages from clients? Establishing password access or encryption protocols may minimize security and privacy risks, but may also make the system less easy for clients to use, as well as require additional staff time to maintain.
- How secure are the data lines? Clients not only reveal their companies' research interests by placing orders, but they may also post credit card numbers or other sensitive information.
- Who will create and maintain the service's home page, order forms, and other Web information? Cyberspace offers more and more sophisticated options. If the service does not keep up with current Web capabilities, its old-fashioned entry may not inspire confidence in potential clients.
- Will a Web page open the service to more vocal criticism from competitors in the commercial sector?

Many business owners and managers attest to the fact that Web marketing makes a significant difference in reaching new audiences quickly, cheaply, and effectively. Fee-based information service managers have recently begun exploring this option, too. They assess the advisability of opening up a small, non-profit service to potentially anyone with a credit card. They review these issues of development and maintenance time, as well as of security. They consider the impact of attracting dozens or hundreds of new clients in a short period of time. Can the service handle this influx in a responsive and cost-effective manner?

Radio

Besides experimenting with online marketing, a service may also decide to try nontraditional or innovative approaches to marketing. One service enjoyed some success with marketing by radio. It bought air time for radio spots and also tried an hour-long "Stump the Researcher" phone-in show (Fraser 1994).

Directory Listings

Once the service has established itself, the manager looks for opportunities to add its name to appropriate directory listings.

* Campus phone book;
* Campus directories developed for non-university users;
* Commercial directories listing research centers, consultants, and so forth;
* Directories issued by trade publications or regional business or manufacturing magazines;
* State economic development directories;
* Appropriate electronic directories; and
* Information industry directories.

While it is unlikely that many clients will call the service based on a directory entry, the listings are almost always free. After the first insertion, the directory editors generally send announcements prior to each new edition asking for corrections or updates. In selected cases, the service also advertises in the directory to draw the readers' attention. For example, TIS advertises in *Burwell's World Directory of Information Brokers*.

Decreasing the Marketing Effort

The manager of a mature service may face the decision of stopping, or at least curtailing, marketing activities. TIS reached this point several years ago when a consistently high level of business threatened to outstrip our resources for providing fast and efficient service. Constraints such as finite office space limit many services' ability to continue to grow indefinitely. The goal may be to reach a point at which repeat customers, along with a few new ones who learn about the service by word of mouth or by serendipity, provide sufficient business to maintain the service at a no- or low-growth position.

Even in a no- or low-marketing situation, however, the manager continues to keep current and former clients informed about the service. A small percentage of customers drift away by attrition for various reasons. A low level of continued marketing attracts replacement customers for the ones who are lost. The manager also closely watches indicators such as total monthly income and total documents provided or projects completed. If these numbers decline over several months, it may be time to beef up the marketing effort again, at least until the numbers increase to a satisfactory level. As the manager learned during the start-up phase, it takes several months of marketing before the payoff, in terms of assigned projects and document orders, becomes evident. There is generally a fairly long lead time between, for example, submitting an ad to a trade journal, and noticing its effect when the journal's readers call the service. The manager would by this time, however, have a better idea than a novice counterpart about which kinds of marketing work best for the particular target audience the service seeks to attract.

FINANCIAL

An established fee-based information service periodically reviews some of the same financial considerations mentioned in earlier chapters, but it also faces new challenges. I recommended that a new service make its financial arrangements as simple as possible, such as starting with a straightforward fee schedule and handling one, or at most two, billing and payment methods. After a few years of operation, the manager reviews, and often modifies, these elements.

Costs and Prices

As the staff become more efficient at handling the work, some costs will decline. Other costs will increase. Some increasing costs, such as copyright or database charges, are recovered through direct charge-backs to the client. Other increasing costs, such as for shipping or supplies, will affect the bottom line.

The manager, possibly together with the business officer, reviews these costs at least every other year to be sure that the projected annual cost-recovery income will indeed cover estimated annual expenses. Sooner or later, the answer to this question will be "no." At this point, one solution is to raise prices.

TIS reached this point once in its history so far. We raised the price for a regular delivery Purdue document from $12 to $14 and took the opportunity to enumerate a few other charges at the same time. After revising our brochure to include the new fee schedule, we mailed copies along with an explanatory cover letter to our clients. I had expected some resistance to the new price and was pleasantly surprised when no one called to protest; in fact, demand continued to soar.

Price increases are inevitable. Business clients are neither surprised nor deterred by reasonable increases to cover the same kinds of escalating costs they observe in their own companies. However, the manager should not tinker with the price list too often, nor introduce too many add-on fees that make cost estimates difficult to explain and to understand. Also, give clients plenty of advance warning about changing rates.

Billing

While staff at a new service may have their hands full issuing monthly invoices, after a few years they will have heard several suggestions from clients for alternative billing methods. High-volume clients may prefer deposit accounts, preferably combined with some type of discount for making these advance payments. Other clients propose making payments using one of half a dozen possible credit cards. Yet others claim that their companies require that all their vendors bill them using a single credit card company; if the fee-based service cannot accommodate this request, then the company cannot do business with it.

Most fee-based information services face institutional constraints about employing at least some of these invoicing variations. There is also a realistic limit on the number of billing methods a service can use. Too many methods result in climbing staff costs for processing and monitoring accounts. However, the manager and staff listen to clients, either from comments made during the course of normal transactions or from a client evaluation survey, and explore the feasibility of offering one or two additional options designed to satisfy the highest number of clients without pushing staff costs too high.

Over the years, several firms have asked if they can negotiate an annual contract with the Technical Information Service, usually for research projects. Several large commercial brokers offer this option. For a flat, annually negotiated, prepaid fee, the information provider agrees to handle all the client's information projects. Most library fee-based information services are simply not large enough or well funded enough to take this risk. If a service negotiates a company's fee at $15,000, for example, and the year's total costs came in at $20,000, the budget may not be flexible enough to withstand the loss easily. Because of the way some universities handle payments, the service may not even enjoy the advantage of the interest on the prepayment.

However, TIS has from time to time responded to bids from companies looking for the best cost from an information provider to perform a specific large project or to become the "supplier of choice." In my written responses to these bids, I clearly explain the TIS policy of invoicing the project upon completion and of monthly billing. Several books include helpful tips for preparing proposals or bids for large projects (Warner 1987, pp. 120-123; White 1981, pp. 75-78). If the service is the successful bidder on a major project from a new client, or from a client who has only requested small projects in the past, the manager would be wise to include in the bid a requirement that a certain percentage of the total project cost be remitted in advance. Accepting unusually large projects often means hiring temporary staff and/or acquiring additional equipment and supplies. The service may not be able to gear up easily for the project without an advance payment from the client.

Meeting Financial Obligations

While watching that the service's clients are paying their bills in full and on time, the manager also keeps an eye on the operations that ensure that the service's suppliers are also being paid promptly and accurately. These suppliers vary from database providers, document delivery suppliers, office machine maintenance firms, printers, publications running the service's ads, specialized equipment or supplies vendors, reference book publishers, and so on.

The volume of these invoices increases at about the same rate as the increase in business. As time passes, it will take more and more staff time to reconcile these invoices against internal records to be sure they are accurate and complete.

For instance, TIS receives monthly invoices totaling over $1,000 each from two other fee-based information services on whose collections we draw heavily for special orders. It takes several hours of staff time per invoice to match the suppliers' statement against our internal records and to price out the special order documents as the invoices are reconciled. Dozens of other suppliers also send weekly, monthly, or quarterly invoices or deposit account statements. Only after the staff is satisfied that the invoices are correct will they be forwarded to the library business office for payment. All bills over $50 are forwarded by the library's business office staff to the University's central accounts payable department. The payment path will differ at different institutions, of course, but obviously, the more people who handle different steps of the process, the longer it takes and the more likely it becomes that errors creep in.

Deposit accounts with selected document suppliers shortcut some of the time needed to meet financial obligations. It is certainly more efficient to send a single check for $3,000 than to cut one check each month for $1,000. However, many universities frown on tying up too much money in prepayments. From the service's point of view, reconciliation with internal records is necessary, whether it receives a deposit account statement or an invoice. In addition, it also takes time to keep up with of dozens of deposit account balances and to order and send replenishment checks. Open deposit accounts with handful of organizations with which meet at least several of these criteria:

- The service orders a high volume of documents;
- Ordering is much easier with a deposit account;
- The organization only accepts prepaid orders;
- Paying monthly invoices incurs additional expenses, for example, fluctuating exchange rates or checks in foreign currency; and
- The organization offers a discount for deposit account holders.

An institutional credit card is extremely handy for prepaying document orders from suppliers such as trade associations and small publishers that decline to ship material with invoices. Once the service has established itself and can prove the significant time and cost savings of using a credit card in these circumstances rather than running around campus to obtain rush prepayment checks, the manager requests a major credit card. Some services have also been successful at obtaining check writing privileges or petty cash accounts. With each of these conveniences comes the added responsibility of reconciling more accounts, but the payment flexibility is usually worth it.

The manager learns the quirks of the local institution's accounting practices and procedures. Especially if the service itself does not issue bills or receive payments directly, the manager asks:

- At what point in the billing process are funds deposited in the service's account?
- Are there any restrictions on the use of the income or of any other available funds?
- How long on average does it take for an invoice to be paid?
- How is the service notified of delinquent accounts?
- How does the institution handle delinquent accounts?
- When is the service's account debited for bad debt?
- How are prepayments credited to the service's account?
- How can rush requests for prepayment checks be accommodated?

Cash Flow and Bad Debt

Some institutions do not actually credit the service's account until the clients' checks have been deposited. This practice represents a potential nightmare for the staff. If, for example, a single high-volume client runs an account 90 days in arrears, the service finds itself in the position of having billed $3,000 or $5,000 or $10,000 that it has not yet collected. In the meantime, invoices from document suppliers and other creditors arrive daily. The service may thus find itself in a cash flow bind.

The client should certainly be made aware that the account is in arrears. After establishing that the local institution does not discourage departments from making such calls, a staff member phones clients asking if they know that invoices have not been paid for several months. Many difficulties can be solved with a single call. Usually, the client with whom the service works simply approves the invoices and then forwards them to another department in the firm for payment. In most cases, the client, on investigation, discovers some internal snag that delayed the payment and straightens matters out promptly. After all, a client making heavy use of the fee-based information service does not want to face the possibility that services might be suspended because of a delinquent account.

Tact is essential. While it is important to work to get the account paid, it is equally important not to antagonize the client unnecessarily. Late payments are usually not directly the client's fault. Staff do not want to jeopardize a heavy user's future business.

There is a limit, however. If, after several attempts, the staff have not been successful at encouraging the client's company to pay a substantial balance, then suspend service and notify the client in writing that privileges will be reinstated as soon as payment arrives.

In practice, while some regular clients occasionally exhibit late- or slow-payment behavior, this problem is relatively uncommon. Purdue's Technical Information Service has only had to suspend service for repeat customers on two or three rare occasions each year; one of them was a Fortune 500 company that never paid its bill for a few hundred dollars of document orders.

A more common problem is that of a one-time client, often an entrepreneur or small business owner, who runs up a bill of several hundred dollars for a single project and then disappears from the face of the earth. Circumvent this problem by requiring credit card payment in advance from new clients, especially ones who seem to be establishing a new business. The budget should also be elastic enough to absorb a few percentage points of bad debt each year. It is one of the costs of doing business.

However, despite its being inevitable, the manager's responsibility is to keep bad debt to a minimum. The best way to ensure this is to monitor client accounts carefully, thereby spotting potential problems before they reach disastrous proportions. If the final billing and payment processing take place in another department, the manager arranges to see the monthly account summaries for the fee-based service.

The occurrence of bad debt may actually provide the manager with ammunition for getting approval for deposit accounts or credit card billing. In the case of deposit accounts, the staff keep internal records of a client's balance. With credit card billing, staff can ask the bank if a new client, or a client with a previous history of seriously delinquent payments, has available credit to cover the estimated cost of the project under discussion. If so, staff can ask the bank to place a hold on the funds for the estimated cost in anticipation of the actual bill coming through a few days later.

One way to try to avoid bad debt is to make sure that new clients clearly understand that the service operates on a cost-recovery basis. Every few months, TIS receives a bewildered call from a new client who somehow never realized that we would charge for faxing an article on a rush basis.

If the institution is one of those that does not credit a department until payment is received, the manager works with the library business officer to see if a special exception can be made in the case of the fee-based information service. Virtually all of the invoices sent out, with a very low percentage of bad debt cases, will be paid within a reasonable time frame. The manager asks what arrangements can be made for the institution to cover the service's expenses while it waits for the payments to arrive. Otherwise, cash flow problems may leave the service's income account too low to pay its own creditors. Many of these creditors will not hesitate to cut off service if the accounts fall behind, placing the manager in a very unpleasant and embarrassing situation if major document suppliers or database vendors threaten to "pull the plug."

Funding Sources

If the service depends to any extent on external funding, the manager stays in touch with the funding sources through both formal and informal means. Formal methods include periodic financial or progress reports, while informal ones mean keeping the funding agency or agencies aware of the service through its newsletters and other promotional pieces.

If the funding is unstable, unpredictable, or insufficient, the manager investigates possibilities for supplementing the income. Some funding sources may be available for a few years at start-up, but are designed to disappear after the service establishes itself. Other funding that seemed stable may suddenly fluctuate or look less secure. If continued external funding is essential or highly desirable for the service's continued existence, the manager, in consultation with the library administration, looks for new or supplemental funding.

PROFESSIONAL RELATIONSHIPS

Cultivating a variety of different professional relationships helps the service's staff better meet their clients' needs. Cooperation between a number of different types of information providers proves beneficial in that each provider supplements the resources available to its partners.

Other Library Units

The manager periodically reevaluates the service's relationship with other library units. This process can be an informal one. Many of these relationships evolve over time. As library staff learn more about the fee-based information service and its objectives through the manager's internal marketing efforts, most initial skepticism evaporates.

As examples, Purdue University's Technical Information Service has noticed several changes over the years:

- An increase in the incidence of reference librarians throughout the library system referring non-campus patrons to TIS;
- An increase in the incidence of library referrals of campus patrons needing highly specialized or unusual services, such as obtaining a copy of a Swedish technical report on a rush basis;
- An increase in the number of referrals to handle interlibrary loan requests from non-campus individuals and from international addresses;
- Requests by the Special Collections department to handle rush requests from non-campus researchers; and
- An arrangement whereby TIS fills at its rates all rush ILL requests from other institutions (except those with which Purdue has reciprocal agreements).

Some of these developments, such as the gradual shifting of highly specialized interlibrary loan requests, were partly a natural outcome of another department's increasing workload and static staffing configuration. Other developments reflect an understanding of how TIS' resources can be effectively used to meet customers' non-routine needs.

However, misunderstanding, resentment, or other negative feelings may suddenly erupt. James C. Thompson candidly reviewed a number of staff relations difficulties between his institution's fee-based service and the rest of the library staff. Problems included ideological differences, territoriality, and competition for resources, but most were eventually resolved (Thompson 1983, pp. 66-68). The manager stays alert to potential friction and works to minimize it.

Other University Departments

The manager keeps staff in selected university departments informed about the service's progress. As suggested earlier, adding these employees' names to the mailing list is one way to be sure they receive periodic mailings. The manager also stays alert for changes in key staff or for the creation of new departments whose staff may benefit from learning how the fee-based information service assists off-campus users. A short visit makes a more lasting impression than simply mailing a few promotional flyers. The benefit is generally two-fold; knowing how these departments work with the business community also helps the service's staff make appropriate referrals on campus.

Counterparts

The manager establishes and maintains professional contacts with counterparts at other institutions. Sometimes, a colleague's advice or insight helps solve an unusual challenge. Having made personal contacts often makes it easier to ask for an unusual service. For example, a client might know that an article on a particular subject appeared in 1994 or 1995 in a certain journal but be unsure about the exact article title and not know the authors' names. Standard bibliographic verification having failed, staff can send such a vague citation to another service with which they have established special relations, with a note requesting an extended manual search for which, of course, they are prepared to pay extra. Sending such a request to an organization with which the service does not have an established relationship may not result in a filled order.

Another benefit is that after making a personal assessment of another service's commitment to accurate information products, the staff feel more confident in making occasional referrals to these services. For example, since the Technical Information Service generally does not undertake complex chemical searches, we refer clients with these needs to one of two other well-respected fee-based services whose staffs include information specialists with chemistry degrees. Personal professional knowledge of the staff there makes the referral much better than selecting a few services or information brokers based on entries in a directory. "Subcontracting research work allows libraries to take full advantage of each other's resources and expertise. This results in more efficient service and a better, less-expensive product for the consumer" (Coffman and Josephine 1991, p. 35).

These relationships also evolve over time. Some begin as the staff at a new service approach established services for document delivery special orders. The information specialists meet some of their counterparts at professional meetings, especially the FISCAL (Fee-Based Information Service Centers in Academic Libraries) meetings at the American Library Association's meetings.

Staff are careful to respect their counterparts' time by not calling too frequently, but in most cases, colleagues are glad to spend a few minutes discussing in general terms how they have solved various challenges at their own institutions. Fee-based information services form an informal network of professionals glad to help one another meet their common goal of assisting the business community meet its information needs.

Information Brokers

The concept of regarding information brokers in the light of professional relationships sometimes surprises new managers. After all, fee-based information service and independent information brokers or commercial information delivery firms operate to at least some degree as competitors. However, both brokers and commercial firms can be valuable colleagues and partners both as suppliers and as clients (Bjorner 1993; Park 1994; Ward 1995).

Many of the larger document delivery firms now look outside their internal journal collections and seek to meet their customers' needs by filling all requests using whatever sources are appropriate. University library research collections, with their wealth of conference proceedings, technical reports, and other specialized material, form an important potential source for filling many of these requests. Normal interlibrary loan channels are usually not fast enough to meet these firms' requirements. The local fee-based information service is the ideal unit for handling these requests. A fairly recent development is that of large commercial document delivery firms reaching agreements with fee-based information services to provide large quantities of documents (500 or more a month) at reduced rates based on a guaranteed high volume basis.

Smaller independent brokers also rely on resources other than those locally available for filling their customers' needs. Traditional interlibrary loans take too long for them, too. While commercial firms may meet some of their needs, fee-based services offer another option and different collection strengths.

These relationships work both ways. An established fee-based information service finds that working with several brokers or commercial firms as suppliers solves a number of problems. For example, TIS works with a broker who sends runners to those major Washington, D.C., area libraries that have unacceptably long response times if contacted directly. Other brokers coordinate retrieval from other major research collections. We also work with a Canadian broker by sending her requests for any Canadian documents not readily available in the United States.

Although filling document delivery requests is the usual way that fee-based information services and brokers interact, sometimes research projects are also contracted out. As one example, a TIS client needed copies of some files only available at the National Institute of Occupational Safety and Health (NIOSH) in Cincinnati. We confirmed by phone with NIOSH staff that the files existed but contracted with a broker in Cincinnati to visit the NIOSH archives and make copies of the relevant information. We paid for the project at the broker's hourly rate, plus expenses, and passed the costs on to the client.

Sometimes, having professional relationships with brokers in other countries is the only way to get copies of international documents in a reasonable amount of time. Using an international broker solves many difficulties associated with finding addresses and phone numbers, time zone differences, language barriers, paying invoices in dozens of different currencies, and arriving at mutually acceptable shipping arrangements.

Other Colleagues

Being active in other national, regional, and local groups helps the professional staff stay in touch with colleagues and potential clients. Some fee-based information services, especially those with economic development goals in their missions, join local chambers of commerce. Information professionals attend local online users group meetings and local Special Libraries Association chapter activities. These events not only help staff stay abreast of new trends and developments but also provide informal marketing opportunities and meet some of the staff's professional development needs.

SPACE AND EQUIPMENT

As the service grows and adds staff, its space and equipment requirements change. Space is usually the most difficult issue, requiring months of planning before approval and renovations are complete. The institution may require that the service pay at least a portion of the moving and renovation costs. Moving the office to a new location involves the further expenses of reprinting all promotional pieces, letterhead, envelopes, business cards, and so on, as well as of notifying clients at least several times of the new address. In most cases, the phone and fax numbers remain the same, but staff limit or suspend service for several days during the physical move.

While frequent moves are not recommended, the manager uses the occasion as a marketing opportunity. After the TIS office moved in 1992, we held a punch and cookies reception to invite the library staff to visit us at our new location.

Managing equipment requires constant attention. As time passes, equipment wears out and needs replacement. In other cases, the equipment may still work well, but upgrades or newer, faster equipment provide significant improvements. The addition of new staff may require new equipment (e.g., a microcomputer), as may increased volume (e.g., another fax machine).

Within a few years, a manager may find that an office that opened with identical computer workstations for each staff member has evolved into a patchwork of different models and pieces. The manager is responsible for:

- Keeping track of the equipment;
- Making recommendations for improvements and upgrades;
- Coordinating maintenance agreements;
- Developing a local area network;
- Providing Internet connections;
- Providing routine maintenance and troubleshooting;
- Customizing software for office applications;
- Training staff on using the office software; and
- Installing new equipment.

Most managers do not have the time or the skills to perform all these tasks personally. One of the best solutions is to hire a computer science or computer technology student to work part-time for the service. These students command a higher hourly rate than general student retrievers, but they provide dedicated and ongoing support for all the service's computer-related applications. Due to other commitments and priorities, the library's systems or information technology department sometimes cannot respond fast enough when the inevitable crises occur.

RECORDS MANAGEMENT

Work does not end with the successful completion of billing clients for the search results and documents. Maintaining accurate, complete, and easily accessible records is another important element of organizing an efficient and responsible fee-based information service. As client demand increases, so do the supporting paper and electronic trails.

Paper Files

Despite our increasingly electronic age, paper files will be with us for at least a little while longer. At the Technical Information Service, our institution requires us to retain proof of orders and invoices for seven years. The electronic transaction records in our database do not provide the same level of detail that the client's original order sheet contains. On several occasions, an information specialist's handwritten notes, taken during a reference interview or tracing the phone numbers called to obtain an obscure document, supply important evidence in confirming actions taken months or years in the past. Being able to produce a copy of the client's original request has several times meant the difference between a company's agreeing to pay us or not for work ordered by a since-departed employee.

Other records to consider keeping, although possibly not for as long, include suppliers' invoices, shipping logs, printed copies of client lists, and so on.

Keeping all this paper, whether for institutional, legal, or accounting reasons, presents a monumental storage challenge. Not only must it be kept, but it must be kept in some kind of logical order, be indexed with finding aids, be accessible if needed, and be handled as confidential information.

Staff who worked on the service's planning and implementation stages should have addressed this inevitability and suggested sufficient on-site storage for the most recent four to eight months of records as well as recommending remote storage for older records. The remote storage should not be so inaccessible that it takes more than a day to retrieve items. It is inevitable that at least several times a year, staff will have to dig into sealed boxes to retrieve evidence to support a client's query.

Electronic Files

Back-ups for computer records are also essential. TIS backs up the entire network once a week, and then backs up daily changes. The office's major databases contain records for the past few months' activities; older records are stripped off periodically and saved on disk in a secure place. Besides taking these precautions, staff individually back up on disk any files they feel are particularly important.

Purging Records

The service will eventually reach a point past which older records need no longer be kept. The manager oversees these records' disposal in such as way that they will not compromise the clients' confidentiality.

Besides destroying old records, however, the manager also oversees purging other ones. The client database mushrooms over time with the addition not only of repeat clients but also of people who call once for general information or who place a few orders and then never contact the service again. Left unchecked, the client database can grow to thousands of names, many of which belong to people no longer interested in the service or likely to place further orders.

If the service sends out various quarterly and annual mailings as suggested in the marketing sections earlier in this chapter, it is paying to print and mail hundreds of promotional pieces to people who have moved, gone out of business, died, retired, or lost interest. If the annual reports or quarterly newsletters were shipped using bulk mail, the staff will seldom learn of these changes, since the bulk mail rate does not include return postage to notify the sender of address changes.

TIS solved this challenge by using several different approaches. First, once a year we send out one mailing using first class instead of bulk rate postage. Undeliverable pieces are returned to the office and staff delete these names from the mailing list. The increased cost of this single first class mailing is offset by reduced future costs on printing and mailing future pieces.

Second, once every two to three years we send all clients a special double postcard via first class asking the recipients to:

1. Check that the address information is correct, and indicate any changes if not; and
2. Return the appropriate half of the postage-paid postcard if they wish to remain on our mailing list.

When the postcards pour back into the office, staff correct the client database for changes in company names and addresses, changes in client names, typographical errors, new employees replacing former employees, and other updates. About two months after the deadline stated on the postcard, we purge the mailing list of anyone who did not respond, being careful to retain the names of known clients who forgot to return a card and of important people, such as the director of a funding agency, who did not bother.

Purging the client database is a large, time-consuming project, but it pays off in helping keep the client list whittled down to those people who are either active clients or who have recently expressed an interest in remaining on the mailing list.

REEVALUATING THE MISSION AND GOALS

Every few years, the manager and the library administrators review the fee-based information service's mission and goals. Have any of the needs, expectations, or assumptions that prompted the most recently articulated missions and goals changed? The manager and administrators examine changes in:

- Funding;
- Philosophy;
- Law;
- Client base;
- Customer needs and expectations;

- Economics;
- Financial regulations;
- Institutional environment;
- Policy and practice;
- Competition;
- Technology;
- Staffing; and
- Focus or mission of a funding agency.

Have any of these factors, or a combination of them, changed significantly enough to warrant rewriting the service's missions, goals, and objectives? If so, revise these statements to reflect the current environment.

CITED REFERENCES

Bjorner, S. 1993. "Fee-Based Information Services and Information Brokers: Making the Arrangement Work." *Fee for Service* 1(1): 6-9.

Coffman, S., and H. Josephine. 1991. "Doing It for Money." *Library Journal* 116(17): 32-36.

Ernest, D.J. 1993. "Academic Libraries, Fee-Based Information Services, and the Business Community." *RQ* 32(3): 393-402.

Franks, J.A., and K.K. Montgomery. 1991. "LINE: The Fee-Based Service at the University of Central Florida Library." *Mississippi Libraries* 55(Spring): 15-17.

Fraser, J. 1994. "Talk Radio: Alternative Marketing Techniques at RIS." *Fee for Service* 1(3): 38-40.

Freeman, J.K., and K.A. O'Connell. 1985. "The Marketing of Biomedical Information Service at the University of Minnesota: Creative Error Correction." Pp. 159-171 in *Cost Analysis, Cost Recovery, Marketing and Fee-Based Services: A Guide for the Health Sciences Librarian*, edited by M.S. Wood. New York: Haworth Press.

Gaines, E.J., and M.A. Huttner. 1983. "Fee-Based Services and the Public Library: An Administrative Perspective." *Drexel Library Quarterly* 19(4): 13-22.

George, L.A. 1993. "Fee-Based Information Services and Information Brokers: A Case Study in Collaboration." *Fee for Service* 1(1): 1, 3-5.

Keeler, L. 1995. *Cybermarketing*. New York: Amacom.

Kingman, N.M., and C. Vantine. 1977. "Commentary on the Special Librarian/Fee-based Service Interface." *Special Libraries* 68(9): 320-322.

Maranjian, L., and R.W. Boss. 1980. *Fee-Based Information Services: A Study of a Growing Industry*. New York: Bowker.

Marvin, S. 1988. "ExeLS: Executive Library Services." *The Reference Librarian* 22: 145-160.

Mintz, A.P. 1984. "Information Practice and Malpractice: Do We Need Malpractice Insurance?" *Online* 8(4): 20-26.

Park, M.W. 1994. "The Benefits of Libraries and Independents Working Together." *Fee for Service* 1(2): 26-28.

Sanders, V. 1993. "Of Fee-Based Librarians." *Library Journal* 118(16): 8.

Tertell, S.M. 1983. "Fee-Based Services to Business: Implementation in a Public Library." *Drexel Library Quarterly* 19(4): 37-53.

Thompson, J.C. 1983. "Regional Information and Communication Exchange: A Case Study." Pp. 55-76 in *Conference on Fee Based Research in College and University Libraries*. Greenvale, NY: Long Island University Center for Business Research.

Ward, S.M. 1990. "Using a Newsletter to Promote Information Services." Pp. 121-125 in *The Information Professional: An Unparalleled Resource*. Washington, DC: Special Libraries Association.

Ward, S.M. 1991a. "The Annual Report as a Marketing Tool." *MLS: Marketing Library Services* 5(2): 4-7.
Ward, S.M. 1991b. "Fee-Based Information Services: Gold Mine for Corporate Librarians." *Business Information Alert* 3(7): 1-3, 11.
Ward, S.M. 1995. "Cooperation Between Non-Profit Fee-Based Information Services and For-Profit Brokers." *Information Services and Use* 5: 153-158.
Warner, A.S. 1987. *Mind Your Own Business: A Guide for the Information Entrepreneur.* New York: Neal Schuman.
White, M.S. 1981. *Profit from Information: A Guide to the Establishment, Operation and Use of an Information Consultancy.* London: Andre Deutsch.
Whitmell, V. 1996. "Staffing the Fee-Based Library Service." *Fee for Service* 3(1): 6-12.

FURTHER READING

American Library Association. 1997. *Internet-Plus Directory of Express Library Services: Research and Document Delivery for Hire.* Chicago, IL: American Library Association.
Aspnes, G. 1974. "INFORM: An Evaluation Study." *Minnesota Libraries* 24(Autumn): 171-185.
Burwell, H.P., ed. 1995. *The Burwell World Directory of Information Brokers,* 12th edition. Houston, TX: Burwell Enterprises.
Cavazos, E.A., and G. Morin. 1994. *Cyberspace and the Law: Your Rights and Duties in the On-line World.* Cambridge, MA: MIT Press.
Dillman, D.A. 1978. *Mail and Telephone Surveys: The Total Design Method.* New York: Wiley.
Ellsworth, J.H., and M.V. Ellsworth. 1995. *Marketing on the Internet: Multimedia Strategies for the World Wide Web.* New York: Wiley.
Lunden, E. 1987. "Quality Control in Fee-based Library Services: Who Cares?" Pp. 31-40 in *Fee-based Services: Issues and Answers,* compiled by A.K. Beaubien. Ann Arbor, MI: Michigan Information Transfer Source, University of Michigan Libraries.
Maloff, J. 1995. *net.profit: Expanding Your Business Using the Internet.* Foster City, CA: IDG Books Worldwide.
Salant, P., and D.A. Dillman. 1994. *How to Conduct Your Own Survey.* New York: Wiley.
Settles, C. 1995. *Cybermarketing Essentials for Success.* Emeryville, CA: Ziff-Davis.
Yudkin, M. 1995. *Marketing Online: Low-Cost, High-Yield Strategies for Small Businesses & Professionals.* New York: Plume.

Chapter 8

Managing Change

THE CHANGING INFORMATION ARENA

Fee-based information services find themselves at the forefront of a rapidly changing world. The amount of information created and distributed explodes at a dizzying rate. The number of formats in which the information is stored or otherwise available frequently increases. New technologies outpace older ones within a few years. No longer do information specialists work solely with established database providers or distributors whose uniform file structures and careful indexing assure accuracy, relevancy, and a certain standard of quality control. Today anyone can create a document or build a database and put it on the Web, but the searcher makes a judgment about its accuracy and timeliness. Tomorrow the file may exist in a different version, reside at a different location, or disappear completely.

As the sources change, so do user expectations. The good news for fee-based information services is that as sources change and proliferate, business professionals will probably be even more willingly hire outside assistance to cut through the information maze, filter out the extraneous material, and present relevant search results (Thompson 1983, pp. 75-76; Wilkins 1992, p. 25). The bad news, if it is indeed bad, is that the searchers they hire to do this work must continually hone and upgrade their skills to learn how to extract reliable information from new sources using new technology.

At the same time, other business professionals do the "easy" searches themselves, and outsource only the complex ones. Another consideration is the fact that clients expect faster and faster turnaround times on more and more complex searches.

Also complicating the picture is the fact that not everything is available electronically, and is not likely to be for some time. People still need copies of technical reports, government documents, conference papers, superseded industry standards, and a wide range of older or otherwise low-use or special interest materials that may not see electronic conversion for years, if ever. Other clients,

173

especially lawyers, require copies of the original paper document even if an electronic equivalent is available.

A growing concern involves the fact that, at least for paper-based information, financial reality has forced libraries to depend more and more on access to materials rather than ownership of them. The document delivery implications are that over time, fewer and fewer requests will be satisfied from the local collections of all but the largest libraries. A fee-based service's expertise in obtaining material from increasingly varied sources quickly and efficiently will be a critical factor in its ability to thrive in the new environment.

A fee-based information service is uniquely positioned to take advantage of these changing circumstances. If it flourishes in the right kind of institutional environment, it can quickly adapt to changing circumstances and offer new services to meet its clients' needs.

CHANGING RESOURCES

Many requests can still be fulfilled by photocopying an article or by logging into a database. I predict that over the next few decades these activities will still be an important, if not the major, means by which fee-based information service staff meet most of their clients' information needs. However, it is also clear from the changes in the information arena over the past 20 years that these traditional means of gathering and distributing information will over time play a smaller and smaller role.

Electronic Information Resources

Information professionals have been using electronic resources for years. The availability of databases distributed by bibliographic utilities like Dialog was to reference work as revolutionary as moveable type was to book production a few centuries earlier. Today's information specialists choose from among thousands of databases in virtually all subject areas. And now, besides these databases, searchers have access to thousands more files available on the World Wide Web.

Web files may not all be as carefully indexed and constructed as the ones distributed through the bibliographic utilities, but they have the advantages of:

- Virtually instantaneous accessibility;
- Covering extremely specific subject areas;
- Providing access to the files' creators through electronic mail;
- Frequent updates, if the creator so chooses;
- Providing access to files that it would not be commercially advantageous to develop;
- Containing graphics currently unavailable in most traditional databases;

- Providing links to related files; and
- Sometimes available at no cost.

The disadvantages include:

- Files that disappear from the Web without explanation;
- Files that change addresses unexpectedly;
- The necessity for the searcher to evaluate the source of the information, and therefore its reliability;
- Some files assess fees for access and use;
- Unlike searching a family of files from the same database producer or distributor, each Web file has its own internal indexing and searching arrangements;
- Because of the different structures of these files and their records, it is time-consuming to convert the electronic records into useful paper records for clients' review;
- Potential danger as a seductive time-waster;
- Slow downloading for large files and/or files with complex graphics;
- Unavailability of color printers to capture the color graphics;
- Clutter of files of marginal use or of questionable accuracy;
- Amount of time it may take to locate useful information; and
- Unresolved copyright issues.

Ownership versus Access

Shrinking budgets and rising prices over the past few decades mean that most university libraries have both slashed their serials subscriptions and reduced their book acquisitions. The trend is not likely to reverse soon. The local collection upon which the fee-based information service depends for filling a high percentage of its document orders thus becomes less and less comprehensive.

The slow erosion of the local collection's ability to support a service's document delivery need not be a problem if staff develop efficient and cost-effective ways of tapping the resources of a wide variety of document suppliers.

Distribution

Today information distribution is largely limited to paper copies, either database printouts or photocopies, popped into envelopes or fax machines. Most commercial database suppliers include wording in their annual conditions mailings prohibiting the electronic transmission of search results. This prohibition thus precludes distribution by electronic mail or by disk.

Many libraries use Ariel transmission of documents. This technology currently requires an Ariel workstation on both ends of the transmission, so at the moment this method is not an option for a service working with large numbers of business clients who do not have Ariel in their offices.

The academic library community, often in partnership with commercial document delivery firms, is also experimenting with ways to transmit electronic articles, complete with accompanying graphic images, directly to the scholar's workstation. While this technology is becoming more reliable and sophisticated, it currently requires state-of-the-art equipment as well as special training and systems support. In addition, as publishers move cautiously into this electronic arena, only a relatively small number of journal titles, mainly of very recent vintage and in the sciences, are included in these electronic files. Finally, academic libraries signing licenses for these databases may find that only campus users are eligible to access and download these articles; they are off limits to the fee-based information service staff for distribution to clients in the for-profit sector. Service managers will face further difficulties when libraries begin cancelling equivalent print subscriptions as they acquire access to the electronic versions. Thus issues related to electronic methods of distribution may also blur with issues related to access versus ownership.

CLIENT NEEDS AND EXPECTATIONS

The information industry is not the only one changing. No matter which services or industries clients come from, their jobs, resources, and environments are also changing. Different information needs evolve from these changes. The staff in a responsive fee-based information service stay abreast of changes not only in their own profession, but also of those in the industries that employ their clients.

The electronic revolution has affected virtually all clients. Their need for information to make informed decisions in their workplaces has exploded. They call staff at fee-based services, and in other organizations that provide mediated searching services, because they realize that searchers can find the relevant information faster and more cost-effectively. However, simply because so many sources are now electronic, many clients expect rapid turnaround on their projects. They perceive the process of logging into a database and downloading some records to be fast and easy. And so it usually is, but only to an experienced searcher who has conducted a thorough reference interview and made a complex series of choices about the appropriate databases, the best search strategy, and the elimination of certain groups records based on factors such as duplication, language, publication year or type, and the client's budget.

Document delivery is even more likely to be perceived as a service in which instant gratification is possible. After all, how hard can it be to pull a volume off a shelf, photocopy an article, and then pop it in the fax machine—all in the next 20 minutes? Once again, the process is indeed relatively simple until one factors in issues like the number of rush orders already in the queue, the availability of a retriever, the accuracy of the citation, the length of the lines at the public photo-copy machines, and whether the item is held locally and if so, how far away from the office is it located?

Most requests can be handled within the clients' time frames in an adequately staffed service, so that high client expectations can be routinely met. However, there will sometimes be occasions when it is simply not possible to meet a client's expectations, such as during some combination of equipment failure, unforeseen staff absences, catastrophic weather conditions, or a day of unusually heavy demand. Most clients are understanding (as long as they do not hear a different excuse every time they place a rush order). Some can extend their deadlines. Other appreciate a referral. Almost all of them realize that without the important human element of a skilled staff handling their information needs, quality will deteriorate. The premium prices they pay cover the special handling that each request receives.

TIMES IN THE LIFE OF A FEE-BASED INFORMATION SERVICE

Good Times: Status Quo or Growth?

Having survived the first few critical years of establishing itself, the service and its parent organization face a major decision. Should the service strive to maintain relative stability in terms of number of clients, staff size, office space, and general capacity? Or should the service continue to make formal efforts to attract new business, knowing that increased volume brings with it increased demand for space, staff, and other resources? The manager and administrators remember that even without formal marketing efforts, a well-organized and responsive fee-based information service experiences at least some growth from repeat business and word of mouth referrals. The service also experiences some degree of natural attrition as clients retire, change jobs, or experience declining or changing information needs.

The answers to these questions depend on each institution's commitment to its fee-based information service and to the mission the service fulfills.

Great Times: Explosive Growth

If the service does a superlative job reaching its target audience, filling orders, and encouraging repeat clients, it may find itself flooded with requests. Work levels that meet or sometimes slightly exceed capacity provide a feeling of accomplishment and security. A moderate level of stress may actually be beneficial in motivating staff and creating an exciting, innovative work environment. However, continually excessive workloads that threaten to swamp the staff's capacity to handle work quickly and accurately produce very different feelings and reactions.

Unlike some other kinds of library tasks, orders from paying customers at a fee-based information service must be handled immediately. Many orders require turnaround times of a few hours to accommodate rush handling requests. While there is a little more time to process non-rush orders, staff begin work on them within a few hours of their arrival. Complications such as bad citations and local unavailability add to the fulfillment time. Since client demand does not ebb at predictable times as does demand from the academic community, the staff cannot look forward to lighter "off season" workloads except around the December holidays, a time at which staffing levels generally also decrease due to vacations.

The manager monitors the work levels, usually in terms of monthly statistics on the number of projects completed and the number of document orders handled. A wise practice is to count the number of orders received as well as the number filled; an unfilled rate of anything over a few percent represents significant amount of work needed to receive, check, attempt to obtain or verify, and cancel orders. Tracking the percentage of rush orders is also a good idea; a 30 percent rush document workload requires significantly more special handling than a 10 percent rush workload. Daily, weekly, and monthly variations are normal, but the manager checks to see if the increase is a trickle or a tidal wave. If there is a pattern of significant increases, and if it is also clear that the staff is struggling to keep up with the demand, the manager has several options.

1. Work with the staff to reevaluate procedures to see if any steps can be streamlined or eliminated. This process should be a continual one as the service evolves, but the struggle to keep up with a hectic pace can uncover overlooked options. However, there is usually a point past which few steps can be reduced or cut out.

2. Reduce or eliminate marketing efforts. This action will not result in an immediate drop in orders, since recent marketing will continue to attract new clients for a few more weeks or months. Satisfied clients will also continue to use the service.

3. Consider temporary measures to increase staff and/or to reduce the number of people needing the same pieces of equipment at the same time. Offering overtime or flextime, hiring more student assistants, and/or hiring temporary clerical help are possible options. Sometimes staff from other library units can be borrowed for a brief time or can provide some back-up assistance. Realize that temporary clerks and additional students will probably be able to relieve pressure on the less specialized tasks. The learning curve for temporary staff to perform complex tasks may be too high to be cost-effective, especially considering that the already-overworked regular staff would have to take time away from their already overwhelming duties to provide the training.

4. Investigate whether the addition of one or two key pieces of equipment will alleviate some bottlenecks. For example, using an extra fax machine may improve the turnaround time on transmitting rush documents.

5. Begin the procedure for requesting additional permanent staff, along with any needed space or equipment. Since this option is usually a lengthy procedure at most institutions, do not wait until the work overload reaches critical proportions before starting this step.

The manager usually selects a combination of these suggestions to alleviate the pressure on the staff.

A final method of reducing orders is to provide such poor service that few clients place additional orders. No one does this deliberately, of course, but when staff are drowning in orders, haste and exhaustion inevitably lead to a higher error rate and thus lower customer satisfaction.

Bad Times: Declining Demand

A manager need not be seriously alarmed if orders decline for a month or two. Demand for services naturally fluctuates depending on a large number of factors, very few of which the service controls. However, if the decline continues steadily into the third or fourth month, the manager pays serious attention to the situation and plans countermoves.

Many elements might be contributing factors to a downturn in orders. Some of them may be things over which the service has at least some control. The manager examines factors such as:

- Quality control;
- Error rate;
- Customer service;
- Phone manners;
- Accurate and timely billing;
- General appearance of items shipped to clients;
- Turnaround times;
- Pricing;
- Ability to obtain items unavailable locally; and
- Effectiveness of marketing strategy.

Contributing external factors are sometimes harder to pinpoint, but possibilities include:

- Another information service or broker courting the same target audience and/or offering lower prices, faster turnaround, and so forth;
- A significant economic downturn in the industry that employs a major part of the target audience; or
- A generally bad economy (local, regional, or national).

Whatever the combination of causes, it is the manager's responsibility to act to reverse the decline. Conducting a client satisfaction survey may help identify problem areas. Many of the marketing strategies discussed in earlier chapters can be used to reach new customers. The manager can return to the original business plan and re-think the service's mission and target audience. If in bad times the target audience is focused too narrowly, either by industry or by region, the manager looks for ways to reach potential clients in other industries or locations. The manager also encourages past clients to submit new orders, perhaps even by offering lower prices for a short period of time, or by experimenting with lower per item prices for clients who exceed a certain level of activity each month.

If the service receives outside funding, consider an appeal to the funding agency. Lower workloads result in some lower costs (e.g., fewer filled document orders mean lower total copyright payments), but other costs (e.g., salaries) remain constant. The funding agency may be willing to infuse more money, either as a grant or a loan, into the service to tide it over. Locating new funding sources in hard times will be more challenging.

A different approach to marketing may be helpful. If the major industry is laying off employees, the service suggests to those who are left struggling with increased workloads that outsourcing projects to the fee-based information service would be economically advantageous. As an unfortunate result of downsizing, corporate libraries are often among the first departments to feel the ax. The manager suggests to the remaining library staff, or to other employees suddenly bereft of on-site library services, that the staff at the fee-based information service can help bridge the gap (Lunden 1983, p. 123).

If the service is located at an institution with a major research collection, another way to develop a new revenue stream would be to approach one or more of the large commercial document delivery firms. Many of these firms actively seek partner libraries to provide their clients with photocopies from sources to which they do not otherwise have access. These firms generally expect to negotiate a volume discount rate, but the income may make the critical difference as to whether the service can survive a severe downturn in business. Of course, once having established this relationship, it would not be good practice to drop it as soon as the regular business improves.

The manager grapples with one particularly difficult issue during downturns. A serious decline in orders usually means that there is not enough work to occupy, and therefore not enough revenue to pay, all members of the staff. The institution's policies about laying off staff may preclude downsizing except through attrition. Even if laying off staff is possible, morale will plummet if employees are let go. The manager does everything possible to avoid taking this step. Are there any vacancies or special projects elsewhere in the library system that the staff could fill temporarily on the library's payroll until the service's business improves? One library solved a similar dilemma by integrating the fee-based information service with the interlibrary loan operations.

The Worst Time: Closing the Service

Although some fee-based information services have existed for over 30 years, others sadly never reach their fifth or tenth anniversaries. The reasons for deciding to close are varied. A subsidy on which a service depends for supplementary income may decline or dry up. Business may be good, but not good enough to pay back a start-up loan or to cover all the overhead or other expenses the institution expects the service to pay. Despite the staff's best efforts, the service may not be able to reverse a serious business downturn. A change in institutional policy or administrators may alter the service's position in the parent organization.

With luck, the staff will have at least several months' warning of an impending closure. A good manager does everything possible to ensure the staff's transition into other positions within the library or the institution. Ideally, some staff remain on the payroll for at least two weeks after the official closing date to handle details such as:

- Preparing the final invoices;
- Paying bills;
- Overseeing proper storage of client records;
- Supervising the disposition of office equipment, supplies, and furniture;
- Answering the phone;
- Terminating or transferring equipment maintenance agreements; and
- Disposing of unusable office supplies such as letterhead and brochures.

Written agreements should be approved for the disposition of remaining funds and income, client records, supplies, and equipment. Someone in the library business office assumes responsibility for handling any straggling financial matters such as closing deposit accounts, accepting late payments, paying bills that arrive weeks or months after closing, and answering clients' questions about their invoices.

Do not leave the clients high and dry by closing the service without warning. Call counterparts at several other services that offer a similar service mix and that have proven to be reliable. If these colleagues agree, include these services' names in a letter sent to the entire client list. Send explanatory letters to suppliers and other creditors as well, requesting them to send final invoices as soon as possible.

CITED REFERENCES

Lunden, E. 1983. "Marketing the R.I.C.E. Operation." Pp. 113-127 in *Conference on Fee Based Research in College and University Libraries*. Greenvale, NY: Long Island University Center for Business Research.

Thompson, J.C. 1983. "Regional Information and Communication Exchange: A Case Study." Pp. 55-76 in *Conference on Fee Based Research in College and University Libraries*. Greenvale, NY: Long Island University Center for Business Research.

Wilkins, A. 1992. "The For-Profit Syndrome: Will Libraries Be Next?" *North Carolina Libraries* 50(Special Edition): 24-26.

Chapter 9

Legal and Ethical Issues

It sometimes seems that almost everything the staff do in fee-based information service involves a conscious decision about each action's legal or ethical ramifications. While this comment is a deliberate overstatement, it is true that staff exercise constant vigilance over the legal and ethical issues involved in providing copies or versions of various types of intellectual property to clients.

Many of these issues are the same ones that face colleagues at library public service desks, but often the fact that a fee-based information service's users are mainly customers from for-profit corporations results in different interpretations.

There are few hard answers for the many ethical and legal questions that arise in providing fee-based services. Some issues arise daily, others rarely. Some instances occur frequently enough that the manager covers them with an official policy. Others must be examined individually and decided on a case-by-case basis. The answers to some questions are fairly clearly defined by law, accepted business standards, or institutional policy; others are open to widely varying interpretation. Some issues involve using common sense and good business practice to achieve the ultimate goal of customer satisfaction. Sometimes customer satisfaction takes a back seat to legal mandates or ethical considerations.

Being neither a lawyer nor a philosopher, I cannot provide definitive answers to the questions and issues this chapter raises. By raising the issues, however, I hope to raise planners' and managers' and administrators' consciousness about them. Many of these examples are taken from my experience during 10 years with Purdue University's Technical Information Service (TIS). Other examples reflect conversations with colleagues, and some represent hypothetical situations. At TIS, staff follow the appropriate legal, institutional, and business requirements to resolve these situations.

RESEARCH

Most fee-based services offer research as one of their core services. Information specialists complete the research by accessing electronic information sources and downloading the results, or in some cases by conducting manual searches through printed sources. Ethical and legal issues involving research include:

- A client asks an information specialist to find specific information from other organizations, such as government agencies or other companies, without revealing the client's identity. When the information specialist calls these organizations, staff there assume the specialist is calling on behalf of a university patron. In some cases, these employees respond more positively to a university caller than to a corporate caller. Is it ethical to allow people to make this assumption without attempting to explain the situation?
- In a similar scenario, a client asks an information specialist to visit particular Web sites and download information. The specialist's Internet address, rather than the client's, turns up in the Web sponsor's log. Is this ethical behavior?
- The fine print in a database vendor's annual "Conditions of Use" booklet clearly states that a certain file may only be searched by the end-user or by an employee of the end-user's firm. If the information the fee-based searcher needs to answer a client's question is in this file, should the searcher connect to it?
- A database producer introduces new licensing terms whereby information brokers, including fee-based information services, must pay the producer an annual fee for permission to search the files and to send search results to a third party. The annual fee is $600. Should the service pay this fee, or should specialists continue to search the database anyway?
- Certain online services are priced lower for academic or non-profit users. Should the service take advantage of these lower rates to complete research projects assigned by corporate clients?
- Two different clients request virtually the same information at the same time. Should the information specialist run the same search twice, or run it once and print it twice?
- A client asks for a relatively simple, but labor-intensive manual search, such as copying the page from the *Wall Street Journal* containing the price of a particular stock on the third working day of the month over a period of four years. The information specialist assigns the project to a clerk. Should the search be billed out at the specialist's hourly rate?
- An information specialist misses a deadline. Should the cost of the project be adjusted?
- Before developing a search strategy for an online search, the information specialist spends half an hour reading background information on the subject of the client's project in order to understand the concept better. Should this half hour be included in the final cost of the search?
- The best database for finding information on a topic is one which the searcher has never used before and for which the service has no specialized

thesauri or manuals. Although the searcher's strategy finds some excellent records, nearly half the records are irrelevant. How should the search be billed?

- The client and the specialist agree that a maximum of three hours will be spent on a project. The specialist spends three and a half hours completing the project. For how many hours should the client be billed?
- The information specialist clearly informs a client that the $200 budget available for a project will only cover a brief dip into one or two databases. The client assures the specialist that an overview of the topic will be sufficient. When the bill arrives, the client complains to the manager that the search results were not comprehensive enough and are thus unsatisfactory. Should the manager adjust the price of the search?
- Despite the information specialist having given an accurate cost estimate at the start of a project, when the invoice arrives the client calls to say that the company did not expect the total cost to be so high. What should the manager do?
- A directory database's "Conditions of Use" state that search results can be distributed in paper form only. A client asks the information specialist for a file on a disk. What should the specialist do?
- The specialist suspects that a client might put the search results to an illegal use. Should the specialist accept the assignment?
- A client's information need seems totally irrational or illogical. Should the specialist proceed?
- Although the specialist's search strategy is sound, by the nature of the terms used, a large percentage of the resulting database records are false hits. The specialist removes the irrelevant records from the results, but should the client be billed for them?
- A client loses part of a search printout several weeks after receiving it. The specialist still has a back-up electronic copy of the search. Should the specialist run the search again, or print the missing pages from the back-up? In either case, how should the client be charged?
- Based on search results obtained from the service, a client makes a major business decision. The company subsequently loses money or fails. Is the institution, the service, and/or the information specialist liable?
- A client bases a major business decision on the results of a specialist's database search. The decision turns out to be faulty, and when the client investigates, it is clear that the database producer made several errors in preparing the information on which the decision was based. Who is liable?
- A client bases a major business decision on the results of a specialist's database search. The decision turns out to be faulty, and on investigation, the client discovers that the specialist chose not to search an additional database or neglected to use certain search terms that would have resulted in different information and, thus, a different decision. Who is liable?

- A new client gives plausible reasons about why he cannot pay for information at the service's published rates. Should exceptions be made for lower rates or for free service because a client indicates inability to pay?
- A client asks for information about a company for which a close relative of the information specialist works. Should the information specialist accept the work, decline the assignment, or alert the client to a possible conflict of interest and let the client decide?
- The manager learns that a respected librarian client is seeking a new position. The fee-based information service has an opening for which the client is qualified. Should the manager mention the vacancy to the client?

DOCUMENT DELIVERY

Many document delivery issues also present knotty problems. A separate section addresses issues related to copyright.

- To what extent will the service order documents from traditional interlibrary loan departments that charge no fees, low fees, or lower fees for requests from non-profit institutions such as the service's parent organization?
- If the service obtains a document at no charge, how much will it bill the client?
- To verify a bad citation, an information specialist has a choice of logging onto a commercial database or dialing up the university's locally mounted version of the same database. The local version is licensed for use only by the institution's students, faculty, and staff. To which version does the specialist connect?
- A document supplier such as a publisher or trade association provides items to educational institutions at a discount below the price it charges to for-profit organizations. Which price should staff ask for when they order items on clients' behalf?
- Another fee-based service asks the local service to deliver an item directly to one of their clients. Should the supplying service add that client's name to its mailing list and send a brochure?
- Rather than placing a document special order, a client wants to know what nearby libraries hold an item. Should the service charge for providing document location information?
- While searching OCLC to identify potential suppliers for a special order, the clerk notices that the client's corporate library holds a copy. Should the client be notified, or should the clerk proceed with the order?
- A client needs an article on a super rush basis. The staff gives the order top priority and faxes the article in under an hour. Later that day, the staff discover that because the copyright royalty fee for the article is $10 a page, the

total price for the order would be over $100, far more than the client expects to pay. How should the order be billed?

- A client calls to point out that a document was shipped incorrectly. The staff will, of course, fill the order correctly. Should it be handled on a rush basis? Should the final cost of the order be adjusted, even if the client does not suggest this? If so, how much should the adjustment be?
- The library is a U.S. government depository and, as such, agrees to provide public access to government documents at no charge. A client requests a copy of a section from the *Federal Register*. Should the service bill the client for copying the pages and shipping them?
- A staff member wants a to buy a personal copy of a book, and asks the publisher to send it to the office with an invoice. When it arrives, the staff member arranges for the service to bill him at home, but for the invoiced amount only, excluding the usual handling fee added to client special orders. Should the manager allow this practice?
- A client asks for several papers from a conference that the institution does not own. Should the service place a special order for the entire conference proceedings, copy the papers for the client and return the volume to the supplier, thus paying a single loan fee to the supplier but charging the client a fee for each paper? Or should the service order each paper separately from the supplier, resulting in a much higher total cost for the client?

CONFIDENTIALITY

Most fee-based information services either state or imply that they protect their clients' confidentiality. Some clients' requests are sensitive in that should a competitor or other third party learn of a certain research interest, the client's company might lose a business opportunity, face a financial loss, or lose a lawsuit. Most clients are concerned about the confidentiality of the nature of their projects, but some are even sensitive about that fact that they have sought outside assistance at all.

- Does the manager have an obligation to warn colleagues about a company that has run up bills of hundreds or thousands of dollars that it refuses to pay?
- Colleagues at another service call to say they have had trouble getting a certain client to pay invoices or to return books. Does the manager admit that the service also serves the same client on occasion? Should the manager act on the colleagues' information?
- The organizer of a local conference on finding start-up funding for small businesses calls. The conference would certainly interest many of the service's local clients. Should the service sell or give relevant portions of its mailing list to the conference organizer?

- While handling a document order, the fee-based service clerk notices that it is exactly the same item that another researcher at the same company ordered the previous day. Would it be a breach of confidentiality to contact the client and reveal that a colleague will shortly receive the same article? If not, are there any copyright implications in the likely scenario that the first client will probably make a photocopy of the article for the second one?
- A service publishes a newsletter, annual report, or other promotional piece briefly stating the types of questions its specialists have answered successfully. No client names or affiliations appear with the questions. Does this practice violate client confidentiality?

COPYRIGHT

Each year, dozens of books, articles, and papers about copyright appear. Technological advances change or increase the number of ways that information can be used, transferred, stored, or adapted. National and international copyright laws struggle to keep up with these changing formats and channels of distribution, while at the same time, basic interpretation of existing laws seems foggy at best.

Since nearly all the resources that fee-based information services provide are protected by copyright, managers face frequent dilemmas about providing services to satisfy customer demand while at the same time avoiding potential copyright infringement. These questions assume that staff carefully report all copyright transactions to the Copyright Clearance Center (CCC) whenever the relevant titles or publishers are listed in the CCC's print or electronic lists. If the service believes it is exempt from paying copyright under the provisions of either the library copying section or the fair use section (or both) of the law, then the potential answers to some of these questions may be different.

- What is the procedure for materials apparently protected by copyright, but not registered with the CCC?
- A client asks for copies of five of seven articles in single journal issue. Is it legal to copy all the articles since the service is paying copyright on each of them? Does the answer change depending on whether the issue is still available for purchase from the publisher?
- A client orders copies of five of seven articles in a single journal issue. Since the issue is bound in a volume over 20 years old, the library allows the service to lend the volume. Should the service copy the articles anyway, thus generating fees on five items instead of one? Or should staff lend the volume, knowing that the client will probably copy the five articles without paying copyright fees on them? Is the service, the client, or both liable for possible infringement?

- A few special order documents arrive from suppliers that the staff suspect or know do not pay copyright royalties. The suppliers may be ignorant of the law, may have ignored the law, or may have supplied items under the assumption or belief that they were exempt under the fair use or library copying provisions of the law. Is the service responsible for identifying these items and paying copyright royalties on them?
- A client asks for a lot of detailed information about a particular industry. The specialist decides that the best way to handle the question is to refer the client to a market research firm experienced in that industry. Although the specialist will not charge the client for the referral, the specialist photocopies a few pages from a consultants' directory to send to the client. Each page of the directory states that a copyright fee should be paid to the publisher for each photocopy made. Should the specialist pay the fee?

MARKETING

Most marketing texts admonish readers to avoid deceptive marketing practices. A fee-based service's institutional parent to some degree monitors its advertising to prevent inadvertent blunders. Common sense and standard business practice also provide basic guidelines for truthful advertising and aboveboard marketing techniques. Electronic marketing has recently added a new twist to the formula, but responsible cybermarketing follows the same general principles as traditional marketing practice.

- Should the manager post an electronic advertisement for the service on a listserv to which potential clients subscribe?
- A mailing list provider supplies names in an electronic format. Should the manager use the list more than once?
- What are reasonable limits for soliciting business on the Internet?
- What should the manager do when a marketing effort is so successful that it generates far more orders than the staff can complete within the turnaround time advertised?
- A subscriber to an interlibrary loan listserv posts a plea for help to obtain an obscure international document. Should an information specialist reply privately with an offer to obtain it on a cost-recovery basis from one of the service's international document suppliers?
- A manager hires a student assistant to send introductory letters and brochures to all the executives listed in a directory published by a trade association. Is this practice ethical if the trade association also sells expensive mailing lists?

CONSULTING

As a service matures, and as the manager and the information specialists become active and known in the profession, at least a few clients or start-up operations will call to discuss consulting opportunities.

- A start-up service contacts the manager to establish a consulting relationship. Should the manager accept the assignment as one to be billed by the institution, or as a freelance assignment? If freelance, is it ethical for the manager to use any institutional supplies, equipment, or time to work on the project?
- A client asks if an information specialist would be interested in handling a project as an independent consultant. The client is willing to pay the specialist directly, but at lower hourly rates than the service advertises. Should the specialist accept?
- A client contacts the service to discuss volume pricing arrangements for substantial and ongoing information needs. For institutional reasons, the manager cannot offer any special pricing, but offers to handle the requests on a freelance consulting basis. Is this ethical?

These examples cover most of the types of legal and ethical questions faced by fee-based information services today. With constant technological changes, there will probably be even more questions tomorrow. I do not want to give the impression that managing a fee-based information service is daily fraught with legal and ethical peril. Many of these situations occur very rarely. Some legal issues, such as those associated with copyright, are still at least partly unresolved or untested. However, with input from university administrators and legal advisers, managers develop guidelines to apply consistently.

In the case of ethical issues, one manager might deplore a certain practice, another tolerate it, and a third invite it. While it sometimes seems that these legal and ethical considerations collude to prevent timely response to client demands, it is possible to manage an efficient, responsive fee-based information service and both comply with the law and simultaneously meet personal, institutional, and social ethical standards.

FURTHER READING

Fong, Y.S. 1995. "The Copyright Quandary: Copyright Practices in Fee-Based Services." *Fee for Service* 2(2): 11-15.

Shaver, D.B., N.S. Hewison, and L.W. Wykoff. 1985. "Ethics for Online Intermediaries." *Special Libraries* 76(4): 238-245.

Chapter 10

Professional Issues

Managing or working in a fee-based information service is an extremely reward-ing professional challenge. However, it is also not a career path that many librari-ans choose as a conscious objective. Nor is it one that colleagues always understand, appreciate, or in some cases, even condone. In addition, the rest of the organizational structure often regards a fee-based information service, espe-cially in its planning stages and infancy, as an experimental oddity.

MEETING CAREER OBJECTIVES

Working as a manager or information specialist in a fee-based information ser-vice offers a wide array of opportunities for professional growth. Some of these opportunities are inherent in the very nature of a fee-based information service. Others are optional benefits sought by some professionals who wish to enrich their professional careers further. These opportunities include:

- Developing or improving public speaking skills, not only to groups of potential clients but also to groups of colleagues;
- Gaining marketing expertise;
- Learning the business community's information needs;
- Developing writing skills for several different kinds of work, such as adver-tising, promotional literature, and articles;
- Participating in professional groups, both library-related and industry-related;
- Working in a team environment;
- Asserting control over the job in the sense of making decisions to increase personal ability to meet clients' needs in a timely manner;
- Contemplating some of the major current professional issues, such as intel-lectual property;
- Designing efficient office operations;

- Evaluating services and drawing conclusions from the evaluations' results;
- Providing or experiencing a corporate library atmosphere in an academic setting;
- Employing problem-solving techniques;
- Starting or running a small business;
- Devising creative solutions to meet client's information needs;
- Satisfaction from the intrinsic rewards of helping corporate clients meet their objectives;
- Participation in the university's efforts to share its resources with the business community;
- Consulting;
- Developing and administering a budget; and
- Keeping abreast of and taking advantage of new technology, resources, and/ or other changes that enhance services.

Working in a fee-based information service is not a job every librarian would enjoy, but for those who find the activities on the list above exciting, there is, in my opinion, no other challenge in academic librarianship quite as enjoyable. While understanding that the job and the department will never, by the very nature of the institution, be one of the library's core or fundamental services, the staff enjoy the freedom and challenge of working as intrapreneurs.

WHO MAKES A SUCCESSFUL INTRAPRENEUR?

Intrapreneurs have been described as "those employed by an organization to manage libraries as businesses-within-businesses" (Warner 1990, p. 946). "In libraries, individuals who develop new programs or services that change libraries are intrapreneurs" (Josephine 1989, p. 152).

Library intrapreneurs are nontraditional. They are risk takers. Although they value quality service, they provide and manage those services with an eye on the bottom line. They market services. They sell. They actively pursue new customers. They understand accountability. They have vision and set goals to reach that vision. As leaders, they build teams and instill their vision in those teams. They are practical; they understand the business mentality; and they are decision makers. They view information as a commercially valuable product.

Library intrapreneurs also talk comfortably about money and use money as one means of evaluating their effectiveness. They view fees not as a barrier to information access but as a means of facilitating access for customers who value information enough to pay willingly premium prices for the convenience of fast, professional, reliable service. They derive enormous satisfaction from meeting the business community's information needs. In many ways, they live on the cutting edge of the profession, because they provide services to customers who expect results using the latest technologies, resources, and techniques.

Relatively few librarians possess the combination of personal and professional characteristics that would make working in fee-based information services (or as information brokers or corporate librarians) a happy and successful experience (Warner 1990, p. 948). But for those few who possess the necessary intrapreneurial skills and temperament, working in or managing a fee-based information service is one of the most rewarding positions in the profession. The experience is often also one that, after a few successful years, provides a springboard into higher administrative positions either in the same institution or elsewhere. Skills developed in a successful fee-based information service can then be used in bringing an intrapreneurial spirit and vision to more traditional library services. As our profession grapples with its image and its role, these skills are essential for positioning libraries and librarians as leaders and partners in the information industry in the new century.

CITED REFERENCES

Josephine, H.B. 1989. "Intrapreneurship in Fee-Based Information Services." *Journal of Library Administration* 10(2-3): 151-158.

Warner, A.S. 1990. "Librarians as Money Makers: The Bottom Line." *American Libraries* 21(10): 946-948.

FURTHER READING

St. Clair, G. 1996. *Entrepreneurial Librarianship: The Key to Effective Information Services Management.* London: Bowker-Saur.

Appendices

APPENDIX A:
SAMPLE BUDGET OUTLINE FOR
AN ESTABLISHED SERVICE

I. Salaries and Wages

	FTE	Amount
Manager	1.0	$
Information Specialist	1.0	
Information Specialist	1.0	
Accounting Clerk	1.0	
Document Clerk	1.0	
Document Clerk	1.0	
Document Clerk	1.0	
Computer Support	0.5	
Student Assistants	4.0	
Total Salaries and Wages		$

II. Fringe Benefits

	F/B Rate	Amount
Manager		$
Information Specialist		
Information Specialist		
Accounting Clerk		
Document Clerk		
Document Clerk		
Document Clerk		
Computer Support		
Student Assistants		
Total Fringe Benefits		$

III. Salaries and Wages/Fringe Benefits $

IV. Supplies and Expenses

	Amount
A. Software	$
B. Manuals (database)	
C. Service Contracts—Equipment	
D. Travel	
E. Telephone Rentals	
F. Telephone Tolls	
G. General Supplies	

H. Marketing and Promotion
    (printing, graphic arts,
    advertising, annual report)
I. Copy Machine Charges
J. UPS/Federal Express
K. Postage
L. Database Vendor Charges
M. Document Vendor Charges
N. Copyright Fees
    Total Supplies and Expenses $

V. Equipment
    Replacement parts $

VI. Total Project Funding $

VII. Estimated Annual Income $

APPENDIX B:
SAMPLE JOB DESCRIPTIONS

I. Document Clerk

Position Summary:

Performs a variety of tasks required to provide confidential information services to companies on a cost-recovery basis. Major tasks are preparing item retrieval forms; retrieving items from campus libraries; data entry; filing; and general clerical support.

Knowledge, Skills, and Ability:

Skills in typing, word processing, data entry, file organization, good written/oral comprehension, and telephone etiquette required. Ability to work under pressure and meet deadlines.

Essential Duties:

Handles incoming document orders by checking the online catalog as well as other sources if required. Prepares item retrieval forms. Places special orders with document suppliers for items not owned locally.	30%
Retrieves documents from library.	20%
Performs data entry for order tracking, pre-billing, and client list maintenance; records information manually in office logs.	15%
Oversees some student assistant activities.	10%
Maintains and organizes confidential client files.	10%
Answers the phone; contacts clients and suppliers about document orders.	10%
Prepares documents for shipping via UPS, fax, Federal Express, or U.S. mail.	5%

II. Information Specialist

Position Summary:

Under the direction of the manager, undertakes research projects for corporate clients. Assists in problem solving for document delivery. Maintains reports and compiles statistics.

Knowledge, Skills, and Ability:

Ability to develop expertise with a wide array of computer-based sources. Knowledge of business and/or technical information sources. Good communications and organizational skills. Experience with microcomputers. Ability to meet deadlines.

Essential Duties:

Conduct reference interviews with clients, usually by phone, and handle or refer as appropriate. Handle clients' information requests using online databases, print sources, or other appropriate sources within clients' deadlines. Assist in bibliographic verification in support of special orders for document delivery.	80%
Complete billing forms and assist with keeping other office records current, including documenting work performed for clients. Prepare reports and compile statistics as requested	20%

III. Manager

Position Summary:

In a team environment, provide leadership for and manage all aspects of a fee-based information service, including reference interviews; online searching; hiring, training, and supervising staff; marketing; billing operations; and reports preparation. Explore nontraditional sources for document delivery. Formulate and implement policies and procedures.

Knowledge, Skills, and Ability:

Ability to develop expertise with a wide array of computer-based sources. Knowledge of business and/or technical information sources. Good communications and organizational skills. Experience with microcomputers. Ability to meet deadlines. Document delivery and marketing experience helpful.

Essential Duties:

Provide information services to non-university clients. Conduct reference interviews, provide cost quotes, and establish project turnaround time. Complete research requests using print or online sources and provide information packet by clients' deadlines. Make information referrals as appropriate. Supervise and advice office staff in providing information services.	50%

Administer the fee-based information service.
Hire, train and supervise the staff. Oversee
business activities such as pre-billing, copyright
payments, approval of vendor invoices, etc.
Provide written and oral reports. Compile
statistics. Oversee marketing activities, such as
attracting new clients, writing a client
newsletter, etc. Initiate strategic planning
activities.   25%

Provide document delivery service to non-university
clients. Verify bibliographic citations using online
databases. Identify and select document suppliers
and place special orders for documents. Prepare
item retrieval forms for document orders. Supervise
and advise office staff in providing document delivery
services.   25%

APPENDIX C:
SAMPLE RESEARCH QUESTIONS

- Buying power of several U.S. ethnic groups
- Reports in the regional press of union activity at a particular company
- Use of a soybean product as a dust inhibitor on gravel roads
- Livestock odor management
- Use of a drug in goats
- Golf instruction video sales
- Toxicity of a chemical
- A rental car company's operational strategies
- List of wig distributors, importers, and wholesalers
- Use of lightweight aggregate concrete in highway bridges
- Seasonal sales statistics for bath spas
- Cellulose gels and gums in food products
- Industry standards about locating and removing large underground pipes
- Thermophysical properties of air at elevated temperatures
- Biographical information about a nineteenth-century French psychiatrist
- Starting salaries for pharmaceutical scientists
- Market information about smart valves
- Patents for wheelchair attachments
- Top 500 U.S. colleges and universities ranked by enrollment
- Maps of Guantanamo Bay
- Fatigue data for stainless steel wire
- Electrical corona effects on transformers
- Airbag deployment injuries
- Sales statistics for charcoal, electric, and gas grills
- Subsidiaries of a German company
- Golf trade associations
- Internal dimensions of an aircraft engine
- Agricultural regulations in Iowa and Missouri
- Wholesale suppliers for garbanzo beans
- Polymer coatings for the interior of metal cans
- Popcorn seed exports to South America
- Accidents involving temporary guardrails and barriers around roadside construction sites
- Projected prices of fresh vegetables for the next six months

APPENDIX D:
SAMPLE QUICK SURVEY

TECHNICAL INFORMATION SERVICE
Evaluation of Services

Our records show that Purdue's Technical Information Service
completed one or more information orders for you in 1990. Please
take a few minutes to evaluate our services so we can serve you
better in the future. Thank you.

1. (Please check one)

    ____ I ordered article photocopies and book loans
         (document delivery).
    ____ I requested an in-depth information search.
    ____ I used both the document delivery <u>and</u> research
         services.

2. Was the information provided within a reasonable time frame?

3. Were you satisfied with the service?

4. Is your organization using the information TIS provided?

5. How will the information you received benefit your
organization?

6. Do you expect to use TIS again within the next six months?

7. Would you recommend TIS to colleagues?

8. Additional comments:

Thank you!

Please return this form in the   Optional:
enclosed stamped, addressed
envelope to: Name: _____
                                        Organization:_____
Technical Information Service   _____
Potter Building, Room 364M
Purdue University
West Lafayette, IN 47907

APPENDIX E:
SAMPLE CLIENT EVALUATION SURVEY

PURDUE UNIVERSITY

TECHNICAL INFORMATION
SERVICE

January 10, 1992

Dear TIS Client:

Will you do me a favor?

Purdue's Technical Information Service is conducting a survey of our Indiana clients. The purpose of the study is to determine current client satisfaction and any areas which may need improvement. We are conducting this survey to better serve our clients—you!

Your name appeared on our client list. Your answers are important even if you haven't used TIS services for some time. It will take only a short time to answer the enclosed questionnaire and return it in the self-addressed stamped envelope provided. Your answers will remain confidential and will only be used in combination with those from our other Indiana clients. When mentioned in the questionnaire, "information" can be described in the following three categories: documents, facts, and research items.

Please return the completed questionnaire using the enclosed self-addressed stamped envelope by January 29, 1992. Thank you for your help.

Sincerely,

Suzanne Ward

Suzanne Ward
Manager

Purdue University's TIS Client Survey

I. CLIENT SATISFACTION

1. How long have you used TIS services? (circle one)
   1   Less than 6 months
   2   6 months to 1 year
   3   More than a year

2. In the last year, which of the following TIS services have you used?
   1   Document delivery (ie: you ordered specific articles, etc.)
   2   Research services (ie: TIS conducted an information search on a subject)
   3   Both
   4   Have not used TIS services in the last year

3. How many times do you contact TIS? (Circle whichever is most appropriate.)
   1   Weekly
   2   2-3 times a month
   3   Monthly
   4   2-3 times a year
   5   Less than 2 times a year

4. How many times have you referred a friend or colleague to TIS in the last six months:
   1   Never
   2   Once
   3   Two times
   4   Three times
   5   Other (please specify the number of times _____)

5. Which two of the following reasons are the most important in your decision to use TIS services?
   List "1" as most important and "2" as second most important. (Mark two responses only.)
   __ Speed of response
   __ Quality of information provided
   __ Ability to assign information requests to a professional who knows your field
   __ Cost of services
   __ Ability to obtain materials not readily available in your area.
   __ Lack of time to obtain information yourself
   __ Other (please specify) _____

6. How satisfied have you been with the speed of response to your requests for information from TIS?
   1   Very satisfied
   2   Satisfied
   3   Neither satisfied nor dissatisfied
   4   Dissatisfied
   5   Very dissatisfied

7. How important is the speed of the response to your requests for information from TIS?
   1   Very important
   2   Important
   3   Neither important nor unimportant
   4   Unimportant
   5   Very unimportant

8. Does TIS meet your deadlines?
   1   All of the time
   2   Most of the time
   3   Sometimes
   4   Rarely

9. When you request documents from TIS, on the average, how soon do you need the material?
   1   Within 5 hours
   2   Within 24 hours
   3   Within 48 hours
   4   Within a week
   5   Within 2 weeks
   6   Other (please specify _____)

10. On average, how many hours of time does TIS save you in obtaining information? (Complete only one category, depending on how often you use our services. Enter the number of hours saved.)
    TIS saves me ___ hours per week
    or
    TIS saves me ___ hours per month
    or
    TIS saves me ___ hours per year

11. Is the value of the information/services provided by TIS: equal to the amount you are billed, greater than the amount you are billed, or less than the amount you are billed?
    1   Equal to
    2   Greater than
    3   Less than
    4   Don't know

12. Can you estimate the amount of money your firm has saved because you obtained information from TIS?
    1   Yes ———> what is the estimated amount? $_____
    2   No
    3   Don't know

13. Have you used any other information service besides TIS?
    1   Yes (Answer Question 13a)
    2   No (Skip to Question 14)

   13a. How would you compare the other information service's performance with TIS regarding the following features?

	Strongly Agree	Agree	Neither Agree nor Disagree	Disagree	Strongly Disagree
TIS' speed of response is better than other service	1	2	3	4	5
TIS has a better price than other service	1	2	3	4	5
TIS has better quality of service than other service	1	2	3	4	5
TIS has better quality of information than other service	1	2	3	4	5
The TIS staff is more helpful than other service	1	2	3	4	5
TIS has better overall service than other service	1	2	3	4	5

14. When you gather information, is it . . .
    1   primarily for your own use
    2   primarily for the use of others in your company
    3   both of the above

II. CLIENT INFORMATION

The following information is for classification purposes only.

15. What is the primary product or service offered by your firm?
_____
_____

16. What is your position/job title within your organization/company?
_____
_____

17. How many years experience do you have in your current field of employment?
   1   Less than 3 years
   2   3 years to less than 6 years
   3   6 years to less than 9 years
   4   9 years to less than 12 years
   5   12 or more years

18. How long have you been with your present employer?
   1   Less than a year
   2   1 to 5 years
   3   6 to 10 years
   4   More than 10 years

19. Check the highest level of education completed:
   1   High school
   2   Bachelors
   3   Masters
   4   Doctoral
   5   Other (please specify _____)

20. What is your company's zip code? _____

III. COMMENTS

20. What else could TIS do to improve services for you?
_____
_____
_____
_____

21. Please share any other comments you may have about TIS with us:
_____
_____
_____
_____
_____

Thank you for your participation!!

Reminder: Please return this questionnaire by January 29, 1992.

SELECTED BIBLIOGRAPHY

This bibliography lists some of the most helpful references for starting and operating a fee-based information service. It is not intended as a comprehensive bibliography. It purposely omits many general references on topics such as the fee-or-free debate, marketing library services, providing information services to primary users, evaluating services, operating small businesses, pricing online search services, information brokers, marketing for non-profit organizations, and consulting. It includes all the chapter references, plus some additional citations. The bibliography emphasizes listing practical, rather than theoretical, references with a major focus on, or a relevance for, academic fee-based information services.

Allen, B., and K.Corley. 1990. "Information Brokers in Illinois Academic Libraries." *Illinois Libraries* 72(8): 596-600.

American Library Association. 1997. *Internet-Plus Directory of Express Library Services: Research and Document Delivery for Hire.* Chicago, IL: American Library Association.

Aspnes, G. 1974. "INFORM: An Evaluation Study." *Minnesota Libraries* 24(Autumn): 171-185.

Association of Research Libraries. 1989. "Fee-Based Services in ARL Libraries. SPEC Kit 157. Washington, DC: Association of Research Libraries.

Baker, S.K. 1984. "Fee-Based Services in the M.I.T. Libraries." *Science and Technology Libraries* 5(2): 15-21.

Balachandran, S., and V. Witte. 1987. "The Off-Campus On-Line Computerized Literature Search Service." Pp. 24-36 in *The Off-Campus Library Services Conference Proceedings*, edited by B.M. Lessin. Mount Pleasant, MI: Central Michigan University Press.

Beaubien, A.K. 1983. "Michigan Information Transfer Source: Fee-Based Information Service." *Library Hi Tech* 1(Fall): 69-71.

Beaubien, A.K., compiler. 1987. *Fee-Based Services: Issues and Answers.* Ann Arbor, MI: Michigan Information Transfer Source, University of Michigan Libraries.

Beecher, J.W. 1985. "Implementing and Managing a Fee-Based Information Service in an Academic Library." Pp. 199-207 in *Cost Analysis, Cost Recovery, Marketing and Fee-Based Services: A Guide for the Health Sciences Librarian*, edited by M.S. Wood. New York: Haworth Press.

Beeler, R.J., and A.L. Lueck. 1984. "Pricing of Online Services for Nonprimary Clientele." *Journal of Academic Librarianship* 10(2): 69-72.

212 / *Fee-Based Information Services*

Bjorner, S. 1993. "Fee-Based Information Services and Information Brokers: Making the Arrangement Work." *Fee for Service* 1(1): 6-9.

Boss, R.W. 1979. "The Library as an Information Broker." *College and Research Libraries* 40(2): 136-140.

Broadbent, H.E. 1981. "Pricing Information Products and Services." *Drexel Library Quarterly* 17(2): 99-107.

Bunting, A. 1994. "Legal Considerations for Document Delivery Services." *Bulletin of the Medical Library Association* 82(2): 183-187.

Burrows, S., and A. LaRocca. 1983. "Fees for Automated Reference Services in Academic Health Science Libraries: No Free Lunches." *Medical Reference Services Quarterly* 2(2): 1-15.

Burwell, H.P., ed. 1995. *The Burwell World Directory of Information Brokers.* 12th edition. Houston, TX: Burwell Enterprises.

Cady, S.A., and B.G. Richards. 1982. "The One-Thousand-Dollar Alternative: How One University Structures a Fee-Based Information Service for Local Industry." *American Libraries* 14(3): 175-176.

Caren, L., and A. Somerville. 1988. "Issues Facing Private Academic Libraries Considering Fee-Based Programs." *The Reference Librarian* (22): 37-49.

Carter, N.C., and S.B. Pagel. 1984. "Fees for Service: The Golden Gate University Law Library Membership Plan." *Law Library Journal* 77(2): 243-274.

Casorso, T.M., and S.J. Rogers. 1987. "Targeting Your Market." Pp. 1-9 in *Fee-Based Services: Issues and Answers,* compiled by A.K. Beaubien. Ann Arbor, MI: Michigan Information Transfer Source, University of Michigan Libraries.

Cavazos, E.A., and G. Morin. 1994. *Cyberspace and the Law: Your Rights and Duties in the On-Line World.* Cambridge, MA: MIT Press.

Clark, M.S. 1986. "Fees for Library and Information Services in Libraries: A Bibliography." *Collection Building* 8(1): 57-61.

Coffman, S., and H. Josephine. 1991. "Doing It for Money." *Library Journal* 116(17): 32-36.

Cool, L.C. 1988. *How to Give Good Phone: Telephone Techniques to Increase Your Power, Profits, and Performance.* New York: D.I. Fine.

Cooper, L. 1988. *How Much Will It Cost Me? Estimating Costs and Preparing Bids for Fee-Based Information Services.* Washington, DC: American Society of Indexers.

Covello, J.A., and B.J. Hazelgren. 1993. *The Complete Book of Business Plans.* Naperville, IL: Sourcebooks Trade.

Dillman, D.A. 1978. *Mail and Telephone Surveys: The Total Design Method.* New York: Wiley.

DiMattia, S. 1993. "Arizona State Folds Fee-Based Service." *Library Journal* 118(6): 24, 29.

Dodd, J.B. 1974. "Pay-As-You-Go Plan for Satellite Industrial Libraries Using Academic Facilities." *Special Libraries* 65(1): 66-72.

Donnellan, A.M., and L. Rasmussen. 1983. "Fee-Based Services in Academic Libraries: Preliminary Results of a Survey." *Drexel Library Quarterly* 19(4): 68-79.

Downing, A. 1990. "The Consequences of Offering Fee-Based Services in a Medical Library." *Bulletin of the Medical Library Association* 78(1): 57-63.

du Toit, A.S.A. 1994. "Developing a Price Strategy for Information Products." *South African Journal of Library and Information Science* 62(December): 162-167.

"Economic Barriers to Information Access: An Interpretation of the Library Bill of Rights." 1993. *Newsletter on Intellectual Freedom* 42(5): 137.

Elliott de Saez, E. 1993. *Marketing Concepts for Libraries and Information Services.* London: Library Association.

Ellsworth, J.H., and M.V. Ellsworth. 1995. *Marketing on the Internet: Multimedia Strategies for the World Wide Web.* New York: Wiley.

Ernest, D.J. 1993. "Academic Libraries, Fee-Based Information Services, and the Business Community." *RQ* 32(3): 393-402.

Everett, J.H., and E.P. Crowe. 1988. *Information for Sale: How to Start and Operate Your Own Data Research Service.* Blue Ridge Summit, PA: Tab Books.

Felicetti, B.W. 1982. "Information Brokering: What Is It, Why It Is, and How It Is Done." Pp. 2-19 in *So You Want To Be an Information Broker?*, edited by K. Warnken and B. Felicetti. Chicago, IL: Information Alternative.

Finer, R. 1986. "The Consulting Process." Pp. 131-158 in *Information Consultants in Action*, edited by J.S. Parker. London: Mansell.

Finnigan, G. 1995. "The Rise of Value-Added Document Delivery Services." Pp. 13-30 in *Document Delivery in an Electronic Age*, edited by D. Kaser. Philadelphia, PA: National Federation of Abstracting and Information Services.

Fiscella, J.B., and J.D. Ringel. 1988. "Academic Libraries and Regional Economic Development." Pp. 127-136 in *Libraries and the Search for Academic Excellence*, edited by P.S. Breivik and R. Wedgeworth. Metuchen, NJ: Scarecrow Press.

Folmsbee, M.A., J.M. Murray, and N. Folmsbee. 1990. "A Primer Concerning the Imposition of Fees for Reference and Other Services in Academic Law Libraries." *Legal Reference Services Quarterly* 10(3): 11-26.

Fong, Y.S. 1995. "The Copyright Quandary: Copyright Practices in Fee-Based Services." *Fee for Service* 2(2): 11-15.

Foreman, G.E. 1985. "Fee-for-Service in Publicly Supported Libraries: An Overview." Pp. 175-183 in *Cost Analysis, Cost Recovery, Marketing and Fee-Based Services: A Guide for the Health Sciences Librarian.* New York: Haworth Press.

Franks, J.A., and K.K. Montgomery. 1991. "LINE: The Fee-Based Service at the University of Central Florida Library." *Mississippi Libraries* 55(Spring): 15-17.

Fraser, J. 1994. "Talk Radio: Alternative Marketing Techniques at RIS." *Fee for Service* 1(3): 38-40.

Freeman, J.K., and K.A. O'Connell. 1985. "The Marketing of Biomedical Information Service at the University of Minnesota: Creative Error Correction." Pp. 159-171 in *Cost Analysis, Cost Recovery, Marketing and Fee-Based Services: A Guide for the Health Sciences Librarian*, edited by M.S. Wood. New York: Haworth Press.

Gaffner, H.B. 1976. "The Demand for Information-on-Demand." *Bulletin of the American Society for Information Science* 2(7): 39-40.

Gaines, E.J., and M.A. Huttner. 1983. "Fee-Based Services and the Public Library: An Administrative Perspective." *Drexel Library Quarterly* 19(4): 13-22.

Gasaway, L.N., and S.K. Wiant. 1994. *Libraries and Copyright: A Guide to Copyright Law in the 1990s.* Washington, DC: Special Libraries Association.

George, L.A. 1993a. Fee-Based Information Services and Document Delivery." *Wilson Library Bulletin* 67(6): 41-44, 112.

George, L.A. 1993b. "Fee-Based Information Services and Information Brokers: A Case Study in Collaboration." *Fee for Service* 1(1): 1, 3-5.

George, L.A. 1994. "Taxes and TQM: Taxation of Fee-Based Services in the U.S." *Fee for Service* 1(3): 43-45.

George, L.A. 1996. "The Price is Right: Analyzing Costs in a Fee-Based Information Service." *Fee for Service* 3(2): 7-10.

Gilton, D.L. 1992. "Information Entrepreneurship: Sources for Reference Librarians." *RQ* 31(3): 346-355.

Grant, M.M., and D. Ungarelli. 1987. "Fee-Based Business Research in an Academic Library." *The Reference Librarian* (19): 239-255.

Green, T.C. 1993. "Competencies for Entry-Level Independent Information Professionals: An Assessment by Practitioners." *Journal of Education for Library and Information Science* 34(2): 165-168.

Grund, D. 1992. "Fee-Based Information Services: Serving Business/Strenghening the LRC." Pp. 113-121 in *Community College Reference Services*, edited by B. Katz. Metuchen, NJ: Scarecrow Press.

Gumpert, D.E. 1994. *How to Really Create a Successful Business Plan.* 2nd edition. Boston, MA: Inc. Publishing.

Haswell, H. 1996. "Searcher's Voice: A Customer's Perspective." *Searcher* 4(3): 4, 6.

Heller, J.S. 1986. "Copyright and Fee-Based Copying Services." *College and Research Libraries* 47(1): 28-37.

Herman, L. 1990. "Costing, Charging, and Pricing: Related but Different Decisions." *The Bottom Line* 4(2): 26-29.

Hill, S. 1991. "Charging for Information Services: Is There a Best Way for Internal and External Cost Recoveries?" *New Zealand Libraries* 49(9): 14-16.

Holmes, C.O'C. 1988. "Rensselaer Libraries' Services to Special Users: The Alumni, Local Business Community and Rensselaer Technology Park." *The Bookmark* 47(Fall): 30-32.

Hornbeck, J.W. 1983. "An Academic Library's Experience with Fee-Based Services." *Drexel Library Quarterly* 19(4): 23-26.

Johnson, A.J.H. 1994. *Information Brokers: Case Studies of Successful Ventures.* New York: Haworth Press.

Josephine, H.B. 1989a. "Fee-Based Information Services in Academic Libraries." Pp. 1084-1086 in *Engineering Excellence: People Make the Difference*, edited by L.P. Grayson and J.M. Biedenbach. Washington, DC: American Society for Engineering Education.

Josephine, H.B. 1989b. "Fee-Based Information Services in Academic Libraries: Competitors in the Private Sector? Pp. 213-218 in *National Online Meeting Proceedings*, compiled by C. Nixon and L. Padgett. Medford, NJ: Learned Information.

Josephine, H.B. 1989c. "Intrapreneurship in Fee-Based Information Services." *Journal of Library Administration* 10(2-3): 151-158.

Josephine, H.B. 1989d. "New Clienteles, New Service Needs: Academic Libraries Respond with Fee-Based Information Centers." *Library Issues* 9(3): 1-3.

Josephine, H.B. 1991. "Universities and Economic Development: Playing the Library Card." *Library Issues* 11(3): 1-3.

Josephine, H.B. 1992. "University Libraries and Information Services for the Business Community." Pp. 321-329 in *The Marketing of Library and Information Services*, Vol. 2, edited by B. Cronin. London: Aslib.

Josephine, H.B., and M.H. Reneker. 1989. "In Defense of FIRST and Freedom of Access to Information." *College and Research Libraries News* 50(5): 377-379.

Kallunki, S. 1990. "To Fee or Not To Fee." *The Unabashed Librarian* (75): 19-20.

Kaser, D., ed. 1995. *Document Delivery in an Electronic Age.* Philadelphia, PA: National Federation of Abstracting and Information Services.

Keeler, L. 1995. *Cybermarketing.* New York: Amacom.

Kibirige, H.M. 1983. *The Information Dilemma: A Critical Analysis of Information Pricing and the Fees Controversy.* Westport, CT: Greenwood Press.

Kinder, R., and B. Katz, eds. 1988. *Information Brokers and Reference Services.* New York: Haworth Press.

Kingman, N.M., and C. Vantine. 1977. "Commentary on the Special Librarian/Fee-Based Service Interface." *Special Libraries* 68(9): 320-322.

Kotler, P., and A.R. Andreasen. 1996. *Strategic Marketing for Nonprofit Organizations.* 5th edition. Upper Saddle River, NJ: Prentice Hall.

Kotler, P., and R.A. Connor, Jr. 1977. "Marketing Professional Services." *Journal of Marketing* 41(1): 71-76.

Lemkau, H.L., S. Burrows, and A. La Rocco. 1985. "Marketing Information Services Outside the Medical Center. Pp. 143-157 on *Cost Analysis, Cost Recovery, Marketing and Fee-Based Services: A Guide for the Health Sciences Librarian,* edited by M.S. Wood. New York: Haworth Press.

Levitt, T. 1981. "Marketing Intangible Products and Product Intangibles." *Harvard Business Review* 81(May/June): 94-102.

Lom, J.A. 1986. "Fee-Based Reference Service: A Reevaluation." *RQ* 25(3): 295-299.

Long Island University Center for Business Research. 1983. *Conference on Fee Based Research in College and University Libraries.* Greenvale, NY: Long Island University Center for Business Research.

Lunden, E. 1983. "Marketing the R.I.C.E. Operation." Pp. 113-127 in *Conference on Fee Based Research in College and University Libraries.* Greenvale, NY: Long Island University Center for Business Research

Lunden, E. 1987. "Quality Control in Fee-Based Library Services: Who Cares?: Pp. 31-40 in *Fee-Based Services: Issues and Answers,* compiled by A.K. Beaubien. Ann Arbor, MI: Michigan Information Transfer Source, University of Michigan Libraries.

Machovec, G.S. 1994. "Criteria for Selecting Document Delivery Suppliers." *Information Intelligence, Online Libraries, and Microcomputers* 12(5): 1-5.

Maloff, J. 1995. *net.profit: Expanding your Business Using the Internet.* Foster City, CA: IDG Books Worldwide.

Maranjian, L., and R.W. Boss. 1980. *Fee-Based Information Services: A Study of a Growing Industry.* New York: Bowker.

Marks, K. 1992. "Libraries: No Longer Free or Fee." *North Carolina Libraries* 50(Special Edition): 20-23.

Marvin, S. 1988. "ExeLS: Executive Library Services." *The Reference Librarian* (22): 145-160.

McDonald, E. 1985. "University/Industry Partnerships: Premonitions for Academic Libraries." *Journal of Academic Librarianship* 11(2): 82-87.

McGrath, K. 1992. *Trademark: How to Name Your Business & Product,* 2nd edition. Berkeley, CA: Nolo Press.

McGuire, K. 1993. "Information Direct: Birmingham Library Services' Fee-Based Business Service." *Law Librarian* 24(September): 125-126.

Meader, R. 1991. *Guidelines for Preparing Proposals.* 2nd edition. Chelsea, MI: Lewis Publishers.

Mintz, A.P. 1984. "Information Practice and Malpractice: Do We Need Malpractice Insurance?" *Online* 8(4): 20-26.

Mitchell, E., and S.A. Walters. 1995. *Document Delivery Services: Issues and Answers.* Medford, NJ: Learned Information.

National Commission on New Technological Uses of Copyrighted Works. 1978. *Final Report of the National Commission on New Technological Uses of Copyrighted Works.* Washington, DC: National Commission on New Technological Uses of Copyrighted Works.

Norton, B. 1988. *Charging for Library and Information Services.* London: Library Association.

O'Keeffe, R.L. 1975. "University Library Service to the Industrial and Research Communities." Pp. 46-57 in *Library Lectures Numbers Twenty-One through Twenty-Eight,* edited by C. Wire. Baton Rouge, LA: Louisiana State University Library.

Olaisen, J.L. 1989. "Pricing Strategies for Library and Information Services. *Libri* 39(4): 253-274.

Park, M.W. 1994. "The Benefits of Libraries and Independents Working Together." *Fee for Service* 1(2): 26-28.

Peterson, D.J. 1986. "Profit Is Not a Dirty Word." *Journal of Library Administration* 7(1): 75-81.

Pienaar, R.E. 1994. "The Organization of Fee-Based Services." *Fee for Service* 1(4): 49, 51-53.

Raffin, M., ed. 1978. *The Marketing of Information Services.* London: Aslib.

Rawles, B.A., and M.B. Wessels. 1986. "Library Consulting." Pp. 111-130 in *Information Consultants in Action,* edited by J.S. Parker. London: Mansell.

Richards, B.G., and R. Widdicombe. 1985. "Fee-Based Information Services to Industry." Pp. 59-64 in *The Future of Information Resources for Science and Technology and the Role of Libraries,* edited by N. Fjällbrant. Göteborg, Sweden: Chalmers University Technology Library.

Richards, D. 1991. "Starting a Fee-Based Service in a Rural Area." *The Bottom Line* 5(1): 14-17.

Rochell, C. 1985. "The Knowledge Business: Economic Issues of Access to Bibliographic Information." *Information Reports and Bibliographies* 14(4): 17-23.

Roeder, C.S. 1987. "Access Fees in a Hospital Library: A Program for Pharmaceutical Company Representatives." *Bulletin of the Medical Library Association* 75(2): 171-173.

Rosenberg, J.A. 1986. "User Fees and Library Economics: A Selected, Annotated Bibliography." Pp. 190-208 in *The Economics of Research Libraries,* edited by M.M. Cummings. Washington, DC: Council on Library Resources.

Rubens, D., and J. Wulff. 1989. "Nuts & Bolts Guide to Fee-Based Document Supply in the United States." *Infomediary* 2(3/4): 193-195.

Rugge, S., and A. Glossbrenner. 1995. *The Information Broker's Handbook.* 2nd edition. New York: McGraw Hill.

Salant, P., and D.A. Dillman. 1994. *How to Conduct Your Own Survey.* New York: Wiley.

Sanders, V. 1993. "Of Fee-Based Librarians." *Library Journal* 118(16): 8.

Savolainen, R. 1990. "Fee or Free? The Socio-Economic Dimensions of the Charging Dilemma." *Journal of Information Science* 16(3): 143-153.

Sawyer, D.C. 1995. *Sawyer's Survival Guide for Information Brokers.* Houston, TX: Burwell Enterprises.

Settles, C. 1995. *Cybermarketing Essentials for Success.* Emeryville, CA: Ziff-Davis.

Shannon, Z.J. 1974. "Public Library Service to the Corporate Community." *Special Libraries* 65(1): 12-16.

Shaver, D.B., N.S. Hewison, and L.W. Wykoff. 1985. "Ethics for Online Intermediaries." *Special Libraries* 76(4): 238-245.

Siegel, E.S., B.R. Ford, and J.M. Bornstein. 1993. *The Ernst & Young Business Plan Guide.* 2nd edition. New York: Wiley.

Smith, P.K. 1980. "Marketing Online Services," Part 1. *Online* 4(1):60-62.

Smith, P.K. 1980. "Marketing Online Services," Part 2. *Online* 4(2): 68-69.

Smith, W. 1993. "Fee-Based Services: Are They Worth It?" *Library Journal* 118(11): 40-43.

St. Clair, G. 1993. *Customer Service in the Information Environment.* London: Bowker-Saur.

St. Clair, G. 1996. *Entrepreneurial Librarianship: The Key to Effective Information Services Management.* London: Bowker-Saur.

Stump, B. 1983. *Operating and Marketing Fee-Based Information Services in Academic Libraries: A Small Business Approach.* Chicago, IL: Association of College and Research Libraries.

Talaga, J.A. 1991. "Concept of Price in a Library Context." *Journal of Library Administration* 14(4): 87-101.

Tertell, S.M. 1983. "Fee-Based Services to Business: Implementation in a Public Library." *Drexel Library Quarterly* 19(4): 37-53.

Thompson, J.C. 1983. "Regional Information and Communication Exchange: A Case Study." Pp. 55-76 in *Conference on Fee Based Research in College and University Libraries,* Greenvale, NY: Long Island University Center for Business Research.

Ungarelli, D.L., and M.M. Grant. 1983. "A Fee-Based Model: Administrative Considerations in an Academic Library." *Drexel Library Quarterly* 19(4): 4-12.

United States, Department of Commerce, Patent and Trademark Office. Annual. *Basic Facts about Registering a Trademark.* Washington, DC: U.S. Department of Commerce, Patent and Trademark Office.

Voigt, K.J. 1988. "Computer Search Services and Information Brokering in Academic Libraries." *The Reference Librarian* (22): 17-36.

Ward, S.M. 1989a. "Information Service Can Focus Research Project." *Marketing News* (September 11): 7, 47, 62.

Ward, S.M. 1989b. "Meeting Industry's Information Needs in Indiana: Purdue's Technical Information Service." Pp. 1081-1083 in *Engineering Excellence: People Make the Difference,* edited by L.P. Grayson and J. M. Biedenbach. Washington, DC: American Society for Engineering Education.

Ward, S.M. 1989c. "Purdue's Technical Information Service." *Indiana Business* (November): 90-91.

Ward, S.M. 1990a. "Client Prospecting: Techniques for Fee-Based Services." *MLS: Marketing Library Services* 4(6): 4-6.

Ward, S.M. 1990b. "Using a Newsletter to Promote Information Services." Pp. 121-125 in *The Information Professional: An Unparalleled Resource.* Washington, DC: Special Libraries Association.

Ward, S.M. 1991a. "The Annual Report as a Marketing Tool." *MLS: Marketing Library Services* 5(2): 4-7.

Ward, S.M. 1991b. "Fee-Based Information Services: Gold Mine for Corporate Librarians." *Business Information Alert* 3(7): 1-3, 11.

Ward, S.M. 1992. "Resource Sharing among Library Fee-Based Information Services." Pp. 124-138 in *Advances in Library Resource Sharing,* Vol. 3, edited by J.Cargill and D.J. Graves. Westport, CT: Meckler.

Ward, S.M. 1995a. "Cooperation between Non-Profit Fee-Based Information Services and For-Profit Brokers." *Information Services and Use* 15(2): 153-158.

Ward, S.M. 1995b. "Purdue University's Technical Information Service: Providing Information to Businesses." *International Journal of Special Libraries* 29(2): 127-132.

Warner, A.S. 1983. "Selling Consulting Services, Buying Consulting Services." Pp. 95-105 in *Managing the Electronic Library,* edited by M. Koenig. New York: Special Libraries Association.

Warner, A.S. 1987a. *Mind Your Own Business: A Guide for the Information Entrepreneur.* New York: Neal Schuman.

Warner, A.S. 1987b. "Selling the Service." Pp. 11-17 in *Fee-Based Services: Issues and Answers,* compiled by A.K. Beaubien. Ann Arbor, MI: Michigan Information Transfer Source, University of Michigan Libraries.

Warner, A.S. 1989. *Making Money: Fees for Library Services.* New York: Neal-Schuman.

Warner, A.S. 1990a. "Charging Back, Charging Out, Charging Fees." *The Bottom Line* 4(3): 32-35.

Warner, A.S. 1990b. "Librarians as Money Makers: The Bottom Line." *American Libraries* 21(10): 946-948.

Warnken, K. 1981. *The Information Brokers: How to Start and Operate Your Own Fee-based Service.* New York: Bowker.

Warnken, K., and B. Felicetti, eds. 1982. *So You Want to Be an Information Broker?* Chicago, IL: Information Alternative.

Weingand, D.A., ed. 1995. "Marketing of Library and Information Services." *Library Trends* 43(3): 289-513.

Weinland, J., and C.R. McClure. 1987. "Economic Considerations for Fee Based Library Services: An Administrative Perspective." *Journal of Library Administration* 8(1): 53-68.

White, M.S. 1980. "Information for Industry: The Role of the Information Broker." *Aslib Proceedings* 32(2): 82-86.

White, M.S. 1981. *Profit from Information: A Guide to the Establishment, Operation and Use of an Information Consultancy.* London: Andre Deutsch.

Whitmell, V. 1993. "Establishing Long-Term Relationships with Your Fee-Based Clientele: Agreeing to Agree." *Fee for Service* 1(1): 10-13.

Whitmell, V. 1994. "Establishing Long-Term Relationships with Your Fee-Based Clientele: Costing Issues." *Fee for Service* 1(2): 22-25.

Whitmell, V. 1996. "Staffing the Fee-Based Library Service." *Fee for Service* 3(1): 6-12.

Wilkins, A. 1992. "The For-Profit Syndrome: Will Libraries Be Next?" *North Carolina Libraries* 50(Special Edition): 24-26.

Williams, S.F. 1987. "To Charge or Not to Charge: No Longer a Question?" *The Reference Librarian* 19: 125-136.

Williams, T.L., H.L. Lemkau, and S. Burrows. 1988. "The Economics of Academic Health Science Libraries: Cost Recovery in the Era of Big Science. *Bulletin of the Medical Library Association* 76(4): 317-322.

Wood, E.J. 1983. "Strategic Planning and the Marketing Process: Library Applications." *Journal of Academic Librarianship* 9(1): 15-20.

Wood, F.K. 1987. "When Do Dollars for Information Service Make Sense? The Wisconsin ISD Experience." *The Bottom Line* 1(4): 25-27.

Wood, M.S., ed. 1985. *Cost Analysis, Cost Recovery, Marketing, and Fee-Based Services: A Guide for the Health Sciences Librarian.* New York: Haworth Press.

Wood, W. 1993. "A Librarian's Guide to Fee-Based Services." *The Reference Librarian* (40): 121-129.

Woodsworth, A., and J.F. Williams, II. 1993. *Managing the Economics of Owning, Leasing and Contracting Out Information Services.* Aldershot, UK: Gower.

Yudkin, M. 1995. *Marketing Online: Low-Cost, High-Yield Strategies for Small Businesses & Professionals.* New York: Plume.

Zais, H.W. 1977. "Economic Modeling: An Aid to the Pricing of Information Services." *Journal of the American Society for Information Science* 28(2): 89-95.

HELPFUL NEWSLETTERS

Subscribing to a selection of the following periodicals helps keep practitioners current with developments in fee-based information services and related issues. Consult *Ulrich's International Periodicals Directory* for the publishers' current addresses and call for subscription information.

> Business Information Alert
> Fee for Service
> Information Broker
> Legal Information Alert
> Marketing Treasures
> MLS: Marketing Library Services

FISCAL LIST-SERV

Contact the American Library Association for the name and phone number of the current chair of the Association of College and Research Libraries' (ACRL) discussion group, Fee-Based Information Service Centers in Academic Libraries (FISCAL). The FISCAL chair will provide information about subscribing to FISCAL's listserv, FISC-L.

Index